Make your Last Relapse The Last

Create Your Own Relapse Prevention Plan

USDrugRehabCenters.com
USDR Publications

Publisher's Note

The ideas, procedures, articles and information provided in this publication are not intended as a substitute for consulting directly with a medical, physical or mental health professional nor are they an endorsement of a particular approach or course of action for an individual. If you are unsure as to whether or not you require professional assistance, please contact your family doctor for referral.

This publication is for private, personal use only. NO part of this publication may be copied or altered in any way, either electronically or physically, without express written consent.

Rehab facilities, rehab programs, group leaders, counselors, or other professionals wishing to incorporate our material into their program are permitted when a hard copy is purchased for each client from our publisher. Please click this link to purchase copies.

Distributed in Online by USDrugRehabCenters.com
Copyright 2007 by USDrugRehabCenters.com
sobertools@gmail.com

Cover and page layout design by www.mdesigns.ca

All rights reserved.

FIRST EDITION
Printed from January 2007 to 2009

DIGITAL EDITION
Produced from January 2011 to present
ISBN: 978-0-9809376-2-6

This book is dedicated to

the valiant efforts of the individuals and their families

in the fight against addictions.

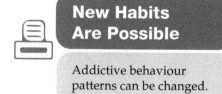

New Habits Are Possible

Addictive behaviour patterns can be changed.

Table Of Contents

Chapter One
Introduction to Relapse Prevention 13
   Leaving Addiction Behind Requires Setting A New Life Course 15
   Finding Personal Incentive To Take Action on Relapse Prevention 16
   Living A Balanced Life Reduces The Risk Of Relapse 17
   Taking Action On Your Relapse Prevention Plan Will Change All Areas Of Your Life 17
   Be Ready To Succeed 19
   » **Commitment To Continued Positive Change In My Life** 20
   » **Relapse Prevention Planning Checklist** 21

Chapter Two
Addiction And Learned Behaviours 23
   How Are Addiction Behaviors Learned? 24
   Why Do People Drink Or Take Drugs In The First Place? 24
   What Do People Learn When Using? 26
   Why Do People Continue To Use? 28
   Why Are People Afraid To Quit Using? 30
   Why Do People Eventually Decide To Quit Using? 30
   Addiction Changed How You Think 32
   Abstinence Allows You Time To Learn 32
   The Power of Using Information To Prevent Relapse 33
   Choosing Information To Support Your New Learning 33

Chapter Three
Getting The Basics Right..39
   Impact of Using Drugs And Alcohol On
      Negative Emotions 41
   Where Do Negative Emotions Come From? 42
   Stopping Automatic And Dysfunctional Thinking 43
   Impact Of Drugs And Alcohol On Your Mental Health 44
   Impact Of Taking Drugs and Alcohol
      On Physical Health 46
   Working On Your Mind And Body To Get Healthy 47
   Sleep And Relapse Prevention 48
   Food And Relapse Prevention 49
   Exercise And Relapse Prevention 50
   Summary 51

Chapter Four
Managing Cues..53
   High-Risk Situations For Relapse 55
   High-Risk Situations Must Be Avoided 56
   Cues: What Are They And How to Manage Them..................................56
   Lower Your Response To Cues And Reduce Cravings By Making A Commitment. 56
   Reduce Cravings By Eliminating Cues..57
   Start Removing Items That Cue You To Drink
      And Use Drugs 59
   Replace Old Cues With Positive Cues..59
   Situations Or Events Are Also Cues...60
   Managing Situation Cues 61
   Location Cues Require You To Stay Away 61
   Common Emotional Cues 62
   Taking Action To Manage Cues Always Includes Creating New Cues......63
   Drug And Alcohol Cues Do Not Last Forever 64
   Summary 64
   » **Personal Cue Inventory And Strategies To Manage Cues** 65

Chapter Five
Managing Cravings 69
   Beliefs Help To Form The Expectation, Which Then Molds The Urge To Use 70
   You Can Control Craving By Using Reasoned Thinking 72
   Taking Action By Developing Your Craving Management Plan 73
   Create A Pocket Helper..74
   Cravings Always Get Weaker If You Don't Respond To The Urge To Use 75
   Practical Techniques For Managing Craving 76
   Developing An Exercise And Relaxation Plan...78
   Boredom Is The Desire For Desire 81
   What Could Be Stopping You?..81

Motivation To Make The Needed Changes 82
Ambivalent Thoughts, Emotions And Behaviors
    Are Normal 84
Summary 84
» **Craving Management Plan** 86
» **Exercise, Recreation And Social Activities Plan** 90

Chapter Six
Coping Skills to Prevent Relapse 93
Managing Anger 95
Managing Depression 98
What Causes Depression? 98
Managing Anxiety 99
Panic Disorder: 100
Generalized Anxiety Disorder: 101
Managing Stress To Reduce The Risk Of Relapse 101
The Balance Sheet In Your Mind: Assigning Meaning To Stressors 104
Do Multiple Stressful Events Add Up? 105
The Balance Sheet In Your Mind & Relapse 105
So Who Decides If An Event Is Stressful? 105
Becoming Stress Resilient By Holding On To Your Values 106
Manage Stress To Prevent Relapse 108
Summary 108
» **Personal Stress Inventory Worksheet** 110

Chapter Seven
Reduce Conflict, Increase Communication, And Decrease Relapse 113
Conflict Is A Source Of Stress.. 114
Conflict And Relapse 114
Conflict, The Basics 114
How We View Conflict 115
Cooperation As An Attitude And Conflict Resolution Tool 116
Communication Skills, A Relapse Prevention Tool 117
How You Look, Talk & Act Is A Large Part Of Communicating 118
Active Listening Is Communicating 120
Take Time To Practice 121
Summary 122

Chapter Eight
Relationships And Relapse 123
Families Impact Addiction Behavior 125
Negative Family And Friend Support 125
Positive Family And Friend Support 126
Guilt, Shame And The Addiction Lifestyle 127
Guilt 127

Shame 128
Simple Actions To Reduce Guilt And Shame 129
Planning For Healthy Relationships To Prevent Relapse 129
Becoming Mentally And Physically Healthier To Build Healthy Relationships 130
Families Need Help Too 130
Social Support And Relapse Prevention 132
Interpersonal Boundary Setting Reduces Risk Of Relapse 134
What Is An Interpersonal Boundary? 135
Living and Enforcing Boundaries 137
Summary 137

» **Guilt and Shame Stress Inventory Worksheet** 139
» **Self Care Recovery Boundaries Worksheet** 141
» **Support Network Worksheet** 145

Chapter Nine

Stay on Track, Develop a Personal Vision 147

What Causes People To Change? 148
Exploring Values 148
Why Is Defining Your Values Important? 149
How Did We Develop Our First Values And Beliefs? 149
Can You Change Your Values And Beliefs? 152
Planned And Controlled Life Change 152
How Do You Raise Your Values And Standards? 153
Meditation, A Simple Tool 153
Creating Your Vision And Establishing Goals 154
Are Your Goals Important Enough To Sustain Change? 155
Tipping Points 157
Your Tipping Point 158
Get Down The Action Details For Each Goal 158
How To Set Goals With Important People In Your Life 159
Life Partners Can Power Change 159
Mutual Goal Setting 160
Summary 161

» **Life Plan And Goals For Next Year Worksheet** 163
» **Goal Planning Worksheet** 168

Chapter Ten

Meaningful Work And Relapse Prevention 169

Mental Roadblocks To Finding The Right Work for You 170
Finding Meaningful Work 172
Use Creative Thinking 174
Create Your Written Vision Of Meaningful Work 174
Making Dreams A Reality 175

Achieving Goals 177
The Catalysts Of Change 178
Increase Your Energy 178
Increase Your Momentum 179
Handle Your Mental Objections To Taking Action 180
Not Enough Time: 180
Not Enough Money: 180
Too Hard For Me To Do: 181
Take Action To Get Ready For That Dream Job 181
Summary 182

Chapter Eleven
Reducing the Risks of Using Again 183
Detecting Your Relapse Setup 185
Habits Or Conditioned Responses 186
A Time Out From Using 186
What Is Substance Dependence? 186
If You Choose To Use Again, Take Precautions 188
A Lapse Can Lead To Greater Commitment 189
Lapse As A Guilt Inducing Event 190
When Can I Go Back To Using Moderately? 191
How About Using Other Drugs And Alcohol Except My Drug Of Choice? 192
Testing the Water 193
Without Drugs And Alcohol, Will My Life Be Perfect? 194
Relationship Problems 195
Financial Problems 195
Peer Pressure Or Social Pressure To Use 196
Daily Life Stressors 196
Health Problems 197
A Balanced Lifestyle 197
Your Future 197
Summary 198

Chapter Twelve
Creating A New Identity 199
Addict As An Identity 200
Identity Expands Or Limits Options 201
Strategies To Change Your Identity 202
Beliefs Can Be Changed 202
Letting Go Of The Past 203
Be The Judge 206
Staying Angry At Someone Else 208
Loneliness And Recovery 208
Loneliness Is Not A Personality Flaw 209
What To Do About Loneliness? 209

Enjoy Being You 210
Beating Boredom 211
Summary 212

Chapter Thirteen
Taking Charge of Your Health And Your Life 215
When Self-Management Doesn't Work 217
An Example Of Self-Management.. 217
Key Tasks To Manage Chronic Health Problems Including Addiction 218
So, What Does The Evidence Mean To You? 219
How To Identify The Resources Required For Your Life Plan 219
Professionals 220
Family Or Friends Who Help 221
Clear Communication With Professionals, Family And Friends.......................... 221
Problem Solving Skills For Health And Life Goals... 221
No Time For Problem Solving? 222
Generating Solutions 222
Addiction Results In Negative Stereotyping 223
Responsible Sharing Of Information 223
Practice What You Will Say... 225
The Stigma of Addiction 226
Where Does The Stigma Around Addiction Come From? 227
What Actions Can You Take To Break Stigma Barriers? 227
Negative Stereotyping Can Be A Two Way Street 228
The Best Tool For Improved Health and Stigma Reduction 229
Summary 229

Chapter Fourteen
Putting All The Pieces Together.. 231
What Is Structure?.. 232
An Example Of The Use Of Structure... 232
What Makes Up Structure? 232
Can Structure Create Helplessness?.. 233
Positive Structure Can Change How You Behave... 233
Structures Can Support Or Deter Sobriety 235
Structure Can Cue You To Succeed 235
When Is It Real Structure? 236
Creating Positive Life Structure Keeps You Safe From Risk 237
Key Points For Your Success 239
Structure Requires And Reinforces Commitment 239
Commitments Build Trust 240
The Commitment Cycle.. 241
Monitoring Your Progress On Your Life Goals... 241
Monitoring Too Late Is Costly 241
Managing Slips, Lapses And Relapses.. 242

Learn Through Honest Appraisal Of The Lapse 242
Reward Yourself For Both Small And Large Successes 243
How Much Time Is Enough For Your Life Plan? 243
Check How You Spend Your Time 243
Making Up For Lost Time 245
Your Time For Recovery 246
You Have The Time ....
» **3 Month Weekly Planner**...**248**

Appendixes

Seeking Further Help 255
Depression, Anxiety, Worry, Relationships 256
Communication 256
Stress & Relaxation 256
Anger Management 256
Counseling & Psychiatry.. 262

New Habits Are Possible

Addictive behaviour patterns can be changed.

You can succeed and make your last relapse the last!

Chapter One

Introduction to Relapse Prevention

Chapter 1

Introduction to Relapse Prevention

You **can** build your own personal relapse prevention plan. This workbook is your guide to creating your plan and putting your plan into action. If you have completed a withdrawal management program and are not actively using drugs and alcohol, you are ready to take immediate action to:

1. Reduce the number of slips or lapses
2. Prevent full relapse or a return to regular using
3. Plan and achieve your life goals.

> **Don't Give Up!**
> It's hard work, but you can finish this book!

The book teaches specific coping skills for relapse prevention, general life skills, and skills to improve health.

To create your comprehensive relapse prevention plan you will need to complete:

- A clear commitment statement and written life goals for the year ahead with compelling reasons for each goal
- A stress inventory with strategies
- A guilt and shame inventory with strategies
- A defined support network with strategies for connection
- A clear boundary-setting plan
- A communications skill improvement plan
- An exercise, recreation, and social activity plan
- A cues and a craving management plan
- A detailed schedule of daily activities for your first three months following withdrawal management (detox) and/or attendance at rehab

The relapse prevention plan components are based on research about what causes relapse and what reduces the risk of relapse. Relapse is a return to using drugs and alcohol at the level of using that existed prior to the period of abstinence. Experts in relapse prevention found relapse is not generally triggered by physical cravings. People, who have been addicted to alcohol and drugs of all types, relapse in response to: stress, feelings of anxiety, fear, anger, frustration or depression; social pressures to use; and interpersonal conflicts (Marlatt, & Gordon, 1985, 2005).

> *People, who have been addicted to alcohol and drugs of all types, relapse in response to: stress, feelings of anxiety, fear, anger, frustration or depression; social pressures to use; and interpersonal conflicts*

Successful relapse prevention is a process of learning, developing, and using new skills, attitudes, beliefs, and values that support you to achieve your new life goals. Relapse prevention begins with you taking the time to describe how you truly want your life to be.

The first step is committing to a life that is self-care centered. To get a sense of what this means, read the following statements out loud.

- I am committed to taking care of myself.
- Achieving the best possible physical and mental health is my first goal.
- Living my life with integrity and to the best advantage for me and those I care about is my second goal.
- I want this above all else because I want to know that when I die I will have lived a life of value to myself and the people I care about. I want to be proud of myself.

How did that feel? Now in your own words, write your commitment to yourself and why you want this **above anything else** in the world. Work on your commitment statement frequently over the next few days until you have the one you would be willing to sign and have your closest family and friends sign as witnesses. Put it on the wall of your home for all who enter to see. Start now with your first draft and use the form at the end of this chapter, "Commitment to Continued Positive Change in My Life."

Don't Give Up!

It's hard work, but you can finish this book!

Leaving Addiction Behind Requires Setting A New Life Course

Your relapse prevention plan is part of a larger plan for your life. With a life plan you cannot fail by making a single mistake. You can only fail by not correcting your mistakes and getting back on your life course. Recognize a mistake, learn from it, and keep moving forward toward your life goals.

It isn't a plan if it's not written. An unwritten plan is difficult to follow and unlikely to be successful. A few fleeting thoughts are not sufficient to keep you on track. Written life goals are essential to creating the path you want to walk. Clear life goals are based on the vision you have for your life. It takes courage to sit down and thoughtfully consider what you really want out of your life. A one year plan is a good start. In your head and heart, you know you need a written life plan.

Get Real Motivation!

What are your reasons for quitting? Are they strong enough? Revisit page 18.

Finding Personal Incentive To Take Action on Relapse Prevention

To abstain, to take enough time and energy to develop a plan, and to take action on your relapse prevention plan requires you to develop strong incentives for you to keep moving forward on your path. Your most powerful incentives for changing your life are not usually material things like buying a car or house, although they can be good motivators. Your big incentives are usually defined by the values you choose to live by.

Incentives need to be real. *Quickly write down three incentives you have for no longer using drugs and alcohol. They can be stated in any format you like. Examples: I never want to overdose and wake up in ICU again; I don't want to go back to jail; I want to keep practicing law and make a difference in people's lives.*

1. _____

2. _____

3. _____

Are your incentive statements important enough to justify a lifetime of work? Incentives to stop using are not necessarily the same ones that will help you to maintain focus on your life goals. Change can be a wonderful experience if your incentives are important enough to make it worth the effort. Write three incentive statements you believe will make it worthwhile for you to change your life forever. They need to be important enough that you can keep them in your pocket and use them as a motivator on those days when you have second thoughts. *If the one's you have written don't inspire and motivate you, work on them over the next few days to make them more powerful.*

1. _____

2. _____

_____

3. _____

_____

Living A Balanced Life Reduces The Risk Of Relapse

How do you create a balanced life? You need a life plan that has concrete goals in five areas:

- Relationships,
- Work/ school,
- Home/ community,
- Physical and mental health, and
- Communication.

As you work through this book, you will develop goals in each area to achieve a balanced lifestyle. Living a balanced life style is one of the most effective strategies to prevent relapse.

Use the "Relapse Prevention Planning Checklist" at the end of this section to keep track of your progress as you complete each required part of your relapse prevention plan.

Taking Action On Your Relapse Prevention Plan Will Change All Areas Of Your Life

As you progress through this book you will have all the information you need to write your balanced life plan. By carrying out your plan you can:

- <u>Improve Physical and Mental Health</u>

    Relapse prevention requires physical health and stamina, and mental health and stamina. As part of your relapse prevention plan you will set goals to develop skills and to take actions to improve your mental and physical health. Mental and physical health are critical components in your plan for successfully remaining abstinent and achieving your goals.

Don't Give Up!

It's hard work, but you can finish this book!

Chapter One: Introduction to Relapse Prevention

- Manage Cravings and Cues to Use

You will create your plan for managing cravings, cues and your responses to cues. Taking immediate action to reduce cravings and manage cues will help keep you safe from drugs and alcohol while you write your total plan and put the other parts of your relapse prevention plan in place. For some this means attending an abstinence based program while getting the rest of their plan working. For others, it is possible to carry out the planning process at home in an alcohol and drug free environment with the support of non-using family and friends.

- Use Coping Skills to Reduce Stress and Negative Emotions

Relapse prevention requires learning and practicing positive coping skills. Coping skills will help you to manage craving, stress, anger, depression, and anxiety. There are resources and techniques that are perfect for your individual plan. A written plan is essential so when you are stressed or experiencing negative emotions you can just look at your plan and use one of the techniques.

Don't Give Up!

It's hard work, but you can finish this book!

- Set Boundaries With Other People

The skill of setting and maintaining boundaries is essential to relapse prevention. Social pressure to use is a main cause of relapse. It's the people you allow in your life who will either support you in your new life goals or pressure you to use through their behavior or by providing access to drugs and alcohol. To keep yourself safe, you will need to complete and follow your boundary setting plan.

- Develop a Positive Social Support Network

Relapse prevention **always** requires a supportive ring of friends, family, and professionals in your life. They will assist you in meeting your goals and provide meaning, help, guidance, fun, and friendship in your life.

- Develop Communication Skills

Relapse prevention requires effective communication skills to manage interpersonal conflict and social pressure to use. Also, these skills will help you to achieve the life goals that are your incentive to remain abstinent. Your ability to communicate well can decrease your stress and increase your work and social opportunities.

Communication skills can also increase your ability to maintain and build a positive support network of relationships. They can increase your success in maintaining positive and healthy intimate partner relationships.

Most importantly they can increase your success at relapse prevention. It's easy to see why communication skills are so important to your plan.

- Put Positive Structure into Your Life

    Positive structure and time-management is core to any successful relapse prevention plan. Boredom, loneliness, empty slots in your day, and lack of positive activities to replace drug and alcohol activities leads to relapse. Relapse prevention requires clear, concrete structure and positive activities for every day. They must be planned well in advance.

Be Ready To Succeed

When you complete the required work in this book, you will be confident and ready to succeed. You will have created an organized written plan so you can become:

- Knowledgeable about addiction and relapse prevention
- Stronger and healthier both physically and mentally
- Skilled in problem solving and clear thinking
- Skilled in using positive relaxation techniques
- An expert communicator

You will be ready to succeed!

References For Chapter One

Marlatt, G.A., & Gordon, J.R., (Eds.). (1985). Relapse prevention: Maintenance Strategies in the Treatment of Addictive Behaviours (1st edition). New York. The Guilford Press. 39.

Marlatt, G.A., & Gordon, J.R., (Eds.). (2005). Relapse Prevention: Maintenance Strategies in the Treatment of Addictive Behaviours (2nd edition). New York. The Guilford Press. 8-21.

Silberman, Mel & Hansburg, Freda, (2000). PeopleSmart, Developing Your Interpersonal Intelligence. San Francisco. Berrett-Koehler Publishers Inc. 37-39.

National Center For Chronic Disease Prevention and Health Promotion. (1996). Physical Activity and Health, A Report of the Surgeon General. Chapter 4. Retrieved from http://www.surgeongeneral.gov/library/reports.htm

Don't Give Up!

It's hard work, but you can finish this book!

Commitment

to Continued Positive Change in My Life

I, _____ am committed to include more:

_____ in my life, and refrain from using _____ this date of _____ .

I want continued change and personal growth because:

_____

Signature

We the undersigned have heard _____ state their commitment and support their decision toward improving their life. We believe in them and their commitment.

_____ _____
Name and Signature   Name and Signature

_____ _____
Name and Signature   Name and Signature

_____ _____
Name and Signature   Name and Signature

_____ _____
Name and Signature   Name and Signature

Relapse Prevention Planning Checklist

Chapter	Compulsory Forms / Exercises	Target Completion Date	Date Done
One	1. Clear commitment statement		
	2. This checklist, Relapse Prevention Planning Checklist		
Two	3. Problem list worksheet		
Four	4. Personal Cue Inventory and Strategies to Manage Cues		
Five	5. Cravings management plan		
	6. Exercise, Relaxation and Social Activity Plans		
Six	7. Personal Stress Inventory Worksheet		
Eight	8. Guilt and Shame Stress Inventory Worksheet		
	9. Self Care Recovery Boundaries Worksheet		
	10. Support Network Worksheet		
Nine	11. Life Plan and Goals for Next Year Worksheet, and Goal Planning Worksheet		
Fourteen	12. Three Month Weekly Planner		

Chapter One: Introduction to Relapse Prevention

Chapter Two

Addiction And Learned Behaviours

You can succeed and make your last relapse the last!

> **Don't Give Up!**
>
> It's hard work, but you can finish this book!

Chapter 2

Addiction And Learned Behaviours

How Are Addiction Behaviors Learned?

Addiction can be viewed as a learning experience because it results in the development and use of a unique set of skills, knowledge, beliefs, and behaviors. Individuals do not intuitively know the effects of drugs and alcohol or how to obtain and use drugs. The addiction lifestyle teaches and reinforces a complex set of behaviors, beliefs, knowledge, and skills.

The experience of addiction is influenced by many factors in an individual's life. These include their: physiology and inherited genes, gender identity, family experience and life experiences, level of poverty or affluence, cultural expectations, level of life skills, total community environment, and immediate personal surroundings. This book focuses on the positive and negative influences on lapse and relapse that are within an individual's control. It gives practical examples and information on how to make life changes that increase the probability of leaving addiction behind.

Why Do People Drink Or Take Drugs In The First Place?

Imagine walking into a bakery for the first time. What influences your behavior? The answer is more complex than you may think. The total environment, the sounds, sights, and smells are all saying, *try this*. Other people in the store are saying, *try this* through their behavior (they are buying) and their conversations about what they like best (verifying the food is good).

But what else influences you? Your own physical state, whether you are hungry or have just eaten a big meal; your personal goals, whether you are trying to lose or gain weight; your beliefs and knowledge about food; your financial state, whether you have enough money to buy something; all play a part in determining your decisions and behavior.

Personal decisions about drug and alcohol use are also influenced by many things. Individuals are influenced by the information they have about drugs and alcohol; what people tell them about the effects they will experience; and the setting in which they receive that information. In addition, their mental, emotional and physical state, their personal needs and goals, their family background and culture, and the ease of availability and affordability of drugs and alcohol; all play a part in decision making. **Your environment was filled with**

cues to use or not to use and you were probably not aware of many of them.

The most powerful influence in your life when it comes to choices about drugs and alcohol are people: the people that you believe in, the people who are your role models, the people who have power in your life, the people you spend time with, and the people you admire. These are the people whom you are most likely to believe, emulate, and copy. Peers and "heroes" influence us. Not only do peers provide information, they influence our moment to moment choices and have a high degree of power over us because we want to belong and have their approval. Peers exert pressure on our choices when we are young and in school and as adults in university and the workplace.

People with power influence us. If your boss wants you to go for a drink and you really want that promotion, what are you going to do? People who lack confidence in the security of their position or lack job options may go for a drink. They're being influenced by a force that they perceive as powerful -- their boss -- and by a personal goal that is important to them -- success at work. **Who we think is important and what we think is important (our goals) influence our choices about drugs and alcohol.**

A positive example of people in power who have influence over choices is physicians. They can exert a powerful influence on our decision to quit using because we see them as knowledgeable and able to help us heal our illnesses.

The positive reasons to try using alcohol or drugs are common across most individuals (Beck, Wright, Newman, & Liese, 1993). *Place a check mark beside any of the following positive reasons for drinking or using drugs that are the same as your reasons.*

☐ 1. To get pleasure and to share in the excitement and activity of using with other people. At first, drink or drug use is most often a shared experience and the goal is to have fun with others.

☐ 2. To improve how you feel. People take drugs to positively change how they feel; to help them feel happier, more energetic, sexier or more relaxed. They do not expect drugs to make them feel unhappy, confused, angry, uptight, sad and depressed. People are always positive that with using they will feel better.

☐ 3. To change your perceptions and physical sensations such as to reduce sensitivity to emotions and physical pain or to increase sensitivity to experiences of sound (music), sight (color) or touch and taste.

Chapter Two: Addiction and Learned Behaviors

☐ 4. To change how you perform or act such as to improve sexual performance, talk more confidently, and reduce inhibitions or to be more creative.

☐ 5. To relieve boredom, experience excitement or celebrate.

☐ 6. Your own unique positive reasons were:

_____

_____

_____

_____

It's important to spend some time thinking about and making your list of your positive reasons for drinking or using drugs. **There were some positive benefits or you would not have taken them.** Once you identify your positive reasons for using, as you go through this book, you will learn other ways to achieve those positive outcomes.

What Do People Learn When Using?

Once a person has started to use, the social experience reinforces using. Individuals who use become part of a unique group, just because they use. You became part of a special group, different from what you had experienced before. Through watching, listening, and participating, you learned what to expect and how to behave when using. Addiction is a social and group learning experience.

Get Real Motivation!

What are your reasons for quitting? Are they strong enough? Revisit page 18.

People learn from other users about the different routes and methods of taking drugs and alcohol and what to expect. If they drink alcohol they learn to expect relaxation. If they inject amphetamines they learn to expect hyperactivity. They also learn about bad experiences or negative side effects (such as nausea or paranoia) and how to reduce them. Individuals come to believe they are in total control of their use. They are confident they can continue to take drugs and alcohol, handle the bad effects, and easily stop using at any time in the future.

People rarely confine their use to only drinking or a single drug. Using two or three different drugs at the same time is a common practice. Alcohol and some combination of drugs including nicotine is the most common addiction experience for those who enter addiction treatment (Frances, Miller, Sheldon, & Mack, 2005).

People do not intuitively know where to get illicit drugs and the required drug paraphernalia such as pipes or syringes. They meet people who give them instructions, advice, and who act as teachers. They are taught where to buy drugs, what drugs to substitute when they can't get their drug of choice, and how to use other drugs to compensate for the bad effects of the alcohol or drugs already taken. Is this similar to your experience? Did somebody help you at each step along the way?

Don't Give Up!

It's hard work, but you can finish this book!

Accessing multiple drugs and using them for a positive emotional effect is complex. The negative side effects can be quite devastating for the novice user. Think about your personal experience. Who taught you and encouraged you to expand the variety of drugs that you used? The teachers are usually experienced users who are actively and regularly using. **People who are actively using are a high risk to people who don't use and to people who have quit using. People who use frequently also encourage and support the use of drugs and alcohol by others.** This is social pressure to use: when others offer, encourage and make available drugs and alcohol or when they discourage, ridicule or belittle those who choose not to use.

Take a moment and list all the drugs and types of alcohol you tried and put a check mark beside those that you have used regularly. Include nicotine if applicable.

Are you beginning to think that the use of drugs and alcohol

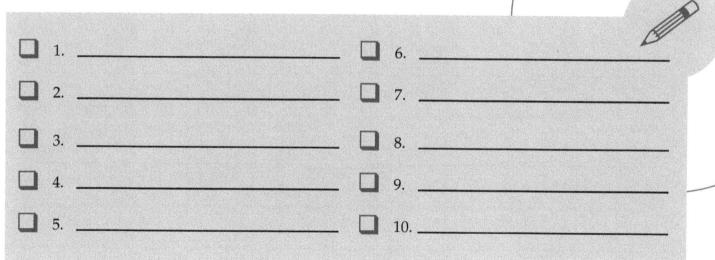

☐ 1. _____   ☐ 6. _____
☐ 2. _____   ☐ 7. _____
☐ 3. _____   ☐ 8. _____
☐ 4. _____   ☐ 9. _____
☐ 5. _____   ☐ 10. _____

required effort and learning on your part and help from other people? Addiction didn't just happen to you. Other people played a role and <u>you</u> made many small decisions and took many actions to get to where you are today. It took considerable effort and time to change your life to include addiction.

Most people who become addicted gradually gravitate to places

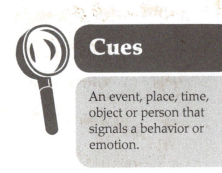

Cues

An event, place, time, object or person that signals a behavior or emotion.

where they can:

- Readily access drugs and alcohol
- Use without being seen or bothered by people who don't use or drink
- Buy, use, and feel relatively safe from police
- Be around people for whom using is the norm and their major purpose in life
- Replace work or school with a role in the drug economy as a drug seller or a drug producer.

In the end, the person addicted to drugs and alcohol behaves differently than non users in all spheres of their life. They express different values, and are part of a group that has a unique language, unique things to do, and shared experiences. They are part of a unique culture of sellers, producers and users. Drug and alcohol addiction becomes a total life experience. It surrounds, restricts, and negatively changes all aspects of your life. **The addiction lifestyle and environment constantly cues you to use and reinforces you to continue using!**

Take a moment and list all the people who taught you to use drugs and alcohol. Start with the people who first got you to try it, those who taught you along the way, and those who used with you and encouraged you to continue using. These are the people who pose a high risk to your continued abstinence.

1. _____
2. _____
3. _____
4. _____
5. _____
6. _____
7. _____
8. _____
9. _____
10. _____

Why Do People Continue To Use?

When individuals use, they find temporary relief from negative emotions such as anxiety, tension, anger, sadness or boredom. In addition they develop a belief that using drugs or alcohol helps them to reduce the frustrations and stressors in life. The primary reason to continue using is that people find relief (Beck et al., 1993).

For individuals with a difficult life, sometimes using drugs and alcohol actually makes life seem better. There are people who have extremely difficult lives. They experience poverty, violence, abuse, depression, anxiety, and a sense of not knowing who they are. At certain times and stages in life, such as adolescence, individuals feel the changes occurring in their lives are out of their control. When they take drugs and alcohol, they experience their difficult life as not so difficult. They feel more in control, more positive. With drug or alcohol use, they experience short periods of time when their life actually feels good.

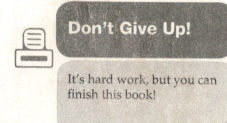

Don't Give Up!

It's hard work, but you can finish this book!

Using boosts confidence. Individuals with low self-confidence find taking drugs or alcohol boosts their self-esteem in the short-run. This is a very common reason for alcohol use. Why do some people want a drink when they go out socially? Many drink because alcohol eases things. It eases the tension, lowers inhibitions, and causes people to be less sensitive to their internal fears. They become more confident for a little while. As people with low self-confidence continue to use alcohol and drugs, it becomes a temporary solution to more and more difficult situations.

Using gives people admission to new social groups in which using is the only requirement to be a part of the group. If you want to be part of a social group that uses, you can go to bars, raves, clubs, lounges, pubs, parks, or any place where alcohol and multiple substances are used and sold. It's an easy way to get social acceptance.

Identify the reasons on the following list that kept you using and

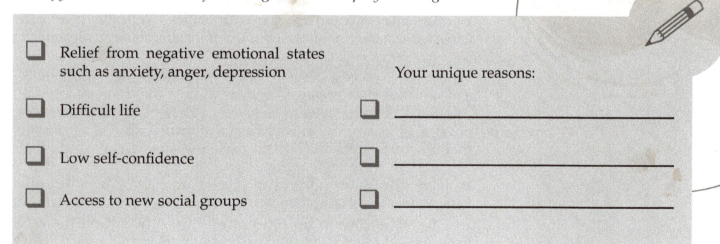

- ☐ Relief from negative emotional states such as anxiety, anger, depression
- ☐ Difficult life
- ☐ Low self-confidence
- ☐ Access to new social groups

Your unique reasons:
- ☐ _____
- ☐ _____
- ☐ _____

add your own unique reasons:

As you go through this book, you will learn positive solutions to meet the needs that alcohol and drugs met in your life.

Chapter Two: Addiction and Learned Behaviors

> **MYTH:**
> *A person with the experience of addiction lacks control over their own actions.*

> **Don't Give Up!**
> It's hard work, but you can finish this book!

Why Are People Afraid To Quit Using?

People fear quitting because they are told about the physical experience of withdrawal. Even before a person experiences total withdrawal, they have had periods of time when they couldn't get drugs or alcohol. As a result, they experienced cravings and felt very physically and emotionally ill. Their own personal experience taught them that quitting was not going to be a pleasant experience. The expected unpleasant experience of withdrawal is a big barrier to quitting. Media and movies exaggerate the experience of withdrawal and reinforce fearful expectations. In reality, withdrawal is not nearly as bad as the serious physical and mental illness that results from continuous heavy use of drugs and alcohol. People learn through personal experience that withdrawal is tolerable and safe if **you are under good medical care or if you go to a facility with knowledgeable staff.**

The second damaging and false belief is that people who become addicted to drugs and alcohol can never leave the drug and alcohol experience behind. Sadly this myth stops some people from making the decision to quit. It is used to convince themselves that they have a good reason for still using or for starting to use again after a short period of abstinence. It is the myth that you lack any control over your own actions.

Why Do People Eventually Decide To Quit Using?

Continued use for the person who is addicted to drugs and alcohol eventually overwhelms all parts of their life. With continued use, they lose personal goals and dreams. Their values and health deteriorate. Often relationships with the people who matter most are destroyed.

People who are addicted eventually feel constantly out of control and can no longer manage their own lives. The drink or the drug drives the very thoughts in their mind. They experience increasing physical illness as well as emotional and mental distress. Eventually they always feel sick.

Individuals who are addicted become burdened by huge financial costs, risk or loss of employment, loss of freedom if incarcerated, and loss of relationships with family or partners. There is often a great financial cost to the family and partner, as well as for the user. People who are addicted find themselves doing things they would never have done before their addiction, to get the money to continue using alcohol and drugs. Family and friends also feel more out of control as they find themselves doing things they would never have done before, as they try everything and anything to help the person who is addicted and to stop them from using.

In the last stages of addiction many individuals experience the stigma of being called a lush, a drunk or a loser. People with addiction always have a part of them that can't be numbed by drugs and alcohol. And they are hurt by harsh words and treatment. Eventually they may even feel self disdain or hatred. Stigma, combined with all the negative effects of using, finally causes them to stand up and say, "I've had enough."

Some individuals only decide to quit once they are experiencing life threatening medical problems and fear of imminent death. They have experienced multiple overdoses and have come very close to dying. They are in liver, kidney or heart failure. They have HIV (Human immunodeficiency virus) or HCV (hepatitis C virus). They carry the fear inside them that their life will end if they don't change. So they decide to quit.

You may be like most people and have decided to quit because you had lost large pieces of your life to drugs and alcohol. You may have felt more and more out of control, and had increasing emotional and mental distress. The enormous financial costs may have become unmanageable and the stigma of being an addict may have felt devastating (Beck et al., 1993).

These many problems can feel overwhelming and distract you from the work you need to do to prevent relapse. Now is the time to make a list of the definable problems you will face in the next three months. As you work through this book, you will have opportunities to develop solutions to some of these problems. It is important to make your list now so you can concentrate on learning the skills you need to carry out your relapse prevention plan.

Use the "Problem List Worksheet" at the end of this chapter and identify the most pressing problems you will face with relationships, work/school, home /community, physical/mental health and in communication. List them using simple concise language. Getting them onto paper helps you stop worrying about them. Listing the problems will help you to start focusing on the actions required to manage them. **Take time now to complete your "Problem List Worksheet."**

Get Real Motivation!

What are your reasons for quitting? Are they strong enough? Revisit page 18.

Your problem list may be a good motivator to stay clean. But it's not enough just to quit using. As you learned through previous attempts to quit, the single action of stopping use doesn't end the total life experience of addiction. If you don't want to relapse and start drinking or using again, you need to take positive action and change your life. You will need to learn new skills to make major life changes. Where do you start? This book will take you through the steps to create your own unique relapse prevention plan. You learned how to become an addict and now you will learn how to leave addiction behind.

Chapter Two: Addiction and Learned Behaviors

Addiction Changed How You Think

Dysfunctional

Ineffective, having negative results.

Remember, much of the addiction experience is learned. Eventually the person using learns from their personal experience that the continued use of drugs and alcohol is not worth the physical and mental illness and pain. It is not worth the total life destruction that is occurring. *Even more damaging to the individual trying to leave addiction behind is the fact that the experience of addiction results in the development and reinforcement of distorted thinking patterns and dishonest communication with self and others. The dysfunctional thinking patterns and inadequate communication styles put the individual at a high risk for continued use and relapse.*

The steps to sobriety sound deceptively simple. The individual recognizes there is a problem. The individual is supported by family and friends to attend detox. They stop using. Then the individual usually attends some form of ongoing counseling or rehab program. And, through these experiences, the successful individual learns the coping skills required to get on with their life and to prevent relapse.

In reality, there are many specific actions, small and large, that you will need to take to successfully change your life and prevent relapse. Also, changing the way you think and the way you behave will take time. The information in this book will help you to increase your knowledge, to take action and to change how you behave and even how you think. *Recovery is just the start of your life-long journey of continuously learning new coping skills to achieve your life goals.*

Don't Give Up!

It's hard work, but you can finish this book!

Abstinence Allows You Time To Learn

When you have a prolonged period of abstinence, you experience increased positive mental and physical health. Abstinence allows you to immediately increase your capacity to learn new skills, begin to positively manage problems, and to experience a reduction in new problems. As you continue reading this book, you will experience increased happiness, physical health, and emotional health as long as you do not use. This is true even if you do nothing else. **More importantly, the probability of not using and maintaining sobriety increases every time you learn a new coping skill, and each time you make the effort to apply that new skill in your daily life.**

Nobody wants their whole life to be *about not using*. You have other goals. You may want better relationships, peace of mind, a new house, or car. Maybe you just want to walk along the street and have people see you as a person who is happy and healthy. Whatever they are, you have goals beyond not using. **Abstinence is like breathing. Everyone has to breathe to live, but breathing isn't what you want to think about all the time nor is it a way to measure your success in life.** People concentrate on their breath when they have a respiratory problem. People count their success in days abstinent when they are leaving the problems of the addiction lifestyle behind. But you have to count more than days abstinent or your life will still be only about addiction and not about living. Eventually, if you use abstinence as your only goal, you will experience frustration, anger, depression, anxiety, and negative emotions that can lead to lapse or relapse. There has to be more.

The Power of Using Information To Prevent Relapse

Addiction can be ended by learning new life and coping skills to help you positively manage cues, cravings, negative emotions, interpersonal conflict, and social pressure to use. These skills can help you to develop a balanced lifestyle. To do this successfully you need quality information. Information based on best evidence is quality information. It is not hearsay, supposition or urban legend. You can use quality information to plan and take actions that will work for you. With quality information you can change your life. You can learn to make good decisions about what to believe, what not to believe, and what to do to prevent relapse. You can learn how to succeed in your life.

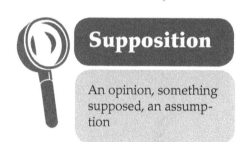

Supposition

An opinion, something supposed, an assumption

Choosing Information To Support Your New Learning

All addiction and mental health books and programs reflect the underlying beliefs of the author or program designers. Whether you're choosing self-help books on mental health and addiction, a rehabilitation program or a counselor, first find out what model of addiction treatment is being used. To make a good choice, you will want detailed information about the evidence, rationale, and principles underlying the program or resource. Knowing the general models used by addiction self help books and programs can help you to start asking good questions (BC Ministry of Health, 2004; Frances, Miller, Sheldon, & Mack, 2005).

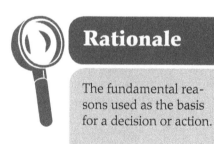

Rationale

The fundamental reasons used as the basis for a decision or action.

1. *Moral model:* This is the simplest model. Using is considered morally wrong. People are responsible for their behavior. Good behavior is praised and bad behavior is discouraged. Practicing a particular religious belief is often the major focus for cure or treatment.

2. *Disease Model:* Addiction is caused by genetic and biological factors. Addiction is considered to be a progressive disease and may require the individual to take medication to reduce the rate of relapse.

3. *Behavior Model:* Addiction has multiple components. Habit formation and habit change are primarily influenced by cognitive (thinking) and behavior principles. Cognitive behavior therapy or similar approaches are used to reduce relapse.

4. *Holistic Model:* This is the most complex and recent model developed. A complex set of factors cause relapse. Individuals have unique strengths and risks arising from gender, sexual orientation, age and cultural identity. Recognizing and working with individual differences and characteristics, the individual is taught skills to prevent and respond to individual problems in their life and to improve physical, mental, social and economic status.

In your recovery and all aspects of your life, you can improve your decision-making by becoming informed. Use this book as a starting point to guide your risk reduction and relapse prevention planning. Constantly search for quality information to support you to move ahead in your life and to live your values.

There are many studies on addiction causes and treatments and some present conflicting conclusions. It is up to you to determine which studies and information you will use to guide your actions. Some studies may reveal that the odds are against a person with your personal history and substance use pattern, in succeeding in abstinence. **Always remember, no study can accurately predict a negative outcome for a specific individual, such as you.**

Always use quality information to reduce your risk of using again. Never use it as an excuse not to try to succeed in achieving your goals. Use information to help you end your experience with addiction. No matter what type of addiction treatment you choose, you can increase its effectiveness by creating your own unique relapse prevention program based on continuous learning, challenging your old ideas about addiction, and taking concrete action to create a positive lifestyle.

Reference For Chapter Two

Beck, Aaron T., Wright, Fred D., Newman, Cory F. & Liese, Bruce S. (1993). *Cognitive Therapy of Substance Abuse.* New York. The Guilford Press. 22-23.

BC Ministry of Health. (2004). *Every Door Is The Right Door, A British Columbia Planning Framework to Address Problematic Substance Use and Addic*tion. 71-75.

Frances, Richard J., Miller, Sheldon I. & Mack, Avram H. (Eds.). (2005). *Clinical Textbook of Addictive Disorders* (3rd edition). New York. The Guilford Press.13-14, 21-32, 259-251.

Marlatt, G.A., & Gordon, J.R. (Eds.). (1985). *Relapse prevention: Maintenance Strategies in the Treatment of Addictive Behaviours* (1st edition). New York. Guilford Press. 39.

Marlatt, G.A., & Gordon, J.R., (Eds.). (2005). *Relapse Prevention: Maintenance Strategies in the Treatment of Addictive Behaviours* (2nd edition). New York. The Guilford Press. 8-21.

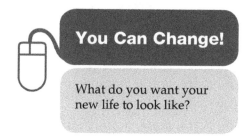

You Can Change!

What do you want your new life to look like?

Chapter Two: Problem List Worksheet

Problem List Worksheet

For each of the following areas write out the clearly definable problems that you will face within the next 3 months, i.e. the ones you can define easily and know the cause(s).

Relationships: such as girlfriend is pregnant, friend wants money back

- _____
- _____
- _____
- _____
- _____
- _____
- _____

Work/school: such as on probation at work, failed grade twelve

- _____
- _____
- _____
- _____
- _____
- _____

Home/community: such as have no place to live, evicted and have no references

- _____
- _____
- _____
- _____

Problem List Worksheet

- _____
- _____
- _____

Physical health/Mental health: such as depression, anger problems, decayed teeth

- _____
- _____
- _____
- _____
- _____
- _____
- _____

Communication: such as can't take negative feedback, use blaming and hidden agendas, have a reputation for lying

- _____
- _____
- _____
- _____
- _____
- _____
- _____

Other:

- _____
- _____

You can succeed and make your last relapse the last!

Chapter Two: Addiction and Learned Behaviors

Chapter Three

Getting The Basics Right

Chapter 3

Getting The Basics Right

Often on the road to recovery and health, people become overwhelmed. They don't know what to do first. They may believe there are too many complex things to be done, medications to take or professionals to see. Do not be discouraged. There are some simple things you can do to help keep yourself on the road to recovery and feeling better. You can reduce worry and anxiety by getting answers to basic questions.

Since I've quit using, why do I feel so badly? After going through detox and withdrawal, you may feel confused because you still feel anxious, lost, out of control or even depressed. You may have insomnia or emotional and physical symptoms. You are craving drugs and alcohol. You are worried. There is a strong temptation to return to using because you think if you use you may just feel better.

It's important to keep in mind that the drugs you took were toxic to your mind and body. Alcohol is a poison. Drugs when abused are toxic to your body. The damage caused by months or years of use takes time to heal. The longer you used and the more different kinds of drugs you used, the longer it will take for your body to heal and return to full normal functioning. Drugs and alcohol changed how you felt by physically altering the chemistry in your brain. Depending on the route you used to take the drug and the side effects of the drug, there was also damage to you physically. Your brain, lungs, nose, veins, skin, heart, and digestive organs may each have been affected. Just like a broken bone, the damage done by drugs and alcohol takes time to heal.

> **Since I've quit using, why do I feel so badly?**

During this time of healing, you may be under a lot of stress. You now experience the stress of coping every day without using drugs and alcohol. If you are attending a rehabilitation program or counseling, you have emotional, mental, and even physical fatigue from learning new things as you work on yourself. Change is stressful, even if you are moving toward success. It's hard work getting up every day and working to change your life. And to make it even more challenging, during the first few weeks and months, you may experience some disturbing symptoms (Ketcham, & Pace, 2003).

1. *Foggy thinking, difficulty concentrating, and some memory problems may occur:* Drugs or alcohol disrupted the normal balances of chemicals made by your brain that are essential to healthy brain functioning. A return to normal balances takes time.

2. *Difficulty learning new things:* The more drugs you have used, the more likely you will experience some short term memory

loss. Here's the good news: for most people, short term memory is restored. The more drugs you have used, the longer you used, the longer it may take to recover. For most people short term memory returns in six to eight weeks. Short term memory loss means you may not be able to learn new skills easily. It does not mean you are incapable of learning new skills. However, you may not remember all the details as easily as you once did. Give yourself extra time to learn.

3. *Over sensitivity:* You may find yourself reacting strongly to things you never would have blinked an eye at before. When a little thing happens such as your zipper won't go up on your jacket, you find yourself filled with rage. This is a side effect resulting from the damage the drugs have done in your brain. As you are going through these ups and downs, you may even find yourself on the verge of tears. Then suddenly you will feel okay. This is also a normal part of recovery and will end with time and abstinence.

Don't Give Up!

It's hard work, but you can finish this book!

4. *Sleep problems:* Lack of sleep is often a big issue for people who have come through withdrawal and are in recovery. Erratic sleep patterns are one of the side effects of the drugs you have taken and of the erratic lifestyle you led when drinking or using. During recovery you may experience disturbing dreams and the inability to fall asleep. When you do fall asleep, you may wake up frequently throughout the night, and be unable to relax. Again, these are the result of damage caused by the drugs, and the lifestyle of addiction. You can learn ways to reduce your sleep problems.

5. *Physical coordination problems:* You may experience difficulty with hand and eye coordination and balance. Your reflexes may be slower. Be a little more careful during the early weeks of recovery because coordination *could* be a problem particularly if you used alcohol heavily.

All these symptoms may make you believe you are not making progress. In reality your body is going through physical changes to adjust to the lack of a high level of toxic chemicals in your body. Knowing that you are experiencing a normal recovery process can reduce anxiety.

Impact of Using Drugs And Alcohol On Negative Emotions

Remember, a lapse is a single use after a period of sobriety. A relapse is a full return to a pattern of repeated use. A lapse does not always result in a return to previous levels of use and can be a learning experience to reduce the probability of another lapse. There is evidence that a lapse or relapse is commonly preceded by the individual experiencing negative emotions.

Based on interviews with people who have experienced addiction, when they chose to use again, it was most often because they were experiencing negative emotions. They felt increasing anger, frustration, depression and/or anxiety. They used drugs or alcohol in response to these unpleasant and negative emotional states (Marlatt & Gordon, 1985, 2005). Even though you have stopped drinking or using, you will still at times experience negative emotions. You can develop a different solution to anger, frustration, depression or anxiety than returning to use. You have the opportunity to learn positive coping skills to manage your negative emotions.

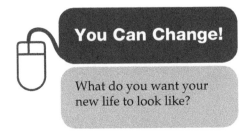

You Can Change!

What do you want your new life to look like?

Where Do Negative Emotions Come From?

Negative emotions do not just arise within you. Your individual world is made up of a series of events. Some of them are positive, some of them are negative and some of them have nothing to do with you, even though you may think they do. You interpret these events through a series of thoughts and an internal dialogue (Burns, *The Feeling Good Handbook*, 1999).

You may look at an event and think, "*Aha, I know what this means.*" Then you talk to yourself inside your head. And, depending on what you say to yourself, your mood changes based on your interpretation of that event and the emotions that came from that interpretation. You may think, "*Oh-oh, this is going to be bad. It's real bad.*" Based on your interpretation, you start to feel sad or angry and experience what is called a negative emotional state. These emotions are often the cue for an addicted person to use alcohol or drugs to feel better or to try to feel nothing.

You may think, "*Wow, this is great that this happened.*" Then you feel happiness and you experience what is called a positive emotional state. <u>Feelings are always created by thoughts.</u> First you experience the event, then the thoughts or interpretation of the event, and finally the positive or negative feelings. Your emotions come entirely from the way you look at or interpret things.

Before you can experience any event, you have to process it and assign some meaning (Burns, *The Feeling Good Handbook*, 1999). For example, you get a job interview. Immediately a series of thoughts run through your mind interpreting the event of being called for an interview. "I'm probably the last on the list," or "They just need to make it look good for someone they have already decided to hire." Negative thoughts or interpretations will lead to negative emotional states such as anger, depression, resentment or anxiety. Your interpretation of the event has changed how you feel and how you will behave when you go to the interview. Your emotions and subsequent behaviors are driven by your *interpretation* of the events in your life (Burns, *The Feeling Good Handbook*, 1999).

Moods do not arrive independently of our interpretation of the events in our lives (Burns, Feeling Good, The New Mood Therapy, 1999). The wonderful thing is, just by recognizing this fact you can take action to become more aware of your thoughts. You can learn the skills to reduce the frequency of negative emotions and to manage your negative emotions without resorting to drinking or using.

Stopping Automatic And Dysfunctional Thinking

Start changing the way you feel by learning practical and straightforward techniques called "cognitive behavior therapy." You can learn to change the way you think, the way you feel, and how you behave. To begin developing your knowledge of cognitive therapy, a recommended book to read is, *"The Feeling Good Handbook," by Dr. David D. Burns.* This book can help you to learn to manage the most common negative emotions experienced during withdrawal and recovery. These include depression, anxiety, frustration, and anger.

For people who have experienced addiction, it is essential that they learn to recognize the automatic self-defeating negative thoughts that make them feel miserable. Negative thoughts lead to painful emotions. These painful emotions in turn convince them that their thoughts are valid. People actually trick themselves. When we have a negative emotion about an event, we experience an internal feeling of unhappiness. The feeling of unhappiness reinforces our belief that all our negative feelings must be accurate interpretations of the events in our lives (Burns, *The Feeling Good Handbook*, 1999).

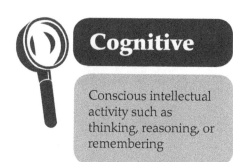

Cognitive

Conscious intellectual activity such as thinking, reasoning, or remembering

If we believe all our negative thoughts, we behave like a hamster on a tread wheel. We don't just stop at labeling one event as negative. Because we're feeling sad and depressed, every event starts to look negative. We have our sad lens on, and we start looking for other things that are going wrong. Feeling badly leads to even more negative interpretations which lead to more negative thoughts and more negative emotions (Burns, *The Feeling Good Handbook*, 1999). Now you're on the path that spirals down into lapse or relapse.

"Cognitive approaches" are new thinking techniques to help stop the negative spiral. You can begin with learning the techniques yourself and then you can get professional support and training for new thinking skills if you decide you need the extra help. Cognitive therapy teaches you how to think more rationally and to stop the unhelpful treadmill of negative and distorted thoughts. Distorted thinking often sounds like this.

- I'm no good at any thing so I might as well use.
- Everyone relapses and I'm no different.
- One more drink will make me feel even better.

- I have the right to be sad and angry.
- I can't enjoy myself without using.

Alcohol and drugs are often used as a solution to negative emotions that arise from dysfunctional or distorted thinking. Begin reading "The Feeling Good Handbook," by Dr. David Burns to start the work required to increase your rational thinking skills and reduce negative thinking.

Impact Of Drugs And Alcohol On Your Mental Health

When you put drugs or alcohol into your body, by whatever means, they eventually entered your bloodstream. They entered your brain and affected how you felt. That's why you took the drug. The reason why most drugs work is that they imitate the naturally occurring substances that the brain produces. These natural substances produce the feelings of well-being, relaxation, pleasure, excitement, pain or a state of alertness or drowsiness. For example, heroin works on the brain receptor sites that alter the sensation of pain. Amphetamines and cocaine cause the brain to release dopamine. Dopamine is the brain chemical that produces the sensation of pleasure. So basically, drugs and alcohol mimic certain chemicals in your brain (Frances, & First, 1998).

Don't Give Up!

It's hard work, but you can finish this book!

Drugs and alcohol affect your brain; they not only cause positive feelings, but often mimic the symptoms of psychiatric illnesses. Depression, mania, anxiety, delusions, and hallucinations can be triggered by intoxication *or* withdrawal from the drugs or alcohol. Severe depression following long-term cocaine use resembles major depressive disorder. The effects of amphetamines can mimic mania. The side effects of withdrawal from benzodiazepines can look and feel exactly like a panic disorder. It is important to remember that psychological and behavioral problems are caused directly by the effects of drugs and alcohol on your brain chemistry (Frances, & First, 1998).

Whenever a psychiatric problem occurs during intoxication or within a month of withdrawal, it is probably due to the side effects of the drug. Each class of drugs can result in mental health problems. If you have quit using *and* your depression gradually lifts, that depression was likely a side effect of the drug. If it does not lift, then you need to contact your physician to assess your depression (Frances, & First, 1998).

The evidence about drugs, alcohol, and their effect on mental health provides you with a good reason to stay sober and a great reason to learn relapse prevention coping skills.

1. *Drugs add up.* Using more than one drug increases the probability that you will experience a serious mental health problem. The more you take, the worse it gets.

2. *Time makes a difference.* The longer you use, the greater the probability you will experience mental health problems.

3. *Drugs worsen existing mental health problems.* If you already have depression, anxiety or other mental health problems using drugs or alcohol *will* make them worse.

4. *Addiction always goes hand-in-hand with mental health problems* (Jiwani, & Somers, 2004). Those who experience addiction are also more likely to have a mental health problem. People who have mental health problems are more likely to develop an addiction if they haven't developed coping skills.

5. *Depression and anxiety are the most frequently triggered mental health problems when using drugs and alcohol.* Using substances can trigger or worsen anxiety or depression. Depression and anxiety are associated *with* the use of drugs and alcohol. Withdrawal from drugs and alcohol often has a side effect of depression and anxiety.

Depression, anxiety, and drug and alcohol use can all result in negative thoughts and feelings. They lead to avoidance behaviors and isolation because you don't feel like being with other people. They can strain personal relationships and the coping skills you do have. To make it worse, it's often difficult for others to be around people who have untreated and unmanaged addiction, depression and anxiety, so people may avoid you (Frances, & First, 1998).

If you have had an addiction experience, it makes *good* sense to evaluate your mental health and pay particular attention to depression and anxiety. Becoming knowledgeable about mental health, and seeking timely professional help if you are troubled by mental health problems also makes good sense. It reduces the likelihood of relapse. *Take time now to list the mental health problems you experienced before and while using drugs or alcohol.*

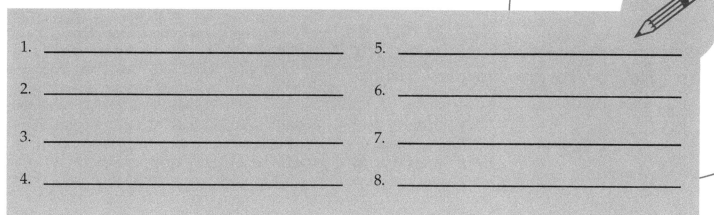

1. _____   5. _____

2. _____   6. _____

3. _____   7. _____

4. _____   8. _____

If you are experiencing troubling mental health problems, take time right now and add them to your "Problem List Worksheet," located at the end of Chapter One.

Chapter 3: Getting The Basics Right

Impact Of Taking Drugs and Alcohol On Physical Health

Taking drugs and alcohol negatively impacts your physical health. Except for alcohol and cocaine, the addiction lifestyle causes **more** physical health damage than the actual drugs.

Alcohol: Alcohol is the most damaging drug and the most toxic. Alcohol contributes to the majority of highway accidents, accidents at home, and violence-related injury. It is truly the most dangerous drug for families. Heavy alcohol consumption and resulting poor diet harms the entire body. The liver is progressively damaged (cirrhosis) and may lead to liver failure and death. Alcohol damages the brain and nervous system resulting in poor memory, poor problem solving skills, confusion, dementia, loss of balance, impotence, numbness of the feet and hands, tremor, and blindness. Alcohol also plays a role in many other diseases such as heart disease, high blood pressure, stroke, and diabetes. Alcohol is clearly harmful in developing pregnancies and damages the unborn child leading to a life time of problems (Goodwin, 2000; NIDA Info Facts: Science-Based Facts on Drug Abuse and Addiction).

Cocaine: **Co**caine constricts the blood vessels and raises blood pressure. It can lead to heart problems including stroke and sudden death. The extent of nasal inhalation can destroy the cartilage in the nose causing huge holes in the nasal passage (NIDA Info Facts: Science-Based Facts on Drug Abuse and Addiction).

Heroin: Heroin is a good example of a drug where much of the damage arises from the addiction lifestyle. Street heroin is cut with harmful substances and injecting heroin can result in extensive brain damage. Serious infectious diseases result from dirty equipment or sharing injecting equipment and include HIV (Human immunodeficiency virus) and Hepatitis C. Sexually transmitted diseases from unsafe sex practices, head injuries, and general infections can also result from the lifestyle. Long-term use leads to extensive tooth decay and gum disease (Rosenstein, 1975). Heroin use reduces the body's ability to produce its own natural painkillers. When heroin use stops, the sensitivity to pain increases. Heroin destroys appetite, disrupts the menstrual cycle, weakens the immune system and reduces the ability to fight off infection (Simpson, 1997).

Amazingly, Normal Functions Will Return As You Do These Four Simple Things

Information about drugs that are commonly abused is readily available through quality web sites such as those maintained by the National Institute on Drug Abuse (USA) found at http://www.nida.nih.gov/. It is well worth your time to research the specific drugs you have used and to become knowledgeable about their short and long term effects, withdrawal symptoms, and treatment so you can make concrete plans to improve your physical health.

The addiction lifestyle: Results in increased stress, lack of quality, regular sleep, poor nutrition, and irregular or no exercise. This leads to the increased risk of dying prematurely, dying from heart disease, developing diabetes, high blood pressure, colon cancer, depression and anxiety, and obesity (NIDA Info Facts: Science-Based Facts on Drug Abuse and Addiction). These risks are all good reasons for you to refuse to return to the addiction lifestyle and to focus on developing your relapse prevention plan.

Take time now and list all the physical health problems you have experienced as a result of using and drinking. Think carefully about the health problems that have resulted from your addiction lifestyle (e.g. sexually transmitted diseases, weight loss or weight gain) and add those to your list.

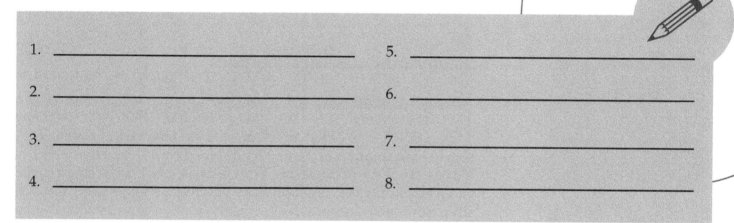

1. _____
2. _____
3. _____
4. _____
5. _____
6. _____
7. _____
8. _____

If you are currently experiencing physical health problems that you need to address add them to your "Problem List Worksheet" at the end of Chapter One.

Working On Your Mind And Body To Get Healthy

The major problems experienced in early recovery are the result of changes to the chemical balance in your brain now that you have stopped using. Alcohol and other drugs disrupted the normal production and actions of the "feel good" brain chemicals. These imbalances cause anxiety, irritability, depression, sleep disturbances, and cravings for drugs and alcohol. Poor nutrition and lack of exercise have left your body in poor shape to function normally.

Amazingly, normal functions will return as you do these four simple things:

1. Sleep well
2. Eat well and take a quality vitamin pill daily

3. Exercise vigorously every day
4. Use daily relaxation techniques.

Your brain will recover its capability to make the needed chemicals. Simply by not using over a period of time, your symptoms will decrease as the period of abstinence continues. If you learn and use coping mechanisms, your reduction of negative symptoms will be even faster. Some symptoms will persist longer than others depending on the intensity and duration of your past drug and alcohol use.

You **can learn** how to manage symptoms while they are with you and to live a lifestyle that supports your body to continue healing. Feeling better physically and emotionally will take time. How much time depends on how you much work you do to help your body heal. Your body will heal faster and your mind will respond more reliably with quality rest, regular exercise, and good nutrition.

Sleep And Relapse Prevention

Sleep is a natural state and must occur daily. It is as natural and essential as eating. It is a response to fatigue. While you sleep, the body tissue, brain, blood and skin cells are renewed. Infections are fought. The immune system — white blood cells — are strengthened. No one can live without sleep. Most people sleep an average of seven and a half hours per day. You may require more or less. How much sleep you need depends on your genetics and your health. While recovering from illness and addiction, you may require more sleep.

Too little sleep causes a lack of concentration, poor judgment, and a decrease in your decision making skills. You can become increasingly irritable, have memory loss, depression, and experience stress. Research also shows that too much sleep can cause similar effects as too little sleep. They include irritability, lack of concentration, and poor judgement (Lavery, 1997).

Be persistent in keeping to your sleep routines.

When you were taking drugs, you ended up losing sleep and the negative effects of both sleep loss and drug taking were compounded. *Now*, it's time to reverse those effects. What you need is balance, not too little and not too much sleep. Depending on the type and degree of your addiction, your patterns of waking and sleeping may have been severely disrupted. You may be more susceptible to illness. You may feel exhausted in your mind and body. Your will power and self control may be weak. Lack of sleep may have negatively impacted your daily patterns such as work, eating, exercise, and interacting with others. Your recovery is jeopardized *until* you develop a healthy sleep pattern.

During recovery the common sleep problems are: increased time to fall asleep, frequent waking up, difficulty getting to sleep, poor overall sleep quality, and sleep deprivation or not enough sleep (Gordis, 1998).

For everyone, certain things make it harder to get quality sleep such as (Lavery, 1997):

- Lack of daily physical exercise.
- Lack of mental activity.
- Lack of motivation and fulfillment in your life.
- Anxiety and depression.
- Using alcohol or drugs.
- Snoring.
- Noise, temperature changes and light exposure.

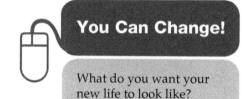

You Can Change!

What do you want your new life to look like?

Here are a few simple ways to begin to improve your sleep (Lavery, 1997):

1. *Establish a regular time to get to sleep and to get up.* Regularity is very important to getting your body back in synch with its rhythm. Get up and go to bed early. Going to bed or getting up late interferes with your body's natural rhythm and you won't be able to get enough sleep.

2. *Eat a balanced diet.* Have breakfast, lunch, and dinner. Eat lightly or not at all before bedtime and avoid alcohol and drugs.

3. *Be physically active* during the day. Quality exercise and quality sleep go hand in hand.

4. *Make the area where you sleep restful.* Ensure it is quiet, able to be kept dark when you are sleeping, well aired, and at a comfortable temperature. Keep your room neat and clean with a comfortable bed and clean bedding.

5. *Create relaxing bedtime rituals.* Listen to calming music, take a warm bath or meditate.

Sleep patterns can be disrupted during immediate recovery for some people and may last up to two years. If you have sleep problems, use the above suggestions, get additional tips on the internet, read some books on sleep, and be persistent in keeping to your sleep routines.

Food And Relapse Prevention

Most people who have been addicted to alcohol or drugs suffer some degree of malnourishment. You can be underweight or overweight. As a result, your body does not have the materials required for normal repair, growth, and functioning of your body and mind. For your body to repair itself you need a balanced diet of nutritious foods. The temptation to eat sugary foods and high caffeine drinks to stave off cravings leads to more problems.

The importance of eating three regular balanced meals and a healthy snack in the morning, afternoon, and evening cannot be over emphasized. Avoiding high sugar foods and replacing them with healthy fruit or other carbohydrates will help to keep your blood sugar from suddenly spiking and dropping.

Eating irregularly and eating foods high in sugar results in mood swings that mimic the mood swings that occurred when you were using drugs. The brain depends on glucose for its energy. When blood glucose drops abruptly, the brain signals distress by symptoms such as mental confusion, headaches, irritability, nervousness, depression, and an intense craving for alcohol or high sugar foods. If you eat foods with high sugar content, the blood sugar rises quickly. It will temporarily relieve those symptoms of low blood sugar. But what goes up must come down and the symptoms return (Ketcham, & Pace, 2003).

> **Don't Give Up!**
>
> It's hard work, but you can finish this book!

If you rely on sweets and other high sugar foods during recovery to reduce your craving for alcohol and drugs, you will actually create *greater* cravings. When your blood sugar drops, you may experience nervousness, insomnia, panic, fear, nausea, mental confusion, irritability, depression *and* your old friend: craving for more alcohol and drugs.

The solution is to eat well and eat regularly throughout the day.

Exercise And Relapse Prevention

Exercise is any activity performed to develop or maintain your physical fitness. It's worth doing because it's fun and a way to be with friends, to challenge yourself, and to learn new things. It's worth doing because people who engage in regular exercise are less likely to relapse and more likely to succeed at their goals. Start a regular exercise routine and improve:

- Your physical health and your energy level.
- Your body's ability to fight disease.
- Your personal appearance, physical strength, and sexual energy.
- Your emotional health, self-esteem, confidence, and overall mental health.

- Your attitude toward yourself and to others around you.
- Your ability to control your moods and manage anxiety and depression (National Center For Chronic Disease Prevention and Health Promotion, 1996).

In fact, you will just plain feel better. Exercise will provide a distraction from the things that cause you to feel angry, anxious or depressed. It will give you the opportunity to increase your social activity with others in a healthy way that does **not** involve alcohol or drug use.

One final important point: **exercise helps reduce relapse**. Exercise reduces stress. Exercising itself is incompatible with active drug use or alcohol use. Exercise enthusiasts choose not to waste their time or money on things that stop them from succeeding. Begin your exercise plan today and get moving. Keep it simple at first; it doesn't have to be expensive to get you moving. It will keep you on the road of relapse prevention and on your way to becoming your own champion. Go to the end of Chapter 5, and add at least one activity to your "Exercise, Recreation and Social Activities Plan."

Exercise helps reduce relapse!!

Summary

So start with the basics:

1. Evaluate your mental health. When in doubt, get professional help.
2. Eat well and take a quality vitamin pill daily.
3. Sleep well.
4. Exercise vigorously every day.
5. Use daily relaxation techniques.
6. Learn and practice cognitive techniques to change negative thinking and feeling.

While you are taking care of the basics there is more to learn to build your relapse prevention plan. The following chapters will help guide you on your way.

• •

References

Burns, David D. (1999). *Feeling Good, The New Mood Therapy* (revised). New York. Harper Collins Publishers. 29-30, 87,121.

Burns, David D. (1999). *The Feeling Good Handbook.* New York. Plume, Penguin Group. 3-11.

Frances, Allen & First, Michael B. (1998). *Your Mental Health, A Layman's Guide to the Psychiatrist's Bible.* New York. Scribner. 119.

Goodwin, Donald W. (2000). *Alcoholism, the facts.* Oxford. Oxford University Press.

Gordis, Enoch. (1998). *Alcohol And Sleep – Alcohol Alert #41, Alcohol and Sleep – A Commentary.* Retrieved from http//www.niaaa.nih.gov/publications

Jiwani, Gulrose & Somers, Julian. (Winter 2004) Concurrent Disorders, Considerations for Evidence Based Policy. *Visions: BC's Mental Health and Addictions Journal, Concurrent Disorders,* Vol. 2 No.1. 10.

Ketcham, Katherine & Pace, Nicholas A. (2003). *Teens Under The Influence, The Truth About Kids, Alcohol, and Other Drugs-How to Recognize the Problem and What to Do About It.* New York. Ballentine Books. 304-309.

Lavery, Sheila. (1997). *The Healing Power of Sleep, How to Achieve Restorative Sleep Naturally.* New York. Simon & Schuster Inc. 16-17, 34, 37, 94-125.

Marlatt, G.A., & Gordon, J.R. (Eds.). (1985). *Relapse prevention: Maintenance strategies in the treatment of addictive behaviours* (1st edition). New York. Guilford Press. 39.

Marlatt, G.A., & Gordon, J.R., (Eds.). (2005). *Relapse Prevention: Maintenance Strategies in the Treatment of Addictive Behaviours* (2nd edition). New York. The Guilford Press. 8-21.

National Center For Chronic Disease Prevention and Health Promotion. (1996). *Physical Activity and Health, A Report of the Surgeon General.* Chapter 4. Retrieved from http://www.surgeongeneral.gov/library/reports.htm

NIDA InfoFacts: Science-Based Facts on Drug Abuse and Addiction. Retrieved from http://www.nida.nih.gov/Infofacts/Infofaxindex.html

Rosenstein, D.I. (Spring 1975) Effect of long-term addiction to heroin on oral tissues. *J Public Health Dent.* 35(2). 118-22.

Simpson, Carolyn. (1997). *Methadone.* The Drug Abuse Prevention Library. New York. The Rosen Publishing Group, Inc. 20-23.

Chapter Four

Managing Cues

You can succeed and make your last relapse the last!

Chapter 4

Managing Cues

You have read about what happens to your body and mind as a result of addiction and some simple ways to begin immediately to improve your health. This chapter will provide strategies to reduce craving, manage cues, and provide you with some specific ways to prevent lapse and relapse.

Based on relapse prevention research, it has been found that relapse is not generally triggered by physical cravings for drugs, alcohol and cigarettes. So what determines when people relapse? A determinant is a factor that causes or influences something. A determinant of relapse can be something that's inside or outside of you (Marlatt, & Donovan, 2005). A determinant can be a skill that you possess or lack. It can be the experience of an emotion such as anger. For example, an angry person has poorer recall of a disagreement than a calmer person. Anger can be called a determinant of memory. A depressed person experiences reduced motivation to exercise. Depression can be called a determinant of motivation. An anxious person worries about social interactions and avoids meeting people. They become lonely or isolated. Anxiety, therefore, can be a determinant of social interactions.

Relapse Determinant

A factor that causes or influences relapse, can be inside or outside self, a skill or lack of a skill, or an emotion.

The determinants that are inside you can be strengthened to reduce risk of relapse. Self-confidence is one example. People who leave addiction behind have an awareness and belief in their ability to manage high-risk situations for using. Self-confidence is more than a display of courage. It is having the coping skills required to succeed. Other examples of internal determinants are (Marlatt, & Donovan, 2005):

- Your <u>expectations</u> of using or not using. If you expect to use, you will. If you expect not to use, you won't.

- Your level of <u>motivation</u> to maintain abstinence and achieve goals. Increased motivation leads to decreased risk of relapse.

Don't Give Up!

It's hard work, but you can finish this book!

- <u>Coping skills</u> such as problem-solving and conflict resolution. These basic skills help you manage your life and reduce risk of relapse.

- <u>Skills to manage negative emotions</u> such as anger, sadness or anxiety are very important. If these emotions are not recognized and positively managed, they can lead to relapse.

- <u>Craving recognition and coping skills</u>. Craving is the experience or desire for the effects of drugs or alcohol *and if unrecognized and not managed* will lead to relapse.

In summary, the internal determinants that influence whether you will maintain abstinence include (Marlatt, & Donovan, 2005):

- Your level of self-confidence in managing high risk situations and life problems.
- Your expectations of using or not using.
- Your level of motivation.
- Your coping skills.
- Your experience of negative emotions such as anxiety, anger, and depression.
- Your management of craving.

These determinants of lapse and relapse can be positively influenced once you learn to recognize them and take action to develop the required coping skills.

> **You Have the Power to Change**
>
> Whether you think you can, or think you can't, you're right. Henry Ford

High-Risk Situations For Relapse

When are you most at risk for relapse? Research shows that high-risk situations are those activities and places that have *many cues to use drugs or alcohol*. High-risk situations are always individual, that is specific to you, and should be avoided. If they cannot be avoided, then you must learn to cope with them. What is high-risk for you may not be high risk for another person (Marlatt, & Donovan, 2005).

The first step is to recognize when you are in or close to a risky situation. It is important to learn to pay attention to the situations you find yourself in and practice being aware of changes in your thoughts and feelings. This will help you detect warning signs as soon as possible (Marlatt, & Donovan, 2005). Take ten minutes now and identify three high-risk situations for yourself. These are situations where there are cues for drinking and drug using as well as social pressure for drinking and using drugs. Consider social occasions such as watching the playoffs on TV with a group of friends or entering a local bar near your home or a particular time you frequently argue with your partner. It may help to think back to your last relapse and picture the situation just before you decided to use again. *List and describe your high risk situations below:*

1. _____   4. _____

2. _____   5. _____

3. _____   6. _____

Cue

A stimulus that signals you to carry out a particular behavior. Leads to cravings.

Craving

A strong desire for something.

High-Risk Situations Must Be Avoided

Lack of coping skills, low self-confidence, and limited knowledge puts you at risk of using again when you are faced with any of your high-risk situations. *Avoidance is always the best choice in the early stages of recovery.* Avoidance will keep you safe while you learn a variety of ways and skills to manage high risk situations. Avoidance of high risk situations is the first and simplest coping mechanism. Stay away from all drugs and alcohol, stay away from people who use, and avoid places where people use. You must take these actions now while you learn additional ways to keep yourself safe.

Cues: What Are They And How to Manage Them

A cue is a stimulus that signals you to carry out a particular behavior. For example, the smells from a restaurant can trigger the feeling of hunger and signal you to get something to eat. A sudden loud noise can cue you to seek safety and as a result you may duck your head. Smells, sights, sounds, things, and places can all be cues that signal you to drink or use. Remember, addiction is based on learning to react in specific ways to specific cues. Your cues to drink or use drugs can be identified and managed to change or extinguish your response to the cues. This means *you can stop* yourself from responding automatically to a specific set of cues.

Cues can lead to craving. Craving is a strong desire for something. Craving is commonly used to describe the feeling experienced prior to drinking or taking a drug and prior to beginning to look for a drink or a drug. Craving can be made more powerful by your thoughts, surroundings or a particular event. Your craving for a cigarette will be felt more strongly when you enter the bar where you always smoked; and less strongly or not at all, when you enter the kitchen of a friend who never allowed you to smoke in their house.

Addiction is based on learning to react in specific ways to specific cues.

Lower Your Response To Cues And Reduce Cravings By Making A Commitment

Research shows the expectation of drug-taking increases craving. Clients in treatment or about to enter treatment experience less intense craving because they do not expect to be taking drugs or alcohol. If you expect not to use and plan not to use, you will decrease your reactivity (reacting spontaneously) to cues and decrease the intensity of the cravings (Wilson, Sayette, & Fiez, 2004). *This means that committing not to use and expecting not to use can result in lowered response to your cues and less intense cravings when they do occur.* That is why you were asked to write your commitment statement as your first action in creating your relapse prevention plan. If you haven't done this yet, now is the time. Go back to Chapter One Introduction To Relapse Prevention and complete your "Commitment to Continued Positive Change in My Life."

The first step to reducing your cravings and sensitivity to your cues is deciding you aren't going to use. Making the commitment not to use and creating a cue reduced, drug and alcohol free environment is the key to relapse prevention. The more you expect not to use, the less you will crave and the less responsive you will be to unexpected cues. You won't allow yourself to relapse in large part because you will have *planned* not to use and you *expect not* to use. You are more confident because you have a plan and expect to succeed.

> **Committing not to use and expecting not to use can result in lowered response to your cues and less intense cravings**

Reduce Cravings By Eliminating Cues

Studies show that cravings can be set off by external cues such as sights, sounds, and smells previously associated with drug-use. Even internal cues can act as a trigger. For a drinker, looking at a clock can remind him it is time for a drink. Food, sex, holidays, and sporting events may have nothing directly to do with using, but for some individuals, they remind them of using. Anger, sadness or even extreme happiness can be a reminder of using and when you feel these emotions, they may be a cue to use if that was your chosen response when you were actively using drugs or drinking (Goodwin, 2000).

To take action on cues, you need to identify them. There are four kinds of cues (Marlatt, & Donovan, 2005):

1. *Things*: The things you surround yourself with, such as a favorite tee shirt you wore to get high with friends, a spoon and a piece of mirror, a mug or a chair.

2. *Gatherings, occasions or events*: Work, hobbies, holidays, family gatherings or the sports you associate with using.

3. *Places and locations*: It's the places you associate with buying and using such as a particular street, bar, liquor store, cafe, club, alley, house or corner.

4. *Emotional states*: Emotions you associate with using such as sadness, anger, desire, and depression. For example, when you felt anger, you headed out the door and used or got drunk. When you felt sad, you took a drug or drank. These negative emotional states became your cues to use.

Don't Give Up!

It's hard work, but you can finish this book!

To begin identifying cues, it's often easiest to start by making a list of your cues that are *things*. These cues are the particular objects that for you have become closely associated with specific activities related to drinking and using drugs.

Chapter 4: Managing Cues

Check any items on the following list that are cues for you.

- ☐ A special case for your drugs
- ☐ Clothes you specifically wore to the bar
- ☐ A favorite pipe for crack or marijuana
- ☐ A special chair you always sat in when you drank
- ☐ A special piece of glass for your cocaine
- ☐ Posters, hats or T-shirts about alcohol or drug use
- ☐ Music you always listened to when drinking or using drugs
- ☐ A private supply of alcohol or drugs that only you knew about
- ☐ A favorite beer mug or wine glass
- ☐ A lucky key chain that doubles as a corkscrew or a bottle opener

These are examples of things that may cause you to think about using. Using the "Personal Cue Inventory and Strategies to Manage Cues" form at the end of this chapter, make a list of your unique cues that are things, and then keep adding to this list. In your mind, walk through your home, your neighborhood, and the homes of your friends. As you mentally walk through each place, add cues to your list. <u>**Do it now.**</u>

Think about it. When you were using and drinking, you surrounded yourself with items that supported your beliefs about your life as a user. These symbols gave meaning to using. It made drinking or using drugs feel special. These items may have signaled to others that you were one of them or to your family that you were not one of them. Now you need to take action and remove these reminders (Marlatt, & Donovan, 2005).

Most likely, you are reading this book because you want to make a life change. To do that, you must give up the symbols and things from your old life that cued you to your old using habits and beliefs. You can't make this life change without giving up some things. Change requires new symbols and new things. *You can't succeed at relapse prevention and meet your life goals if you don't remove and replace your using cues.*

The good news is you get to replace old things with new things and create new meanings for yourself. You can create positive, safe spaces in your life by creating positive cues. This will reduce your craving and your choice not to use will automatically be reinforced by the cues around you. Stress and being around things that are drug related cues are critical factors to relapse and drug use.

Start Removing Items That Cue You To Drink And Use Drugs

Begin planning for how you are going to remove the cues on your list from your life. It's not enough to just make a list of your cues, **you must remove them**. If you think this is not necessary, remember the previous times you tried to reduce or stop using. This time you will succeed, you are going to take all the necessary steps, one at a time. Begin by removing or having a trusted friend remove your cue items from your home, car, and place of work. This positive action will reduce your risk of relapse.

Start with your personal belongings. How many of them are cues? Get rid of them, whether they are the key chain, the CD you love to get high to or the movie you watched over and over while you drank. Ditch them. Throw them out. They aren't worth keeping. Your health, happiness, and success are so much more important now.

If you don't want to be exposed to some cues, get a friend to remove cues from your home, work or school. Think about the people who are most supportive of you and your goal to build a new life. Choose one or two of these people with whom you feel it is safe to share your cue list. Call them and ask them to go to your home, and get rid of these things on your list. Do the same for work or school. Tell these "helping people" that you never want to see these items again. Have them get rid of your stash of drugs, posters, or ashtrays. Empty the alcohol cupboard. It's your list. Don't delay, get on with it.

Replace Old Cues With Positive Cues

Begin to replace the old cues with positive cues that have meaning to you. Take the time to reward yourself and replace old belongings with a positive lifestyle cue. For example, when you throw out your drinking shirt and replace it with your new *exercise shirt*. Throw out your bottle of alcohol and replace it with a *bottle of vitamin B complex* for increased resistance to depression. Throw out your poster of the Rolling Stones and replace it with your *poster of a mountain climber*. Get going. Create those positive cues. For each cue identified on page 1 of your list at the end of this chapter, identify the person assigned to remove the cue. If the person you have identified to get rid of the cues is you; <u>start now</u>, get up, and go get rid of the items that are your cues.

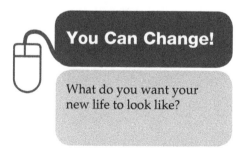

You Can Change!

What do you want your new life to look like?

Situations Or Events Are Also Cues

A situation is a circumstance you are in at a particular moment. A situation, gathering or event can be a cue to using. The situations that cause you to begin thinking about using will be unique to you and require more action than simply removing an object. Situation cues are best identified by remembering your past experiences of particular situations that you usually responded to by:

1. *Using before* the event, such as drinking before a dance, date, or difficult meeting.

2. *Using during* an event or situation to get extra enjoyment, such as holiday celebration, sporting event, relaxing at the beach or having sex.

3. *Using after* an event or situation is over to manage the feelings leftover from the situation such as a family argument or a stressful day at work or school.

Take time now and begin your list of situational cues. For a start, check any of the following that apply to you:

- ☐ Family gatherings such as Sunday dinners
- ☐ Birthday parties
- ☐ Concerts
- ☐ Sporting events
- ☐ Work gatherings such as picnics, house parties, retirements
- ☐ Fishing or camping
- ☐ Social events held after tennis, golf, bowling, attending movies
- ☐ Particular holiday
- ☐ Payday
- ☐ Sex
- ☐ Watching TV
- ☐ Barbeques
- ☐ Lunches with your boss or coworkers
- ☐ School parties
- ☐ Being alone

Take ten minutes now and using page 2 of your "Personal Cue Inventory and Strategies to Manage Cues," start writing your list of events or situations that cue you to use.

Managing Situation Cues

Family or friend gatherings that involve alcohol or drug use are cues for many people and may be for you. You will need to think of options to manage these situations and enlist the help of supportive friends and family. Managing these situation cues can be handled in two ways.

1. Share your decision not to use with supportive family and friends and ask them to assist you by not using around you. Ask them to ensure gatherings are drug and alcohol free when you are invited. Ask them to help you to talk to other family or friends about supporting your decision not to use and not to be around those who use. Ask them to hold separate gatherings for those who refuse to support your non-drinking or using plan. Getting family and friends to support you to develop non-using friendships can be a real help in preventing relapse.

2. Learn to manage situation cues and stressful events that cue you to use or drink by:

   - Declining or refusing to attend those events.

   - Using stress management and relaxation techniques before, during, and after the event.

   - Limiting the time you attend stressful events to twenty or thirty minutes and then excusing your self.

   - Explaining to family or friends that you no longer wish to participate in events that cause you to experience stress or anger.

In summary, cue situations can be managed through non-attendance, changing your role in the situation, and by preparing and practicing coping skills to manage the stress of the cue situation before, during and after the event. Effective coping skills can include relaxation techniques, stress management, anger management, conflict management and cognitive or clear thinking skills. If sex is a particular cue for you, then you may wish to seek advice from a counselor who has expertise in this particular area. Take a few minutes now and using the Strategies to Manage column on page 2 of your "Personal Cue Inventory and Strategies to Manage Cues," start listing your chosen strategies next to the events or situations you identified as cues for you to use.

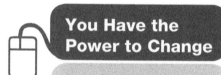

You Have the Power to Change

Whether you think you can, or think you can't, you're right. Henry Ford

Location Cues Require You To Stay Away

Location cues are usually specific locations, such as the sign on your favorite bar that when you drive past and see it, starts you craving a drink. As you walk near your former dealer's corner, you feel the need for some coke. Passing by a friend's apartment, where the two of you always used together, starts you thinking about smoking grass. Using page three on your "Personal Cue Inventory and Strategies to Manage Cues," worksheet, begin your list of high-risk locations. Download a map from the Internet or buy a detailed map of the city or town where you live. Take a red pen and mark in the places that cue you to use. Draw a red line four blocks wide around each of these places. Inside this line is your red zone. Do not go inside that red zone and you won't be cued. Besides avoidance you may need other strategies, such as buying your food at a different market that does not also sell alcohol. You may need to drive to school or work by a different route that avoids taking you past your former dealer's home or a liquor store you used to frequent. Get very specific on your actions to keep you away from high risk locations.

Common Emotional Cues

What's going on in your mind can strongly cue you to use if using has been part of your response to particular negative emotions. Remember, anger, depression, anxiety, fear, frustration, stress, boredom, and loneliness can all be cues to use. Emotional cues are rarely managed with a single action. Just like your car needs a tune-up and your body needs regular physical exercise to stay in shape, your mind also needs tune-ups, to recognize, decrease, and manage emotional cues. *Take a few minutes now and list the negative emotions you commonly felt before using.*

1. _____
2. _____
3. _____
4. _____
5. _____
6. _____
7. _____
8. _____
9. _____
10. _____

To learn to recognize your negative emotions early and label them accurately as cues, practice listening to the thoughts running through your mind. There are many actions you can take right away to increase your skills in managing your negative emotions. Learn meditation. Buy and read informative mental health books to increase and test your understanding of emotional states. Search the internet for articles or websites that help you increase your understanding. Use quality screening tools for anxiety, depression, anger and relationship problems that can be found in evidence based books such as *"The Feeling Good Handbook"* by Dr. David Burns, to check in with yourself. Use the exercises in self help books on anger management, depression and anxiety. Sharpen your thinking and reasoning. Seek feedback from a professional or friends on how they see you manage negative emotions and to review your progress.

Use physical activity to proactively reduce the frequency of occurrence of your emotional cues. Use physical activity to reduce the impact of an unavoidable negative emotional state, such as when you don't get the job you applied for or your dog dies. Take a walk outside or go for a bike ride when you feel yourself getting angry or blue. Scan your emotional state daily and take action when you notice you are beginning to frequently experience negative emotions.

Don't Give Up!

It's hard work, but you can finish this book!

Use the internet and other sources to learn relaxation techniques such as deep breathing or progressive muscle relaxation. There are many different techniques, so you can try them out and choose the ones that work best for you. Don't wait until you're angry or sad to use relaxation techniques. Start using them every day. Remember, you can become your own best relaxation therapist. Try reading and completing workbooks such as *"The Relaxation & Stress Reduction Workbook,"* by Martha Davis, Elizabeth Robbins Eshelman and Mathew McKay.

Now take ten minutes and do page four of your "Personal Cue Inventory and Strategies to Manage Cues." Make sure you start to fill in your strategies to manage each emotional cue and identify those you need more information about effective ways to manage.

Taking Action To Manage Cues Always Includes Creating New Cues

You have the opportunity to rid your environment of cues that may encourage the choice to use again. You can learn to manage or avoid gatherings or places that may encourage you to use again. You can learn to manage emotional states that may encourage you to use again. Remember you need to go a step further than just thinking about it, you need to take action.

Add positive cues to your life, cues which will support you in meeting your new goals: new clothes, sports equipment, self-help books, inspirational posters, a new calendar, a signed commitment statement to your new life, a poster with your life goals, new furniture, a new apartment, a new town, new music or a new market to buy food *and you will find you have developed a new*

Like Our Book?

You'll love our free online rehab program: USDrugRehabCenters.com *attitude toward your life.*

Drug And Alcohol Cues Do Not Last Forever

The good news is that cues **do extinguish** with time and with less exposure, especially if you don't respond to them. As you progress in your recovery, your old lifestyle cues will have less power and impact.

Summary

Keep creating new cues in your life to support your new way of thinking and being. Don't ever stop getting rid of negative cues. Don't ever stop giving yourself new positive cues. As you create new cues, old cues will begin to fade. When in doubt of your ability to manage a cue, stay away. You have nothing to prove and nothing to gain by testing yourself with old cues. Work to increase your knowledge of your negative emotions and to develop your skills to manage them. Take action on your cues now and you will be on the road to relapse prevention!

. . . .

References

Davis, Martha, Eshelman Robbins, Elizabeth, & McKay, Mathew. (2000). *"The Stress Relaxation & Stress Reduction Workbook."* Oakland California. New Harbinger Publication, Inc.

New Habits Are Possible

Addictive behaviour patterns can be changed.

Goodwin, Donald W. (2000). *"Alcoholism, the facts."* Oxford. Oxford University Press. 91.

Marlatt, G.A., & Donovan, D.M., (Eds.). (2005). *"Relapse Prevention Maintenance Strategies in the Treatment of Addictive Behaviours."* (2nd Edition). New York. The Guilford Press. 8, 71-72, 138, 158.

Wilson, S.J., Sayette, M.A., & Fiez, J.A. (2004). Prefrontal responses to drug cues: a neurocognitive analysis, *Nature Neuroscience*, Vol. 7 (# 3), 211.

Personal Cue Inventory and Strategies to Manage Cues

Cues: a stimulus that signals you to carry out a particular behavior, such as using drugs	Person requested to remove cues	Strategies: Stay away from cue or implement plan to manage
Things: things, clothes, posters, music		

You can succeed and make your last relapse the last!

Chapter 4: Personal Cue Inventory and Strategies to Manage Cues

Personal Cue Inventory and Strategies to Manage Cues, continued

Cues: a stimulus that signals you to carry out a particular behavior, such as using drugs	Strategies: plan to manage
Gatherings, Occasions, or Events: Christmas, birthdays, celebrations	

Personal Cue Inventory and Strategies to Manage Cues, continued

	Strategies: plan to manage
Cues: a stimulus that signals you to carry out a particular behavior, such as using drugs	
Places and locations: streets, neighbourhoods, cafes, bars	

Chapter 4: Personal Cue Inventory and Strategies to Manage Cues

Strategies: plan to manage												

Cues: a stimulus that signals you to carry out a particular behavior, such as using drugs

Emotional States: twisted thinking

Chapter Five

Managing Cravings

Chapter 5

Managing Cravings

Craving is the desire for a drug or alcohol. An urge is an internal sensation, a subtle pressure pushing you to get ready to act on a craving. Craving is associated with wanting and an urge with doing. The urge is the feeling that comes <u>after</u> you begin experiencing a craving. You experience a craving or a desire to get high and then a desire to feel relief from this discomfort. The urge is the actual internal feeling of pressure to act on the craving. In between your sensation of craving and the urge to use is a moment of time (Beck, Wright, Newman, & Liese, 1993).

An urge is the <u>intention</u> to carry out a specific behavior. The urge can be started by unpleasant feelings such as anger, frustration or anxiety or by the expectation of an unpleasant, stressful event. If you act on your urge, you will use. Using will reduce craving and you will have a <u>momentary</u> reduction of frustration, anger, and anxiety (Beck, Wright, Newman, & Liese, 1993). But, you will also be back on the trail to an addiction lifestyle. That's not what you want.

Active

Defined by following a course of decisive action, not contemplation or speculation. Creates or involving movement or change.

Between cravings and the urge to use is your <u>opportunity for action</u>. There is a time interval or delay between the craving and acting on it to obtain drugs or alcohol. This delay gives you a window of time to use control or willpower. Willpower is active. It is using self-help techniques. It is not simply passive endurance of discomfort.

Extending the time period between the craving and the use of drugs and alcohol creates a <u>natural decrease</u> of the craving episode. It lowers the chance that you will decide to act on the craving. *The longer you don't act on the craving, the less intense the craving is*. Urges to use are about anticipated outcomes. Urges to use anticipate a positive reward for using and feeling high and a negative experience for not doing it, such as experiencing craving (Beck, Wright, Newman, & Liese, 1993).

Some people confuse an urge with a need. They say they need a drink as though they would not be able to function and would die without it. Such a belief is dysfunctional and not reality based. Dysfunctional beliefs play a huge role in the generation of urges. Dysfunctional beliefs fail to perform the function that is normally expected of a realistic belief, that is, to guide you in acting or responding in a way that supports your goals (Beck, Wright, Newman, & Liese, 1993).

Beliefs Help To Form The Expectation, Which Then Molds The Urge To Use

Beliefs help form expectations of what we can and cannot do. Research confirms many addicted individuals hold dysfunctional beliefs that keep them at risk of continued use (Beck, Wright, Newman, & Liese, 1993):

1. General exaggerated sensitivity to unpleasant feelings
2. Low motivation to control behavior
3. Low impulse control
4. Excitement seeking and low tolerance for boredom
5. Low tolerance for frustration
6. A sense of hopelessness for ever achieving pleasure in a way that does not include alcohol or drugs

> *The most commonly held erroneous belief by people who are addicted is they have little or no control over their urges and behaviors.*
>
> *You have been in control and you are in control now.*

Dysfunctional beliefs play a huge role in urges and decisions to use. Recognizing and breaking down your false beliefs will help you manage your cravings. Dysfunctional beliefs fuel cravings. They are often used by individuals to justify continued use of drugs and alcohol. People use dysfunctional beliefs to ignore, minimize, and deny problems arising from their drug use. They often blame problems on something or someone other than the true source of the problems, their use of drugs or alcohol.

Dysfunctional beliefs of people who are addicted are frequently centered on the individual's sense of hopelessness about being able to stop drinking and using. These beliefs develop over time. The individual's original belief, *I should drink or use to relax and be part of the group*, becomes *I need to drink or use to be accepted*. The belief is gradually expanded to include using as a response to a single negative emotion such as feeling angry. This belief is then expanded *to include using as a response to all* negative emotions. *I have to take a snort when I am lonely, unhappy, angry, worried or even a little distressed.* Eventually the person is using whether they are alone, around somebody, happy or sad – it doesn't matter. Dysfunctional beliefs gradually lead to increased use and an increased number of reasons to use (Beck, Wright, Newman, & Liese, 1993).

New Habits Are Possible

Addictive behaviour patterns can be changed.

The depression or sadness that is <u>always</u> experienced <u>after</u> using most drugs including cocaine, heroin, or alcohol results in more craving to counteract this low feeling. The dysfunctional beliefs expand to include, *I need to use just to feel better*. When drugs or alcohol are taken to relieve all stress, all anxiety, all sadness, and all the natural occurring tension in our lives, it reinforces the person's belief that they can't tolerate unpleasant feelings or function without alcohol or drugs (Beck, Wright, Newman, & Liese, 1993).

The most commonly held erroneous belief by people who are addicted is that they have little or no control over their urges and behaviors.

They incorrectly believe that craving is *irresistible*. Unfortunately, this dysfunctional belief leads to the acceptance of and expectation that relapse is inevitable. *I have no choice*. This belief sets up the individual who has experienced addiction, for the continuous expectation of failure and the continuous fear of loss of control. This belief causes a high level of stress that increases alcohol and drug use (Beck, Wright, Newman, & Liese, 1993).

The notion of total loss of control is too simplistic. It does an injustice to you and the internal resources available to you. In fact, all people who use and abuse drugs and alcohol do exercise control <u>most of the time</u>. When the urge is not strong or the substance is not available, you are able to abstain (Beck, Wright, Newman, & Liese, 1993). You have had the experience of craving and not acting on urges to use. You have been in control and <u>you are in control now</u>.

> **You Can Change!**
>
> What do you want your new life to look like?

When you were using, craving led to routine drug taking. You immediately scanned your surroundings to act on your urge. You made a plan: *I'm going to the liquor store* or *I'm going to the corner to get drugs*. You became mobilized to act. You got ready to use. You put on your hat, your coat, found some money, and went on your way to get drugs or alcohol. While acting on the urge you experienced a variety of sensations similar to hunger or yearning for something. You operated under your appetite or pleasure principle. You ignored your reality principle, which is that you really wanted to control the urge. And you really wanted to quit using (Beck, Wright, Newman, & Liese, 1993).

The wish not to use is experienced as a mental state rather than a gut state of craving. The wish not to use has a thinking component (Beck, Wright, Newman, & Liese, 1993). And, it's more than just a feeling of discomfort. What powers the *will not to use* is decision-making and repeated re-commitment to abstinence and your life goals. That is one of the reasons why you need to write your life goals down, keep them in your pocket, and read them frequently.

You Can Control Craving By Using Reasoned Thinking

You can stop cravings in their tracks. You can stop using *permission-giving thoughts* (It's okay to use when things go wrong) and start using *permission refusal thoughts* (I exercise when I am upset, I don't drink when I am upset). This does not require you to suddenly develop super willpower. It does require you to learn and practice new ways of thinking. It requires you to take action to keep yourself safe from cues and from people who put you at risk. There are two ways to increase your control.

1. Identify craving stimulus situations and practice managing them—in advance.

2. Improve your rational thinking to reduce and combat your permission to use, or permission-giving thoughts.

Taking Action By Developing Your Craving Management Plan

Take the time required to identify your permission-giving thoughts and develop your personal rebuttals. Use page 3 of your "Craving Management Plan" at the end of this chapter and list some of your permission-giving thoughts or reasons for using again. Take the time now to begin this list. For every set of permission-giving thoughts, write an effective and strong reason not to use. These reasons will be one tool to use when you start to give yourself a reason to begin drinking or using drugs again. This exercise has been shown in studies to be an effective way to manage cravings and urges to use. If you keep your list current, it becomes a tool to help you prevent lapse and relapse. Here are some examples of permission-giving thoughts.

Rational

Using reasoning skills to replace harmful thoughts with helpful, positive thoughts and actions.

- I stopped once, I can always stop again.
- I can use just a little, one drink won't hurt me.
- I'm young and strong. I can use safely for a few more years.
- I've had a rough day and I deserve just one drink.
- If I have one drink, I can still stay away from cocaine.
- I can handle any drug, except heroin. As long as I stay away from heroin, I'm in control.
- No one will know, so it doesn't matter if I drink and use tonight.

Use your "Craving Management Plan Worksheet" and fill out some of your permission-giving thoughts. Write down all your possible reasons for giving yourself permission to use again. Once you have created that list, write down a rebuttal or reason to deny each permission-giving thought.

Share your best *reason for using* and your best *rebuttal statement* with a non-using friend or a supportive family member. Have them give you feedback. Ask them to help you to strengthen your rebuttal statement. Permission-giving and permission refusal are important gatekeepers for your actions. Even when the urge is strong, you can abstain, particularly if the drug is not readily available. The more clearly you identify your permission-giving thoughts and develop strong rebuttals, the more likely you will prevent a lapse or relapse. The more you identify highly realistic scenarios and practice refusal skills, the safer you are.

New Habits Are Possible

Addictive behaviour patterns can be changed.

Chapter Five: Managing Cravings

Using your "Craving Management Plan" worksheet at the end of this chapter, describe some of the actual situations in the past where you were offered or sold drugs and alcohol or asked to go places where you knew using was going to happen. Imagine realistic and likely situations. Write them down. Now think of <u>realistic ways to refuse</u> those offers. Write them down.

You Can Change!

What do you want your new life to look like?

Get a supportive person to help you. Have them role-play with you and verbally offer you drugs and alcohol or ask you to go to a using event. You role-play turning them down. *Keep it simple.* Do it enough times until it feels natural. You don't have to give an explanation for why you no longer use. Get a person who is willing to help you who is willing to create and practice many different situations. Practice with them over and over until your refusal becomes second nature. Here are some examples:

- Not for me thanks.
- No thanks, I don't drink.
- I'm not interested in going to the bar but I would be up for a movie.

When some one offers you drugs or alcohol, *use your refusal skills to turn them down* and *remove yourself quickly and immediately from the situation*. You are learning and practicing self-defense to tip the balance in your favor. This is not a game. This is your life that you are learning to manage. Don't worry about hurting someone's feelings or what they think about you if you immediately leave a restaurant, a movie or a room. This is not a popularity contest. This is your life.

What else can you do? Create a positive self-image and a balanced lifestyle. A balanced lifestyle includes: regular exercise, healthy diet, quality sleep, and healthy relationships. Reduce the frequency of acting on negative impulses by practicing thinking before acting and using your new coping skills to manage frustration, anxiety, anger, depression, or sadness.

Become more aware of your feelings and your cravings. Try not to react. Just feel them, and note them when they occur. Try many different methods to manage cravings to find those that work best for you. Exercise, meditate, read or go for a walk when you feel cravings. Learn your emotional craving cues: loneliness, sadness, anxiety, boredom, or anger. Learn the times of day cravings most occur. Take action to change that state of being, manage that emotion, and stay active in times of risk.

Create A Pocket Helper

Write down at least five short compelling reasons why you don't want to use again and keep them in your pocket. Some examples are:

I don't want to overdose and die. I don't want to lose my wife. I want to keep my children. I want to succeed at work. I want to be the best at .... I can be. Now write five of your own compelling reasons why you don't want to use again.

1. _____   6. _____

2. _____   7. _____

3. _____   8. _____

4. _____   9. _____

5. _____   10. _____

Whenever you feel cravings, take this list out. Read it out loud and then do something active to take your mind off the craving. Get physically moving, walk or run. Get moving emotionally, laugh or sing. Find your own creative antidotes to cravings and keep several on hand. These can be puzzles, a funny book, spiritual readings or even running shoes. Find whatever it takes to meet your different needs for distraction at different times, and keep different items at work, at home, in your car, in your purse, and in your pocket. They won't help you in the back of your closet. One craving antidote in one location is definitely not enough.

Cravings Always Get Weaker If You Don't Respond To The Urge To Use

Simple waiting and counting can sometimes be effective. Each episode of craving will gradually lessen and fade. That is the way your body works. Taking action to reduce the stimulus or remove the cue will reduce the frequency and the strength of the craving. Leave that movie with graphic drug using. Walk away from detailed discussions on how great crack is. Removing yourself from cues will reduce the frequency of cravings.

As the days and months pass, cravings will occur less and be weaker when they do. As long as you're managing your anxiety, stress, depression, anger, and frustrations by continually improving your coping skills, you can change the outcome of cravings. You can act by using new knowledge to change beliefs. You can act by challenging dysfunctional thinking. You can combat permission to use beliefs. You can keep yourself away from easy access to drugs or alcohol.

You can remove cues and practice managing stimulus to cravings. You can interrupt your relapse cycle. You can succeed.

Practical Techniques For Managing Craving

Reduce cravings by using some simple coping skills. The key goal is to change your focus of attention from inside yourself and your feelings of craving to other sensations. Although the techniques at first glance seem like quite a simple solution, studies show that the following techniques *do reduce* strong cravings.

Remember, the goal is to change your focus and attention from *internal* thoughts and sensations to *external* thoughts and sensations. As you read the techniques, take time to briefly note on your "Craving Management Plan Worksheet," the techniques you would like to try out. It is important that you have several techniques you can practice and use quickly. For starters try some of the following simple techniques to reduce or end cravings (Beck, Wright, Newman, & Liese, 1993).

It's Proven You Can Reduce Strong Cravings!

Use distraction:

Focus your attention on describing your surroundings. The more you can focus on your surroundings, the less you will be focusing on your internal sensation of craving. Use talking to someone to distract you. Remove yourself from a cue-laden place. Go for a walk or a drive. Visit a friend. Go to the library. Do household chores as a part of distraction. This diverts your attention from craving and results in a sense of satisfaction and accomplishment. Recite a favorite poem, meditation or a prayer out loud. Write it down as you recite it. Get involved in a card game, video game, board game or word puzzles. Choose any mentally challenging and pleasurable activity that diverts your focus. Have you got the idea?

Use cue cards:

When cravings are strong in early recovery, you can lose your ability to reason objectively. Prewritten coping statements will help you get through this. Write your statements on an index card and keep it with you. Use your card to list your greatest advantages of not using. Keep this card along with a list of things you can buy with the money you didn't use for drugs or alcohol. Write single, concise statements and update them regularly. Try these:

- I feel saner when I don't use.
- Things are going great with my life. Keep it that way.

- I look physically great. Keep it that way.
- Get out of this situation now!

Use imagery:

Refocus and get your mind off cravings by imagining something outside yourself. Begin by saying: *Stop!* Hold your hand up in stopping motion. Replace thoughts and images of using with images of you running or exercising. You are powerful and strong. Imagine yourself being successful at work or imagine yourself laughing and having fun with your kids. Create your own positive mental images to use when you need them.

Record rational responses:

Carry a note pad with you and jot down the thoughts that go through your mind when you experience cravings or unpleasant thoughts. Write down a description of what you are feeling. Create rational responses for your negative thoughts and write them down such as: *This feeling will pass shortly. I can stand it for a few more minutes.* Then, use a distraction technique to take your mind off your craving.

You Have the Power to Change

Whether you think you can, or think you can't, you're right. Henry Ford

Use relaxation:

Relaxation training can help you cope with anxiety, frustration, anger, and cravings. It will increase your feeling of well-being, reduce stress, as well as reduce the occurrence of cravings. Try these:

- Deep breathing
- Meditation
- Listening to music
- Looking at peaceful pictures
- Watching calming videos of water
- Yoga
- Looking outside at nature
- Guided imagery tapes or CD's

Learn and practice a number of options to meet your varying moods and to carry out in different settings.

Schedule activities:

Always schedule activities for those times when you regularly used, such as after work or on a Friday or Saturday night. Have positive commitments already scheduled for those high-risk times. These

Chapter Five: Managing Cravings

New Habits Are Possible

Addictive behaviour patterns can be changed.

commitments will allow you to move forward quickly with your day when you experience a craving, rather than having to stop and think, *What can I do? What can I do?* Keep a list of activities you can do on short notice when you feel those strong cravings. Keep your relaxation tools with you, wherever you are. For example:

- Keep a pair of walking or running shoes at work.
- Maintain a drop-in membership at an exercise club.
- Keep an updated list of movies you are interested in seeing and that are playing so you can go on a moment's notice.
- Buy a membership card for drop-in swimming and keep your swimming suit in your car or locker.
- Keep the phone number of a good friend in your wallet who is willing to go walking or running at short notice.

Next, use your calendar to book activities for every day, *in advance*. Make a list of short-notice activities for each week that you might need to use to combat sudden urges or cravings. Keep your commitment to abstinence posted with your positive life goals for family, work, education, sports, and whatever you want to accomplish. This will reduce cravings, as *expecting not to use* reduces craving (Beck, Wright, Newman, & Liese, 1993).

Do not test yourself to see if you are cured. You are safer when you don't test yourself. Stay away from cues forever. This is called being smart and taking care of your self. Be an addiction myth destroyer. Total lack of control over drug or alcohol use is a myth. Manage your cues and cravings and live for your life goals. You can choose to never use again. Stay away from all drugs and alcohol, even if you weren't addicted to them, because drugs and alcohol impair your judgment. Keep your mind and body sharp and you will never choose to use again. Now you know the facts.

Developing An Exercise And Relaxation Plan

You are working to develop a relapse prevention plan that will help you move into a new lifestyle, one that involves new people and situations far removed from an addiction-involved lifestyle. Regular exercise and positive recreational and social activities need to be a major part of your relapse prevention plan. They are essential to creating your new balanced lifestyle. You need:

1. *Physical exercise*: Activities and movement intended to keep you fit and healthy.
2. *Recreation*: Activities that you take part in for pleasure or relaxation rather than work.
3. *Social activities*: Activities that allow you to meet and interact

with others in a friendly way and offer you an opportunity for interaction with people who aren't using.

Exercise, recreation and social activities, of course, can be combined in one activity such as hiking. Hiking involves exercise and meeting new people. It is a recreational and a social experience. *Remember, new activities should provide the opportunity for you to engage in a lifestyle that is incompatible with addiction activity and support you in meeting people who are not involved in addiction.*

To create your plan, you will need to take some time to think about new recreational and social activities you want to try and past activities you want to start again now that you are drug and alcohol-free. *To get started answer the following questions:*

1. What is available where you live?

   _____

   _____

2. How much money do you have available to dedicate to your plan?

   _____

   _____

3. What activities or locations should you avoid, even though they are recreational or exercise activities, because they cue you to use again?

   _____

   _____

4. Who else can be a part of your plan?

   _____

   _____

Use the "Exercise, Recreation and Social Activities Plan," at the end of this chapter to begin your personal plan. Start with a formal exercise plan because it's easy and concrete. Exercise will:

1. Keep you in shape and increase your strength for other recreational activities.

2. Improve your physical appearance, which will increase your confidence to try some of those other social activities.

3. Help you manage the stress of trying new social activities.

4. Give you the opportunity to meet new people with similar interests.

5. Give you something to talk about.

6. Help you manage cravings and negative emotions.

You can see why exercise is such a powerful tool for you and is highly recommended. Begin by getting up ten minutes early each day for a brisk walk. Even walking around your living room is a start. Every hour, get up and walk around for five or ten minutes. Get up and walk around during the T.V. commercials. Take the stairs. Find a workout buddy and schedule your activities and workouts. Keep track of your goals and progress. Get professional advice from a personal trainer. Above all get active and make daily choices that increase your physical activity.

Make a specific plan rather than, *"Sometime today I'm going to go for a walk somewhere."* For walkers or runners, pick a time and pick a park or a section of your neighborhood with good paths. Plan for locations that allow for variety and plan for good and bad weather. Find a mall for those winter months. If you're a swimmer, find the nearest pool where you can do your laps or take water aerobics classes. Take action, phone and find out about times and costs. For cycling, plan a route. Obtain a membership at a community gym for working out. Or, begin in your own home with basic exercise equipment. Get started and make your plan specific with days, times, activities, people, and places marked down on your calendar. **Take away all your excuses by planning.**

Today, decide on at least one form of exercise that you are willing to try. Take time now to complete the "Exercise, Recreation and Social Activities Plan" at the end of this chapter. List at least three things to do this week and complete all columns for each of the three activities including:

- Equipment, knowledge, course and/or clothing required
- Place to access or carry out activity
- People who might participate with me
- Start date and times

Boredom Is The Desire For Desire

We're bored when we know we want something, but we don't know what it is. Everyone has the ability to create genuine pleasure in their life. We did it as children and we still have that power inside us as adults. The experience of addiction took your time, money, intellectual energy, and your love. These resources are now available to you again and you can use them to find many avenues of expression. You are free to find joyous activities to fill your life (Chopra, 1997). There are unlimited recreation activities and possibilities. Here are some ideas:

- Camping
- Fishing
- Kite flying
- Rollerblading
- Dancing
- Gardening
- Painting
- Ceramics

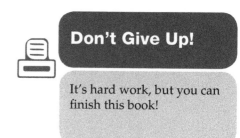

Don't Give Up!

It's hard work, but you can finish this book!

Getting interested? Try to keep an open mind. Find ways to meet new people. It takes effort and courage to find new ways to socialize. Recreation and sports are one way. Joining clubs or groups that share a common interest are another. Try social action and outdoor volunteering, tree planting, ecotourism, historical site restoration or walks to support causes such as cancer research.

What Could Be Stopping You?

Your life can change quickly once you learn and use new skills. Think about it. The only thing stopping you from succeeding in any area of your life is a lack of knowledge. If you commit to learning, you can bridge that gap. If your goal is to have three new social activities and three new friends you truly enjoy being with, what could be stopping you? You can acquire new knowledge, mental skills, people skills, and the ability to handle the stress of meeting new people. You can find new social activities that build on your current interests and abilities. You can have friends and activities that bring you joy and support your success.

How can you quickly acquire the skills you need to move ahead in your new exercise, recreational, and social life? The fastest way is by investing time and money in courses, CD's and books that can help you to get the knowledge and skills you need. Consider: How much money would you spend each year on servicing a car? Include gas, oil changes, new tires, repairs, other insurance and payments. You

need to spend as much time, energy and sometimes money each year improving and upgrading your social and recreational skills.

There are people out there who are physically, recreationally and socially active, and who are having fun and excitement. What separates them from everyone else? It is their lifetime commitment to learning, a willingness to invest in their own personal development, and a willingness to commit time and energy to improving their skills. That's not complex. Do you want to step up and join those people who are happy and reasonably successful? It's easier than you think. Whether people have had the experience of addiction or not, many people prefer to do nothing and hope things will get better.

You can take action and invest today in your new future. Invest your energy, commitment, time, and money. You have everything to gain. You know you can learn to play any sport from tennis to lawn bowling to hockey. You can succeed at any adventurous activity from flying to mountain climbing. You can express yourself creatively from dancing to drawing. You can create your own fun world from a home gym to a garden with a walking path. You can meet people and be a friend who is desired by others. You can learn to communicate with clarity, humor, and interest. You can enjoy being you and find yourself interesting to be with, even when you are alone.

A recent survey (*2004 Alberta Recreation Survey)* asked people about their most important reasons for taking part in leisure activities and they identified:

1. For physical health
2. For pleasure
3. To enjoy nature
4. To relax
5. To be with family

Create your own compelling reasons. Exercise, social, and recreational activities can add the excitement and joy you need in your life, without using alcohol and drugs. Unless you take the time to plan, and the time and energy to take action, you will drift back into negative life patterns. Take action and you can move quickly and safely from the lifestyle of addiction to a comfortable and healthy lifestyle that includes fun and joy.

Motivation To Make The Needed Changes

Motivation is not a personality trait, it is an eagerness to change, a state of readiness. Motivation can change from one situation or time to another. You can influence your own motivation. To decrease the desirability of continued drug and alcohol use:

1. First list all your positive reasons (e.g. to have excitement) for using alcohol and drugs and negative reasons (e.g. to manage anger) for using alcohol and drugs.

2. Then take the time to list <u>in detail all the many benefits for not using</u> (e.g. I will have more money). Then <u>list the disadvantages of not using</u> (e.g. I will have to find new friends).

3. Now go over your lists and tip the balance in your favor by adding more and more positive reasons not to use and benefits of not using.

You Can Change!

What do you want your new life to look like?

Research shows that people who want to increase their motivation to change need to take the time to list the positive and negative reasons for <u>both</u> actions: using and not using. Then they need to **weight reasons in favor of the desired action, not using.** Each individual's tipping point will be different and specific to them (Miller, & Rollick, 1991).

You can increase your motivation for change by developing personal life goals that are realistic, clear, and based on standards of behavior that are normal and praiseworthy. Behaviors that are acceptable and normal among heavily drinking and drug-using friends are not usually acceptable in the wider community and the world of friends you're attempting to enter (Miller, & Rollick, 1991). Share your goals with non-using family and friends, and get feedback. That way, you will know whether they are reasonable and still high enough for you to have some challenge. Goals *and* feedback together will help create your own motivation for change.

Your motivation for change increases as you challenge yourself to consider new options for change in your life and take action to achieve new goals. Clearly, by reading this book, you are opening your mind to options that will decrease the desirability of continuing drug and alcohol abuse. You are making a life plan that includes relapse prevention and excludes activities that place you at risk.

You can increase your self-motivation through action. Action *always precedes* an increase in motivation. Mistakenly, we sometimes think that motivation comes first. It doesn't. Action precedes motivation (Miller, & Rollick, 1991). Take time today to complete and begin your own:

> *Mistakenly, we sometimes think that motivation comes first. It doesn't. Action precedes motivation.*

- Personal Cue Inventory and Strategies to Manage Cues
- Craving Management Plan
- Exercise, Recreation and Social Activities Plan

Start today and exercise every day. Use relaxation techniques every day. Improve your nutrition at every meal. Increase relapse prevention knowledge through reading every day. Take courses. Read and practice increasing problem-solving skills, communication skills, relaxation, exercise skills, and social skills. Increase your nutrition knowledge and maintain your sleep patterns every day.

Work to create a positive attitude and environment for yourself, for your future. Accept that you may feel conflicted and deal with it. Ambivalence plays a central role in changing behaviors in addiction, body weight, and most of the tough changes in life. People recognize the cost, harms, and risks involved in their behavior. But, they are still attracted to the harmful behavior. Ambivalence is about holding *two conflicting* sets of emotions and feelings at the same time (Miller, & Rollick, 1991). Does this sound familiar?

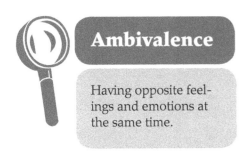

Ambivalence

Having opposite feelings and emotions at the same time.

Learned patterns of alcohol and drug abuse are powerful sources of ambivalence. Habits take time to change and they are powerful sources of ambivalence. Addiction is a classic example of approach avoidance conflict. *I can't live with it; I can't live without it.* Approach avoidance conflict is known as the most difficult type of conflict to resolve for all people, not just people with the experience of addiction. It has the greatest potential for keeping people stuck and creating stress.

Ambivalent Thoughts, Emotions And Behaviors Are Normal

You can learn to manage and resolve ambivalence. You can work through ambivalent thoughts, by completing and keeping with you a list of the costs and benefits of changing your life and not using. Add more reasons every day to keep your list current and to keep the balance in favor of abstinence and getting on with your life goals. You can work through ambivalence by clarifying and challenging values that allowed you to use and that call you back to using. <u>Create new values</u> that will support change. Challenge those erroneous positive expectations of what a return to alcohol or drugs means for you (Miller, & Rollick, 1991).

Summary

You can work through your ambivalence by thoughtfully completing the exercises in this book and by taking action to improve your self-confidence and self-esteem through:

1. Using reasoned thinking to challenge permission-giving thoughts.

2. Learning to manage depression, anxiety, anger, and frustration.

3. Improving your skills to manage your high-risk situations and practicing your drink and drug refusal skills.

4. Improving your communication skills so you can increase your success at those new social activities and make new friends.

5. Getting involved in new exercise, social, and recreational activities.

6. Managing cravings by using distraction, cue cards, imagery, rational responses, relaxation, and positive activity scheduling.

If someone tells you that relapse is probable, so what? *There isn't any research that shows all individuals relapse.* It does not exist. *You are not a statistic.* You are in control of your life. Keep working to increase the probability of your success. Believe in yourself and your ability to master the required skills. Believe in your ability to make a commitment to the required life changes.

> **There isn't any research that shows all individuals relapse. It does not exist. You are not a statistic.**

Take a break now and call a friend to go for a walk or watch a movie. Get your new activities started now to reduce your cravings and exposure to cues.

• •

References

Beck, A.T., Wright, F.D., Newman, C.F., & Liese, B.S. (1993). *"Cognitive Therapy of Substance Abuse."* New York. The Guilford Press. 31, 34-35, 160-168.

Chopra, D. (1997). *"Overcoming Addictions, the spiritual solution."* New York, Harmony Books. 100-101.

"2004 Alberta Recreation Survey." Highlights of Results. 1. Retrieved from http://tprc.alberta.ca/recreation/ars/surveypdf/2004 Survey_Highlights.pdf

Miller, W.R., & Rollick, S. (1991). *"Motivational Interviewing, Preparing People to Change Addictive Behavior,"* New York. The Guilford Press. 14, 21, 29, 38, 40-41, 45.

Don't Give Up!

It's hard work, but you can finish this book!

Chapter Five: Craving Management Plan

Craving Management Plan

Craving is the desire for a drug or alcohol. An urge is an internal sensation pushing you to act on the craving.

Techniques can include:
- distraction
- flashcards
- imagery
- rational responses to automatic thoughts
- relaxation training
- activity scheduling
- your own techniques to tell people you are not interested in alcohol or drugs

Craving Situation Description	Technique For managing
1.	
2.	
3.	
4.	
5.	

Craving Management Plan

Techniques can include:
- distraction
- flashcards
- imagery
- rational responses to automatic thoughts
- relaxation training
- activity scheduling
- your own techniques to tell people you are not interested in alcohol or drugs

6.	
7.	
8.	
9.	
10.	
11.	

You can succeed and make your last relapse the last!

Chapter Five: Craving Management Plan

Permission Giving Thoughts: reasons for using again	Rebuttal: reasons for not using this permission giving thought
1.	
2.	
3.	
4.	
5.	
6.	

Craving Management Plan

Permission Giving Thoughts: reasons for using again	Rebuttal: reasons for not using this permission giving thought
7.	
8.	
9.	
10.	
11.	
12.	

You can succeed and make your last relapse the last!

Chapter Five: Exercise, Recreation And Social Activities Plan

Exercise, Recreation and Social Activities Plan

Recreation, Exercise and Social Activity	Equipment, knowledge, course and/or clothing required	Place to access or carry out activity	People who might participate with me	Start date and times
1)				
2)				
3)				
4)				
5)				

Exercise, Recreation and Social Activities Plan

Recreation, Exercise and Social Activity	Equipment, knowledge, course and/or clothing required	Place to access or carry out activity	People who might participate with me	Start date and times
6)				
7)				
8)				
9)				
10)				

Chapter Five: Managing Cravings

Chapter Six

Coping Skills to Prevent Relapse

You can succeed and make your last relapse the last!

Chapter 6

Coping Skills To Prevent Relapse

No single book or model of relapse prevention can completely portray all the skills required to change all the different types of negative behaviors from over eating to gambling. This book provides a starting point for persons who have abused drugs and alcohol. If you develop positive life skills and implement strategies to achieve a balanced lifestyle you are more likely to succeed in achieving your goals and in overcoming a substance addiction. You will experience fewer lapses, recover from lapses more quickly, and not proceed to full relapse. *Evidence shows that lifestyle balance is a critical factor in decreasing the probability of relapse* (Marlatt, & Donovan, 2005).

Balance

Stability created by working at rational thoughts and helpful actions to counter negative life events. Life events can include feelings, places, people or a course of action taken.

To achieve lifestyle balance, you will need to reduce daily negative stressors and increase daily pleasurable activities so you can experience a *balance* in your life between daily negatives and daily positives. When you are able to balance negative stressors with positive activities in your life, you will be much less likely to relapse.

What are some of the skills that can be learned to reduce the frequency and impact of negative events or stressors? What skills can help you increase the frequency of positives or pleasurable events?

- Rational thinking skills
- Communication skills
- Physical fitness skills
- Stress management skills
- Time management skills
- Relaxation skills

Individuals who make a concrete plan and who also diligently learn and practice a variety of these skills significantly reduce their risk of relapse. Remember, negative emotional states of anger, depression and anxiety, interpersonal conflict, and exposure to social pressure to use are the most commonly identified high-risk situations for relapse (Marlatt, & Donovan, 2005).

New Habits Are Possible

Addictive behaviour patterns can be changed.

Learning to recognize, acknowledge, and manage anger, depression and anxiety will require you to find resources to assist you. You will need to decide which coping skills are priorities for you. The more coping skills you develop, the lower your probability of experiencing relapse. Increasing self-confidence *and* ability to use coping skills predicts successful outcomes. The more motivated you are and ready to change, the more likely you are to try and to regularly use a variety of coping skills. This results in an increased probability for success in achieving your life goals and a decrease in your risk of relapse

(Marlatt, & Donovan, 2005). You will be working on many fronts to put the odds in your favor.

Managing Anger

Anger is a universal, natural and understandable emotion. Anger is an unpleasant feeling often experienced when you perceive an event as unfair or undeserved; after you think you have been mistreated; or when you are involved in a disagreement. Anger can result in a desire to strike back at the assumed cause of this unpleasant feeling. Angry thoughts trigger more angry feelings. Anger has physical signs such as a flushed face, increased heart rate, increased blood pressure, sweating, and the release of stress hormones. It often includes behaviors that are culturally influenced such as yelling, clenching fists or pouting. Anger can involve protecting self-interest or defending causes or principles such as honor. Anger often appears with feelings of depression and anxiety (Schiraldi, & Hallmark Kerr, 2002).

> *You will be working on many fronts to put the odds in your favor.*

The average adult gets angry once a day and irritated about three times a day (Schiraldi, & Hallmark Kerr, 2002). Considering the frequency of the experience of anger and the fact that unmanaged anger *is* a cause of relapse, one can see why learning about anger management is so important to reducing your risk of relapse. Anger is a common response to:

- Other people when they hurt us or don't do what we expect of them

- Situations like traffic jams, a computer glitch or losing something

- Ourselves when we fail to meet personal goals, don't acknowledge our limitations or use negative self talk (Schiraldi, & Hallmark Kerr, 2002).

Certain thinking habits clearly intensify anger. One example is thinking that all offenses are deliberate. *Everything negative that happens is a deliberate jab at me.* The most common explanation for the frequency and intensity of anger is that many people simply have not learned the skills of anger management, and the physiological reasons behind anger (Schiraldi, & Hallmark Kerr, 2002).

You Can Change!

What do you want your new life to look like?

Anger can be a physical response of the body to inadequate rest, inadequate recreation, poor physical or mental health, poor nutrition, and the influence of alcohol or drugs. This is one of the reasons taking care of the basics as outlined in Chapter 3 is so important. Occasional anger causes no lasting harm. Chronic anger keeps the body in a constant state of emergency and may contribute to digestive disorders, hypertension, heart disease, infections, headaches, and

Chapter Six: Coping Skills To Prevent Relapse

more. People may use anger as a defense against; guilt, hurt or loss, feeling helpless or trapped, anxiety or fear, feeling bad, feeling wrong or unworthy, or feeling empty and frustrated (McKay, M., Rogers, & McKay, J., 1989). Everyone has sometimes used anger to defend against painful feelings.

Problems occur when using anger as a response becomes a habit and when the frequency and the intensity of anger begin to negatively affect health and relationships. The person who has low self-esteem and feels worthless may blow up at the slightest provocation rather than face self doubt. The person who has difficulty acknowledging fear may attack and blame rather than face their discomfort. The person whose judgment is clouded by drugs or alcohol turns to anger more frequently. *Think about your experiences of anger and answer the following questions:*

1. How often is anger my first response?

   _____

   _____

2. What about being angry works for me?

   _____

   _____

3. What about my anger does not work for me?

   _____

   _____

4. List the behaviors you most commonly use when you are angry.

   _____

   _____

Now, try to answer the questions again, this time specifically for when you were angry and intoxicated with drugs or alcohol. Then compare your answers to questions 1 to 4 with questions 5 to 8.

5. How often is anger your first response when you are intoxicated?

    _____
    _____

6. What about anger works for you when you are intoxicated?

    _____
    _____

7. What about your anger does not work for you when you are intoxicated?

    _____
    _____

8. List the behaviors you most commonly use when you are intoxicated and angry.

    _____
    _____
    _____

Discuss your anger response with a trusted non-using family member or friend. See if your answers to the above eight questions match theirs. Take the time to learn more about anger and decide if gaining the necessary skills to manage anger will be one of your priority goals. Check out specific anger management resources to assess and improve your skills. Try effective and easy to use evidence based workbooks like "*The Anger Control Workbook, Simple, innovative techniques for managing anger and developing healthier ways of relating,*" by Mathew McKay & Peter Rogers. It is well worth developing increased anger management skills to reduce stress and to become

Chapter Six: Coping Skills To Prevent Relapse

more effective in relationships, even if anger is not a major problem for you. Always seek professional help if anger is a particularly troubling issue for you and if your anger response involves any level of physical violence.

Managing Depression

Depression is the most frequently encountered psychiatric disorder. *Twenty percent of women and ten percent of men* will suffer an episode of depression at some time in their life. At any given time, *five to ten percent of women and three percent of men are depressed*. Unfortunately, four out of five cases of depression go undiagnosed and untreated (Frances, & First, 1998).

So, how do you know if you are depressed? It's mostly a matter of time. How long have you been feeling badly? *Try this depression checklist and check off any symptoms you are experiencing:*

- ☐ Loss of energy, fatigue
- ☐ Feelings of emptiness
- ☐ Loss of interest in pleasurable activities including sex
- ☐ Disturbances in your sleep patterns
- ☐ Appetite and weight changes
- ☐ Recurring thoughts of death or suicide
- ☐ Hopeless feelings
- ☐ Feeling worthless, guilty, trapped
- ☐ Memory lapses, loss of concentration
- ☐ Physical symptoms: headaches, stomach aches

In general, anyone who suffers from five or more symptoms nearly every day, all day, for more than two weeks may have an illness that requires some type of assessment or treatment (Medina, 1998). Remember the key is duration. How long do the symptoms last? Do they interfere with your ability to function? If you are concerned about your symptoms, get an assessment from your physician or a mental health professional. Managing depression is critical to preventing relapse.

What Causes Depression?

Depression has chemical, psychological or biological causes. Chemicals that are in our brain control how we feel emotionally. Depression can be a result or the cause of an imbalance in these chemicals. Alcohol, drug use or withdrawal can cause an imbalance in the chemicals in your brain and result in depression. What does all this mean? It means depression is not a moral flaw or weakness. Depression has some biological causes, some environmental causes, and some learned behaviors as a cause. Depression is treatable. Risk factors for depression are:

1. Using or withdrawing from drugs or alcohol
2. Family history of mood disorders or addiction
3. Recent negative life events such as moving, family problems
4. Divorce
5. Chronic stress: unemployment, illness
6. Having a low to moderate self-esteem
7. Lack of closeness with family and friends
8. Being single
9. Traumatic events, violence or assault
10. Being young, being between the ages of 18 – 24 (BC Partners for Mental Health and Addictions Information, 2006)

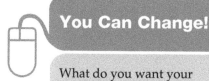

You Can Change!

What do you want your new life to look like?

Cognitive behavioral therapy (learning rational thinking skills) is very effective for depression. Some studies have shown taking vitamin B6 in addition to other treatments combats depression. Regular exercise is very effective in reducing depression. Relaxation, social activities, quality sleep and a healthy diet lessen the overall symptoms of depression. Increasing your pleasurable activities that do not involve drug and alcohol also reduces depression. Sometimes, medications called antidepressants are prescribed. They work in conjunction with cognitive therapy, vitamins, good exercise, relaxation, social activities, sleep, and a healthy diet. There are many positive ways to manage depression, so there isn't a good reason not to get treatment (Medina, 1998).

Managing Anxiety

Responding to danger is the most basic of human survival skills. People with anxiety disorders have fears that occur out of proportion to any realistic danger. Their fear mechanism is over sensitive. *Twelve percent of the general population in any given year will experience an anxiety disorder* (Frances, & First, 1998). Anxiety disorders include panic disorder, generalized anxiety disorder, phobias, obsessive/compulsive disorder, social anxiety, and post-traumatic stress disorder. The two most common anxiety disorders in people who have experienced addiction are panic disorder and generalized anxiety disorder.

Panic Disorder:

The symptoms are: A sudden sensation of dread. Your heart races, you perspire, and have trouble catching your breath. You feel dizzy and very frightened. You feel as if you need air and you are unable to calm yourself (Frances, & First, 1998).

What physically happens during an anxiety attack? Certain organs are geared up, causing increased heart rate and breathing. Other organs are turned off. You feel sick to your stomach because blood is temporarily diverted from your digestive track. Some of the symptoms, lightheadedness, numbness, shortness of breath, are the result of breathing too quickly and shallowly. Sweating results from the temporary gearing up of all your metabolic functions. Pupils can dilate to sharpen your visual acuity. You are ready for fight or flight (Frances, & First, 1998).

People who have panic attacks may have a low body threshold for triggering the fight or flight response so it goes off without reason. Another cause may be that some individuals have an *extra* sensitivity to *any* unusual body sensation and a panic attack is triggered by minor events even when the heart skips a beat or breathing becomes a bit labored. The severity and frequency of panic attacks varies widely from person to person (Frances, & First, 1998).

Don't Give Up!

It's hard work, but you can finish this book!

A number of substances cause panic attacks by their direct effects upon the body or when the body is withdrawing from the substances. Panic attacks can be caused by taking any type of stimulant including diet pills, decongestants, amphetamines, cocaine, and caffeine. Panic attacks can disappear once the stimulant is stopped (Frances, & First, 1998). Substances taken to reduce anxiety such as alcohol, sleeping pills or tranquilizers can cause withdrawal panic attacks when their use is cut down or stopped suddenly. Panic attacks can also be caused by medical conditions such as an overactive thyroid, adrenal glands, asthma or heart arrhythmia. *About twenty five percent of the general population experiences a panic attack at some point in their lives.* If you are having frequent panic attacks, you need to take action (Frances, & First, 1998).

What is the treatment for panic attacks? Some antianxiety medications have a quick positive effect. Unfortunately all are potentially addictive at the dosage required. Once you start, it is often difficult to stop, because the withdrawal symptoms perfectly mimic what it is like to have a panic attack.

Cognitive behavioral therapy can teach you how to prevent uncomfortable sensations from escalating into a full-blown panic attack. Cognitive therapy takes longer and is more work, but the techniques, once learned, can be applied indefinitely and used in other parts of your life such as managing the dysfunctional thinking that maintains addiction. Sometimes, anxiety disorders require a combination of medication and cognitive therapy (Frances, & First, 1998).

Generalized Anxiety Disorder:

This is the second most common disorder among people who experience addiction. Some people are nervous, tense, and anxious most of the time. At the slightest provocation, they experience waves of fear or worry. This chronic state of tension and feeling on edge is exhausting to them and is known as generalized anxiety disorder (Frances, & First, 1998).

Anxiety is a common side effect of stimulants, caffeine, diet pills, cocaine, and speed. The more drugs you use, the higher the risk of experiencing generalized anxiety disorder. As with panic attacks, substances that depress the central nervous system like alcohol, tranquilizers, sleeping pills, and narcotics cause anxiety when they are withdrawn or stopped. Prescription medications are also common causes of anxiety, particularly antidepressant medication.

You Have the Power to Change

Whether you think you can, or think you can't, you're right. Henry Ford

The treatment for generalized anxiety disorder is anti-anxiety medication and cognitive behavioral therapy. They are sometimes used together. Many people with generalized anxiety disorder also have depression and need treatment for both disorders.

Because people who have had the experience of addiction are at higher risk for anxiety disorders, it is important for you to assess your feelings of anxiety and take action to reduce your risk of relapse. Self-assessment tools for anxiety are readily available. When in doubt consult your physician or a mental health professional. The coping skills to manage anxiety are very similar to those for depression. Healthy sleep, diet, and exercise are very helpful. Learning relaxation and distraction techniques are also helpful. Learning the basic symptoms of anxiety disorders, recognizing the symptoms, obtaining an assessment, and taking action are all part of your quality relapse prevention plan.

For both depression and anxiety, *"The Feeling Good Handbook"* by Dr. David Burns has excellent simple assessment tools, exercises and strategies to reduce anxiety and depression. Even if you don't have the experience of depression or anxiety, the tools in Dr. Burns' book are helpful for managing the daily negative emotional stressors that can lead to lapse or relapse if left unmanaged or unacknowledged.

Managing Stress To Reduce The Risk Of Relapse

People who abuse drugs are more vulnerable to stress than the general population and stressors can trigger craving in people who are addicted (Frances, Miller, & Mack, 2005). Relapse can be a response

Chapter Six: Coping Skills To Prevent Relapse

to unrecognized and unmanaged personal irritations, frustrations, and stress. Stress has no biological structure like germs or viruses. It is purely the result of how the mind and body interact. It is a true example of the connection between mind and body, how we think about things, and our body's physical reaction to those thoughts. So what is stress? Stress is an emotional response as well as a physical response. It is characterized by increased heart rate, a rise in blood pressure, muscular tension, irritability, and often, depression. Take a moment and write in your own words your definition of stress on the "Personal Stress Inventory Worksheet" at the end of this chapter.

In the Every Day Stressors and Work Stressors columns, add at least two concrete examples of what causes you to feel stress. An example of an every day stressor could be that your neighbor runs his lawnmower at 6 AM on Sundays. Keep this list beside you and add items as you think of your stressors. You will be building your own stress inventory.

You do have choices as to how you react to daily stressors. For example: You're driving to work on a busy highway in the fast lane. The driver in front of you is driving below the posted speed limit and refuses to get out of your way.

New Habits Are Possible

Addictive behaviour patterns can be changed.

Choices:

1. Follow them until they pull over and yell at them.
2. Exceed the speed limit, change lanes and go around them, while shaking your fist at them.
3. Breathe deeply and calmly and turn on your radio.
4. Decide that they're just another driver on the highway.
5. Slow down and accept that you will get there when you get there.

Another common stressor: you have been having trouble sleeping and you are still tired when your alarm clock goes off.

Choices:

1. Smash your alarm clock; go back to sleep, and miss work.
2. Yell at your partner, get up, and bang drawers and doors.
3. Get up and decide that today you will make a plan to improve your sleep.
4. Get up, eat breakfast, and go to work.
5. Call in sick.

Every stressful situation comes with several solutions. The choices you make can increase your anger, depression, anxiety, and stress. Choices can increase the conflict and problems in your life. Or, choices can calm you, enhance your feelings of well-being, and support you to find solutions that benefit you and those around you. Your solutions can make it more fun to be you. You can teach yourself new ways to solve problems. Life is always filled with stressful situations. Learning to manage stress is about thinking and living with a different frame of mind.

Think back to your most recent relapse. Picture what was happening in your life, the stressors or irritations you were facing in the days leading up to and just before your decision to use again. *Review the following list of items and check off any that apply to your pre-relapse situation. You are identifying the stressors you experienced just before you decided to use again:*

- ☐ Loneliness
- ☐ Feeling manipulated
- ☐ Anxiety
- ☐ Depression
- ☐ Boredom
- ☐ Argument
- ☐ Money problems
- ☐ Too little sleep
- ☐ Illness
- ☐ Problem at work or school
- ☐ Bad or no sex

- ☐ Feeling unvalued, unwanted
- ☐ Insult or criticism
- ☐ Too much time on your hands
- ☐ Offer of drug or alcohol from a friend or relative
- ☐ Girl or boyfriend problems
- ☐ Pencil broke, shoelace broke, tooth broke, multiple little problems
- ☐ Others:
- ☐ _____
- ☐ _____
- ☐ _____
- ☐ _____

Now, take five minutes and go back to your "Personal Stress Inventory Worksheet." Compare the examples of daily stressors that you wrote down previously with the above list of stressors that you experienced before your last relapse. Are they the same or different? *High-risk stressors are the stressors that were present*

You can succeed and make your last relapse the last!

in the days and hours before you relapsed. Add checked items on the above list to your "Personal Stress Inventory Worksheet" and underline any items already on the worksheet that were present prior to your last relapse. These are your high-risk stressors. This is the beginning of a very important part of your relapse prevention plan. You can't manage stress and prevent relapse if you don't take the time to identify the specific high-risk stressors that you frequently face.

The Balance Sheet In Your Mind: Assigning Meaning To Stressors

We all keep a balance sheet of debits and credits in our mind, which can be about life, relationships, work or even the weather. The balance sheet is where we use old information to decide whether a new event in our life is fair or unfair. It's how we make quick judgments. *Why me? Not again. Harry always remembers my birthdays.*

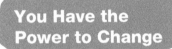

You Have the Power to Change

Whether you think you can, or think you can't, you're right. Henry Ford

Balance sheet examples can be positive or negative. You can count the things that happened or the things that didn't happen, *good things or bad things*. It is whatever you decide to remember. For example:

- For a partner/spouse and you, it can be the number of times each of you has done the dishes this week. Total: three times each.

- With a boss, it can be the number of times they recognized your successes: Total: zero.

- We don't just count; we make judgments and take action based on those judgments.

- With a partner/spouse, it can be the number of times each of you has done the dishes this week: three each. *Judgment*: she carries her fair share. *Action*: Expect she will continue to do her fair share and appreciate her.

- With a boss, it can be the number of times they recognized your successes: zero. *Judgment*: My boss is not fair in how he treats me. *Action*: Become more alert for any slight from my boss and put less effort into my work.

When you start to make judgments about people in your life and attribute meaning to their actions, check for your balance sheets in your mind. Are you keeping tallies that increase your stress? Do they accurately reflect events or are they automatic negative interpretations of events? The way you keep track in your mind can increase stress and negative emotions, which can increase the probability of a lapse or relapse.

Do Multiple Stressful Events Add Up?

Let's say a single stressful or irritating event happens. You notice, react, and then forget it. *Does the stress from that event stick with you and build up? It probably doesn't.* For example, you get up in the morning and find your drawer is empty of work socks. You realize that you forgot to wash your work socks when you did the laundry yesterday. You experience a moment or two of irritation. Then you put on the same socks as yesterday and decide to wash your socks tonight while you are watching TV.

Now let's say a stressful or irritating event occurs and <u>you place special importance on it</u> by adding it to your negative balance sheet in your mind. *You interpret it as <u>more than a single chance event</u>. Is the stress from that event cumulative? It probably is.* Using the sock example, you decide that a lack of clean socks is just one more sign you are a failure and you will never get your life organized. Further, you believe it is probably a sign that you are not meant to go to work today and you call in sick. The way you interpret and react to little life events can lead to increased stress and increased risk of relapse.

The Balance Sheet In Your Mind & Relapse

Keeping a hidden negative mental balance sheet is an insidious way to increase your risk of relapse. For example, Bill has finished rehab and gone back to work. Bill's boss speaks to him about leaving his tools scattered around in the shop. Bill interprets this event as proof that his boss does not like him and that he will get fired in the end no matter what he does. He adds this single event to his *'the world is unfair to me list'* which is actually his *'reasons why I don't have to stay clean'* list. Bill has just moved himself one step closer to giving up on his commitment not to drink or do drugs.

Each stressful event can be seen as a single event and managed poorly so it increases your stress. Or, it can be seen as a single event and managed well so it decreases stress and increases positive outcomes and feelings. A stressful event can also be viewed as part of a succession of stressful events such as partnership/marriage breakdown. The event can be used as a signal to make a plan and take action to decrease stress and increase the chances of solving a larger problem. Or, once again, an event can be seen as part of a larger hidden agenda of an unfair world, a world that is against you. It can be used as an excuse to express anger, to give up on commitments such as exercising, losing weight, and studying, and a reason to start using drugs or alcohol again.

New Habits Are Possible

Addictive behaviour patterns can be changed.

So Who Decides If An Event Is Stressful?

Our families teach us what is acceptable to perceive as stressful and what is acceptable behavior following stressful events. (Remember, "Don't be a baby!") Our friends and family react to stress in particular ways. We may learn to show we are under stress by: crying or silence; yelling or laughing; minimizing or exaggerating events. We learn from news reports as we watch how people react after floods, murders or even winning the lottery.

Ultimately you decide what is stressful. For each person, stress is unique in its causes although some events are common stressors to most people. There are effective ways to increase your resilience to stress and there are good techniques for reducing immediate feelings of stress. To succeed in preventing relapse, you will need to become an expert in detecting and taking action to reduce your stressors in your worlds of work, home, school, and social activities.

> *Only you can decide what is stressful.*

The first step is to learn quick relaxation techniques (such as described in Chapter 5) to reduce stress in specific situations. The second is to check for dysfunctional thinking when you interpret events. Finally, become aware of your own hidden agendas and practice using *accurate language to label events*. For example:

1. *Label some events as just unfortunate irritations* such as a broken shoelace. Put it in perspective as a little irritating event. Take action. Tie the broken shoelace or wear other shoes. Get on with your day. Use humor and laugh about it.

2. *Label a series of events as "one bad day."* Late for work, burnt supper, and tripped over the carpet. Put it in perspective. *Well, it was just a bad day.* Take action to reduce your feelings of stress and irritation. Meditate. Go for a run. Laugh with a friend about it. Recognize that everyone has those stress filled days.

3. *Label events over time as unrelated and unfortunate events.* Get on with solving individual problems. Keep track of successes. Build more resilience by eating right, exercising, developing and revisiting values. Know that change is the only constant. Things will change for you.

Using accurate language requires you to check for dysfunctional thinking and check for automatic assumptions about events or people in your life. It requires you to pause and reflect for a moment before acting. It's a great relapse prevention coping skill.

Becoming Stress Resilient By Holding On To Your Values

Beyond accurate language and dysfunctional thinking, lies the reality of managing real life events that are stressful. Getting through the hard times without drugs or alcohol requires you to develop your own internal standards and to use them as decision making guides and motivators in times of stress.

Take time to rediscover your values. Look back to your life before addiction. What positive ideals did you believe in? Read and talk with others about spiritual and life values to figure out your own value system. Look for events outside yourself that bring up feelings of concern such as poverty or the environment. Are these things you can get involved in and make a difference, events that are outside your own small world? What things are really important in the outside world (Peele, 2004)?

Don't Give Up!

It's hard work, but you can finish this book!

Ask non-using family members or friends about their values and the important events in their lives. Find out how they came to hold those values. What actions do they take to live their values even when things go wrong? Think about famous people who exemplify different value systems, the Dalai Lama, the Pope, Bill Gates or Martin Luther King. Think about different organizations and the values they imply by their group actions: Greenpeace International, Amnesty International or Sierra Club. Living by values reduces stress and increases self-esteem and self-confidence.

Now is the time to start identifying some of your values. Start by creating at least one value statement for yourself. Make it simple so you can easily remember it. A value statement could be: *Do no harm to others or to myself. To act with integrity and honesty in personal relationships. To act with compassion and forgiveness when others or myself make mistakes.* Write a value statement now.

Your Value Statement:

_____

_____

_____

_____

Values can be used to guide small or large decisions: to lie or tell the truth; to use a seatbelt or not; to take a job or attend university; and whether to go for a drink or go for a run. You can revisit value statements as a way of checking in with yourself and making sure you are on track. Always check for dysfunctional thinking and hidden agendas when you find yourself taking actions that conflict with living your positive life values, and reaching your goals.

Manage Stress To Prevent Relapse

Take action to end the stress of boredom and loneliness. If you like excitement and taking risks, find positive activities where risk is part of the adventure, like skydiving. Take action to reduce your stress from depression, anxiety or anger. Find and engage in pleasurable activities to reduce stress like meditation, rollerblading or listening to music.

Summary

Develop positive attitudes and living habits to reduce anger, anxiety, depression, frustration, and stress. Habits precede attitude so start with positive actions and become rigorous in carrying them out until they become habits. Get up early in the morning *without fail*. Make your bed when you get up in the morning, *without fail*. Take a shower in the morning, *without fail*. Eat breakfast, *without fail*. Leave early for work, *without fail*. Meditate for ten minutes every day, *without fail*. Exercise for half an hour every day, *without fail*. You get the idea. Reducing stress is about living your values and values are reflected in every action you take or don't take. **It all starts with developing habits that reflect a positive attitude toward every moment of your life.**

Still worried? Pretend you are calm for long enough, and you will eventually be calm. The hard work is in continuing to be calm when everything around you tells you not to be. Take time to identify which of your stressors are irritations that can be managed through simple stress reduction techniques. Identify which stressors are the results of relationship choices and require a life change, such as ending a high-risk friendship or finding a different peer group through new activities. Identify which of your stressors result from the two big choices you made; where you live and the work you do. Make an action plan for change.

If you find yourself stressed, breathe deeply, in through your nose and out through your mouth, slowly three times. Try this right now and while you are slowly breathing in and out, know you can make changes in your life. You already have evidence of it. You're reading this book and starting a new life. Know you've changed. You've stopped using drugs and alcohol. Close your book and take a break. There is the rest of the day and the rest of your life. You can do this.

• •

References

BC Partners for Mental Health and Addictions Information. (2006). "Depression Fact Sheet." Retrieved from http://www.

heretohelp.bc.ca/self-help-resources/your-results/?f[0]=im_field_story_topics_mh%3A116

Burns, David D. (1999). The Feeling Good Handbook. New York. Plume, Penguin Group. 3-11.

Frances, Allen & First, Michael B. (1998). "Your Mental Health, A Layman's Guide to the Psychiatrist's Bible." New York. Scribner. 12, 32, 79.

Frances, Richard, Miller, Sheldon, & Mack, Avram, (Editors). (2005). "Clinical Textbook of Addictive Disorders." (3rd Edition). New York. The Guilford Press. 12.

Kendall-Reed, P., & Reed, S. (2004). "The Complete Doctor's Stress Solution, Understanding, Treating, and Preventing Stress and Stress-Related Illnesses." Toronto, Ontario. Robert Rose Publishing. 83-85.

Marlatt, G.A., & Donovan, D.M., (Eds.). (2005). "Relapse Prevention Maintenance Strategies in the Treatment of Addictive Behaviours."(2nd Edition). New York. The Guilford Press. 4- 5, 7, 12-15.

McKay, M., & Rogers, P. (2000). "The Anger Control Workbook, Simple, innovative techniques for managing anger and developing healthier ways of relating," Oakland, California. New Harbinger Publications, Inc.

McKay, M., Rogers, Ph.D., & McKay, J. (1989). "When Anger Hurts, Quieting the Storm Within." Oakland, California, New Harbinger Publications Inc. 24 - 32, 218, 220- 221.

Medina, J. (1998). "Depression. How it happens. How it's healed." Oakland California. New Harbinger Publications Inc. 6-7, 32-33, 82-87.

Patterson, K., Grenny, J., McMillan, R., & Switzler, A. (2005). "crucial confrontations, Tools for resolving broken promises, violated expectations, and bad behavior." New York. McGraw-Hill. 84-85.

Peele, Stanton. (2004) "Tools to Combat Addiction." New York. Three Rivers Press. 41.

Schiraldi, G.R., & Hallmark Kerr, M. (2002). "The Anger Management Sourcebook." New York. Contemporary Books. 3, 4, 7, 12-13.

You Have the Power to Change

Whether you think you can, or think you can't, you're right. Henry Ford

Chapter Six: Personal Stress Inventory Worksheet

Personal Stress Inventory Worksheet

Write your personal definition of stress:

My Stressors and Action Plan

Under line or circle high risk stressors, that is those you have identified as occurring in the days prior to and immediately before your last relapse:

Every Day Stressors	Technique to Manage or Life Change Required

Personal Stress Inventory Worksheet

Every Day Stressors Continued	Technique to Manage or Life Change Required Continued

Work or School Stressors	Technique to Manage or Life Change Required

You can succeed and make your last relapse the last!

Chapter Six: Coping Skills To Prevent Relapse

Chapter Seven

Reduce Conflict, Increase Communication, And Decrease Relapse

Chapter 7

Reduce Conflict, Increase Communication, And Decrease Relapse

Conflict Is A Source Of Stress

Conflict may be remembered as the times you were angry at someone, the times you disagreed with someone or times when you stood up for yourself. Conflict often results in unpleasant emotions which is why we try to avoid it.

Interpersonal conflict is frequently the result of broken commitments or broken promises. There is a gap between expectations and what happened. A gap is a difference between what you or the other person expected and what really happened. A gap is missed commitments, disappointed expectations, and often plain bad behavior (Patterson, Grenny, McMillan, & Switzler, 2005). Addiction leads to frequent broken commitments, disappointed expectations, and bad behavior. During addiction, alcohol or drugs are used to avoid conflict or to provide false courage to speak up and say the things that are later regretted. People who use drugs and alcohol often manage conflict badly, which leads to more conflict, which leads to more use of alcohol and drugs.

Conflict And Relapse

Unresolved conflict results in increased stress and negative emotions like anger, depression, fear or anxiety that are often associated with relapse. People who use drugs and alcohol are often involved in conflict, because using drugs and alcohol; dulls mental alertness, reduces awareness of what is happening in one's surroundings, and causes individuals to become self centered. You need to learn to identify conflicts and resolve them early, in a positive way.

Conflict, The Basics

The first rule of conflict resolution is that conflict is inevitable. The second rule is that conflict does not alwasy have to be an unpleasant and relapse provoking event. Even the most compatible people experience conflict. Badly managed conflict leads to worse conflicts. Conflict that is well managed can be constructive. With the right skills, you can face conflict with relative calm, achieve what you need, and become more aware of your own and other people's feelings and needs. You will reduce tension and stress as problems are solved. You'll feel closer to people and better about yourself (Tjosvold, 1993).

Make Your Last Relapse The Last

Take five minutes to think about two conflicts you have recently experienced. Jot down a few lines to tell the story about each situation. Then write a one sentence definition of what conflict means to you.

1. Conflict A:

   _____

   _____

   _____

1. Conflict B:

   _____

   _____

   _____

3. My definition of conflict:

   _____

   _____

   _____

How We View Conflict

Some people see conflict as a competition, *I win or I lose*. Competition increases conflict. Using competition to resolve conflict means we determine exactly what we want to have happen, usually before we even talk to the other person. We draw our line in the sand, present what we want, and set ourselves up for either winning or losing.

Competition in personal relationships means someone always loses and that always means the relationship loses. When self interest is more important than mutual interests, the underlying conflict is rarely resolved. When one person *wins* the conflict, the resolution is rarely satisfying to both people. Someone is always left feeling unfairly treated, injured or hurt. The real conflict or a similar one will come up again (Tjosvold, 1993).

Don't Give Up!

It's hard work, but you can finish this book!

Cooperation As An Attitude And Conflict Resolution Tool

When using a cooperative method to resolve conflict, both people work to:

1. Find the common interest, what both people are interested in having happen.

2. Share the cost and the benefit of the resolution.

3. Agree to contribute something to make the agreed upon outcome happen.

4. Make sure *both* people *really* benefit in some way.

5. Determine how each person will treat the other.

This method is effective, because each person considers the other person's ideas. Both people have worked to discover what each needs or wants and the relationship is strengthened (Tjosvold, 1993).

Solving conflicts positively will decrease your stress and will help you to prevent relapse.

Look back at the two recent conflicts you described. What model did you and the other person use to attempt to resolve the conflict? Mostly cooperation or competition? Had you or they already decided what must happen before you even spoke to each other? Were the conflicts resolved or are you still arguing about them?

If you need to strengthen your partner relationship, conflict resolution skills may be a priority for you. Couples who know how to handle confrontation and handle it well, are more likely to stay together. Couples who rely on contentious facial expressions, hostile stares, and thinly veiled threats, don't stay together. During a study of 700 couples, those couples who stayed together had demonstrated the ability to work through differences by stating their views honestly and respectfully (Tjosvold, 1993).

Interpersonal conflict resolution skills are not learned in one session. The cooperative approach briefly described is one approach. There are different approaches and some are more suitable to certain types of conflict situations than others. You will need a variety of conflict resolution tools. To achieve your life goals and prevent relapse, make a specific goal to: continue reading, practicing, and taking courses until you become an expert in managing interpersonal conflicts in your life. Conflict is inevitable therefore conflict resolution is an essential life skill. Solving conflicts positively will decrease your stress and will help you to prevent relapse.

Communication Skills, A Relapse Prevention Tool

You have quit using and drinking. You are changing your thinking, behavior, and lifestyle. You need to communicate to resolve old conflicts. You need to successfully communicate that you have changed, so the people who support you believe you have changed. Just as important, how you communicate and present yourself gives reinforcing messages to yourself that you have changed and are on a new road to a new life. Communication skills give you increased confidence to solve problems, improve relationships, and get your needs met without taking drugs and alcohol. The common benefits of developing communication skills are (Silberman, & Hansburg, 2000):

1. When you understand someone else, you are appreciated. We like people who take the time to understand us.

2. Being listened to helps us feel important. When you explain yourself clearly, you are understood. If you can make your point clearly the first time, there will be less confusion later. This decreases misunderstandings in your relationships and saves you heartache, energy and time.

3. When you assert yourself, you are respected. People respect forthright individuals. When you are straight forward, other people admire your courage and personal strength. When you exchange feedback, you are enlightened. When you seek feedback, you discover the impact of your behavior on others. When you give feedback to others, you learn whether your views are on target or not. In the exchange, your relationships with others become more meaningful.

4. When you influence others positively, you are valued. Lots of people give advice, but people only welcome and value your advice if you give it in a constructive manner and you are sincere and helpful.

5. When you resolve conflict effectively, you are trusted. If you are kind to people and hard on problems, you won't hurt feelings and make enemies. Others will be inspired by you.

6. When you collaborate with teammates, you are prized. People with good team skills are the employees and clients who are wanted.

7. When you change, your relationships are renewed. The change in your behavior is often the catalyst for change in the other person's behavior. You create an opportunity for problem relationships to be mended.

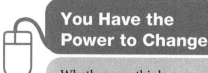

You Have the Power to Change

Whether you think you can, or think you can't, you're right. Henry Ford

Make your communication goals based on what is important to you. Your communication goals can be: understanding people, expressing yourself more clearly, asserting your needs, exchanging feedback, influencing others, resolving conflict, becoming a team player, or changing your own communication style (Silberman, & Hansburg, 2000). Whichever communication goals you choose, there *are* courses, books, and people who can help you to learn and practice those skills. A good place to start is the comprehensive and positive approach presented in "*PeopleSmart Developing Your Interpersonal Intelligence*," by Mel Silberman and Freda Hansburg.

How You Look, Talk & Act Is A Large Part Of Communicating

At school, do people frequently mistake the janitor for the principal? In a doctor's office, is the secretary frequently mistaken for the doctor? At the police station, is the chief of police frequently mistaken for the person in cells? How do you tell who is who when they don't have a name tag? It's the way they look, talk, move, and act. In the workplace, court, school, social situations, everywhere, first impressions are important.

When we see a person for the first time, we look at them to find out what kind of person they are and what they do. When we want to know if someone has changed, we look to see what has changed about them: appearance, composure, facial expression, voice, attitude, behavior or clothes. How will you and other people know you have changed and are no longer using drugs or alcohol?

Your appearance can have a positive or negative effect on your own attitude toward yourself, toward relapse prevention, and your new lifestyle. Check your appearance; eyes, smile and posture. Do you look and move like you have a positive attitude and are trustworthy, confidant, kind, successful? Do you look like you care about yourself?

For relapse prevention, you will need to develop your communication skills. You will need to work to ensure that what you say is well thought out, rational, considerate, and appropriate to the setting. But the greatest element of communication is *how you say your message*. We speak with *words and body language*. Every time we talk, our body gives additional meaning to our words (Wainwright, 1999). You can improve your communication by effectively using body language and ending old habits that no longer match who you want to be and what you want to project to others and yourself. You may no longer want to project the tough guy image or the sexual image.

Facial expression reveals emotion, whether you're sad, bored or happy. It reveals attitudes towards others, whether you're angry or just plain disinterested in a conversation. We make personality and other judgments about people, based on what we think we see in their faces. Simply smiling can change your own outlook and increase your attractiveness to others. Frowning has the reverse effect. A smile can be used to reduce tension and improve the emotional state of people who have depression or anxiety (Wainwright, 1999).

Changing posture is part of changing attitudes and establishing positive relationships. More erect body posture signals a feeling of hopefulness, confidence or dominance. Stooping postures are associated with lack of interest, depression or submissiveness (Wainwright, 1999). Does changing your body posture really change the way you feel? Yes, it does. Here's how you can test it:

- Straighten up in your chair, put your shoulders back.
- Put your hands in front of you, palms up, feet uncrossed, and flat on the floor.
- Hold your head up.
- Now, breathe deeply and slowly and smile.

Get Real Motivation!

What are your reasons for quitting? Are they strong enough? Revisit page 18.

Okay, what are you feeling now? What would someone think if they walked in right now and looked at you? They would think you were interested and positive.

Body size, shape and clothes influence how people perceive us and how much attention they pay to us. We can't give a positive impression of ourselves to others if our clothes don't send a positive message (Wainwright, 1999). *Take a few minutes and write down two or three positive messages that you want to send to yourself and others by the way you dress.*

1. _____

2. _____

3. _____

Now write down one or two simple ways you can change your clothing or appearance to more clearly send a positive message.

1. _____

_____

2. _____

_____

If you want to improve or change your image, start by looking at your reflection in a mirror and by having someone give you feedback. Actions to create a new you can include changing your hairstyle, changing your clothes, and getting in good physical shape. Pay more attention to your face and skincare. Observe others and how their clothes and physique are sending messages and learn from their successes. Avoid using extremes: the heavy sexual message, the tough guy message, the user message or the drug dealer message. How did you dress when you were drinking and using? What messages were *you* sending then? Decide on the changes you want and set about making them in an organized and determined manner.

In conversation, only 7% of the impact is from what you say, 93% of the impact is nonverbal (Wainwright, 1999). So, give lots of eye contact, keep an interested facial expression and smile a lot. Dress to send positive messages, keep healthy, and in good shape physically. Take the time to work on your body language and you will send clear, positive messages to others and to yourself that you are on the road to success. Take the time to learn more by reading books such as "Body Language" by Gordon R. Wainwright. A little extra knowledge can go a long way to learning how to change how you feel about yourself and how others see you.

New Habits Are Possible

Addictive behaviour patterns can be changed.

Active Listening Is Communicating

Active listening is a skill and the basis of effective communication. People who have had the experience of addiction focused on themselves and the drug. They lost the ability and habit of listening to others. Active listening *intentionally* focuses your attention on the person speaking to *understand* what they are saying. As the active listener, you listen, repeat back what you think they have said, and demonstrate you understand what they're saying.

Active listening is a way of *listening and responding* to other people that improves mutual understanding *and* actually reduces conflict. If you are engaged in conflict and are busy formulating a response to what's being said instead of paying attention, then the conflict escalates. If you focus first on hearing what the person is really saying, you can then better respond to reduce the conflict (University of Colorado, 1998). Active listening avoids misunderstanding, because part of active listening is always taking the time to confirm and clarify what the other person said, *and* what emotions they're trying to express. Active listening opens people up and encourages them to say more.

To get others to listen to you, first send clear signals that *you want to listen*. Listen first, then, ask to be heard. It is difficult to accept that someone is listening if they are looking away. So, maintain eye contact and lean slightly toward them. It is common to bring your head closer to the person when you are really listening. Practice sending those listening signals. Physical closeness signals intellectual and emotional closeness. Nodding indicates you understand or agree. Using these behaviors signals you are giving your full and undivided attention (University of Colorado, 1998).

> *Listening is the physical act of hearing.*
>
> *Active listening communicates interest through body language and the ability to explain what you have just heard.*

You need to work to repair relationships that have been impacted by addiction. Remember to use all your communication skills. Use posture, eye contact, head nods, and repeat what you have heard from them in your words. Describe the emotions you think they are projecting. When people are intoxicated, active listening skills disappear which results in misinterpretations of what happened and what was said. When in conflict or under stress, your deliberate use of active listening skills can lower tension and support a positive resolution. Active listening skills can help you get the most out of an educational course. Whether you are beginning a new relationship or working to improve an old relationship, active listening can bring about mutual understanding. Active listening is an effective coping skill to reduce stress, to hear from others, and get your opinion heard in a positive way.

Take Time To Practice

Try this exercise. Find a person to practice with. First, let them take the role of listener and you take the role of the speaker. Share with them in five minutes what you know about active listening. Have them repeat it back to you. Then switch roles. Now, give feedback to each other on the listening skills you both used and your verbal and nonverbal communication. How did it feel to have someone take five minutes to truly listen to what you were saying and try to get the gist of what you were feeling? How did it feel to truly listen to someone else?

You Can Change!

What do you want your new life to look like?

Practice active listening frequently and when you are in relaxed situations so that when you are under stress it will be an easy tool for you to use. Active listening can reduce conflict and increase a sense of trust. Give it a try.

Summary

Now that your experience with addiction has ended, there are many issues that need to be aired, heard, and worked on. Practice your verbal and nonverbal communication skills, and your conflict resolution skills **before** the "big" conversations. Timing for important conversations is everything.

1. Allow enough time to get ready, physically and mentally.
2. Allow enough time to practice what you have learned.
3. Allow enough time for your conversations.
4. Allow enough time to evaluate how the "big" conversation went and to plan for the next time.

There are many conflict resolution and communication courses, pick one that meets your needs. Get going today, you've got a lot to learn and a lot to share with others.

· ·

References

Silberman, Mel, & Hansburg, Freda. (2000). *"PeopleSmart Developing Your Interpersonal Intelligence."* San Francisco. Berrett-Koehler Publishers Inc., 12-18. PeopleSmart Scale, Pages 12 - 18.

Tjosvold, Dean. (1993). *"Learning to Manage Conflict, Getting People to Work Together Productively."* New York. Lexington Books. 4-5, 7-8.

University of Colorado, International Online Training Program On Intractable Conflict (1998) *"Active Listening."* Retrieved from http://www.colorado.edu/conflict/peace/treatment/activel.htm

Wainwright, Gordon R. (1999). *"Body Language."* Illinois. Contemporary Publishing. 1, 21-32, 58-68, 70-82.

Chapter Eight

Relationships And Relapse

You can succeed and make your last relapse the last!

Chapter 8

Relationships And Relapse

Some of your relationships have encouraged you to use drugs and alcohol and supported you to remain stuck in an addiction lifestyle. In this chapter you will find information that helps you to look at what you can do to change the way you relate to family, friends, and acquaintances. Building positive and safe relationships will support you in your relapse prevention plan and in achieving your life goals.

Before reading further, take a few minutes and think of which of your family and friends have been supportive of you and your decision to stop using drugs and alcohol. Then, answer the following questions:

1. Who are the key people who supported you to stop using?

   _____

   _____

2. With whom would you like to build a better relationship now that you are not using?

   _____

   _____

3. List the personality traits people like about the non-using you. Examples of positive personality traits are confidence, sincerity, optimism, warmth, persistence, humor or kindness.

   _____

   _____

4. What are your own positive personality traits that you admire?

   _____

   _____

5. What traits do you feel may have gotten lost or pushed aside by addiction?

   _____

   _____

Use these answers to remind you that you are a person worthy of quality relationships and able to attract others.

Families Impact Addiction Behavior

Families can provide positive support to help you to prevent relapse. They can also play a role in a decision to return to using. *Positive family support is highly predictive of long-term abstinence and takes the form of healthy pressure not to use, participating in your rehab and life goals, participating in reducing your stress, and helping you to reduce interpersonal conflict* (Marlatt, & Donovan, 2005).

Negative Family And Friend Support

Negative family and friend support increases the risk of relapse and takes the form of social pressure to use and increased interpersonal conflict. What does this look like?

- Encouraging you to attend events with drug and alcohol use such as house parties.
- Belittling your attempts to learn new activities and make friends who don't use.
- Discouraging you from returning to abstinence, if you do have a lapse.
- Continuing to offer you alcohol, cigarettes or drugs.
- Tracking your days of abstinence in a negative fashion. *You'll never make it to thirty days.*
- Drinking or using in front of you, leaving drugs or cigarette packages out.
- Talking about how much fun you used to be.

Negative family support takes the form of creating and maintaining interpersonal conflict:

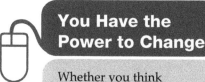

You Have the Power to Change

Whether you think you can, or think you can't, you're right. Henry Ford

Chapter Eight: Relationships And Relapse

- Using anger, threats, and physical aggression during disagreements.

- Instead of resolving disagreements, using nagging, pouting or cold shoulder treatments.

- Repeatedly bringing up past conflicts including your past drug or alcohol use and past behaviors that were part of using such as lying.

Anger is the most common and powerful emotion that must be managed during family conflict. Negative support can be direct or very subtle. If you improve your listening skills and your ability to provide feedback to family members who provide **negative support**, you can subtly change some of their behaviors. When you cannot influence someone's behavior, you can use boundary setting skills that are discussed later in this chapter.

New Habits Are Possible

Addictive behaviour patterns can be changed.

Positive Family And Friend Support

Positive family support comes from those people who trust in your ability to achieve your goals and maintain abstinence. They help you to improve your skills and don't just pat you on the back. Positive support is demonstrated when family and friends take specific actions that help you to achieve your goals. These might include: offering to drive you to a job interview, helping you prep for an exam, helping you stay healthy by running with you or participating in sporting events with you, attending and participating in counseling sessions or communication classes with you.

To prevent relapse you will need to seek out family members or friends who are willing to actively support you in your decision to remain abstinent. To succeed in repairing relationships and developing a more supportive family network you will need to develop communication skills and anger management skills to assist you to resolve interpersonal conflicts. **If you are in a partner or marital relationship you may want to consider relationship or marital therapy. Both have been proven to reduce relapse, particularly for those with alcohol abuse problems.** Your relapse risk is reduced when partners agree to:

- Learn communication skills to give you positive and honest feedback that reinforce your abstinence and life goals.

- Maintain an alcohol and drug free house.

- Learn conflict resolution skills.

- Not associate with former friends or family who are heavy drinkers or drug users.

Partners who actively and positively support you through these types of behaviors will increase the probability of your success and improve the relationship.

Guilt, Shame And The Addiction Lifestyle

Guilt and shame are negative emotions. Guilt is an acute awareness of having done wrong, accompanied by feelings of regret. Shame includes feelings of dishonor, unworthiness, and embarrassment. We all have secrets in our lives, things we are embarrassed about, that make us feel shame or guilt; things we have done to ourselves or others; or things that were done to us by others, although we were not responsible (Potter-Efron, R., & Potter-Efron, P., 1989). Addiction may have resulted in you doing things that left you feeling guilt or shame.

Guilt and shame often exist together. When you are addicted to crack, you feel guilty for falling into this trap. To support your addiction, you sell yourself for sex or steal and you feel shame, because you know you have done something demeaning. You are still addicted and continue to feel guilt over it. Guilt and shame exist together and are sometimes indistinguishable.

Guilt

Pride is a level of respect for yourself, a belief in the value of your personal character, body, life, efforts or achievements. Everyone needs to have a sense of pride about themselves. Shame is a negative feeling about the self. The experience of shame may result in feelings that you are defective, incompetent, weak, inferior or deserving of criticism (Potter-Efron, R., & Potter-Efron, P., 1989). Guilt, on the other hand, is about doing harm or failure of doing. Guilty people may have gone too far and harmed others such as stealing money from their family. They may not have done enough such as failing to take care of and protect their children.

As you have learned, unmanaged negative emotional states are linked to relapse. Guilt and shame are negative emotions. The lifestyle of addiction leads to doing things we would never have done before and will never do again once the experience of addiction is over. Examples include: stealing money, wasting valuable years intoxicated, harming someone in anger, going to jail, performing sexual acts for money or drugs, making promises you never intended to keep, being manipulated or manipulating others. The possibilities are endless.

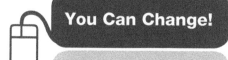

You Can Change!

What do you want your new life to look like?

Using the "Guilt and Shame Stress Inventory Worksheet" at the end of this chapter, write your personal definition of guilt and of shame. Use only a couple words for each entry and record the things you feel most guilty about, and the things you feel most ashamed about. Write down those items where you feel both guilt and shame.

Guilt can be good. It can motivate you to take action and make amends. It can motivate you to change your behavior. It can motivate you to look at your value system and make changes there too. So, guilt can be good if it leads to positive action in your life (Potter-Efron, R., & Potter-Efron, P., 1989). Because guilt is most often found in doing or a failure of doing, it is most easily overcome by action. That's why it's a good motivator. You have begun your guilt inventory, so take a few minutes now and decide for which items it would be easiest to take action. For example: paying back money. That can be a pretty easy action. Other actions may be more difficult, like making amends to a partner or children. Decide what actions you can take to correct or make amends for each problem and end the guilt.

> **Don't Give Up!**
>
> It's hard work, but you can finish this book!

When guilt is managed ineffectively, you can overload yourself with responsibilities and attempt anything to make amends for all your past mistakes, however small or far in the past. You begin to worry about the possible negative consequences of every action you have ever taken. You begin to see only black or white, right or wrong in every part of your life. You may even become immobilized when you can not figure out how to make amends. It is important to be objective with yourself when you're experiencing guilt and be sure your actions to make amends are based on sound and rational thinking. It is helpful to check out your level of guilt, and the decisions related to that guilt, with someone who is supportive and unbiased. It can be a friend, a counselor or person you trust and are confidant will give you quality feedback.

Think carefully about what actions you will take to make amends. Watch out for dysfunctional, all or nothing thinking, and get on with it. Remember, there may not be a way to clean up all the things you feel guilty about. If someone has passed away, they won't ever see how you have changed. You may have to learn to accept what you have done. Often the person you will need to forgive is yourself.

Acceptance is when you realize some things can't be changed and let it be. Acceptance does not mean you're happy about it. It's just that you accept something happened, you did it, it's over, there is nothing more you can do about it now, and you have to let it be. Return to your "Guilt and Shame Stress Inventory Worksheet" at the end of this chapter and next to each guilt stressor you have identified add any strategies, including acceptance, that you want to use.

Shame

Managing shame is sometimes a lot more difficult than guilt. It requires rebuilding your self esteem and faith in yourself. This takes lifestyle change and that takes time. To manage shame, name what you did or what you're still doing to cause you to feel ashamed. First *stop* whatever you are doing that causes you to feel ashamed. Accept that it will take time to work through the feelings you have about yourself. Find a counselor or a trusted friend to talk to. Shame can be isolating. When you begin communicating with others, be cautious about who you talk to. Not everyone should be trusted to hear your story. Talk only to people who will not make you feel more ashamed (Potter-Efron, R., & Potter-Efron, P., 1989). A mental health professional may be the first option to try. Return to the "Guilt and Shame Stress Inventory Worksheet" at the end of the chapter and list any techniques or strategies you would like to use to manage each shame stressor identified on page two of the form.

Simple Actions To Reduce Guilt And Shame

Start with a total health exam from a physician and make sure you address any chronic health issues. Then, begin a regular exercise program to increase your overall health and feelings of well-being. Focus on your positive achievements and get adequate sleep, to increase your ability to overcome negative thinking. Make healthy food choices to increase your energy and positive feelings about yourself. Reduce your stress through using relaxation techniques and being rigorous in your daily life. Keeping to schedules and meeting your commitments will increase your overall feelings of self-worth and competence. Do something every day that makes you feel proud of you. Return to your "Guilt and Shame Stress Inventory Worksheet" at the end of the chapter and add any of the above techniques you want to use next to the specific guilt or shame stressor you have identified.

> *Not everyone should be trusted to hear your story. Talk only to people who will not make you feel more ashamed.*

Guilt and shame can lead to negative thinking that supports a return to use of drugs and alcohol. A good resource for managing guilt and shame is *"The Feeling Good Handbook,"* by Dr. David Burns. It will take time and action to overcome feelings of guilt and shame and rebuild your self esteem. Each small step takes you closer to your life goals.

Planning For Healthy Relationships To Prevent Relapse

People who quit using and drinking and who do not remove drug and alcohol users from their social network (circle of friends, family, and acquaintances) have a very high risk of returning to use or relapse (Marlatt, & Donovan, 2005). Producing, dealing or distributing drugs predicts a lower probability of achieving abstinence and predicts higher levels of use (Marlatt, & Donovan, 2005). If you want

Chapter Eight: Relationships And Relapse

to remain abstinent, you need to end your relationships with people who use or who are in the drug economy. Relationships based on mutual involvement in drug and alcohol use contribute to relapse. The drug is always the most important part of the relationship and the user will continue drinking, using or dealing. When you quit and the other person continues using, you will need to end or set specific limits on the relationship or you will put yourself at a high risk for relapse. Considerable practice is needed to develop the assertive and communication skills required to maintain safe relationships with people who have destructive behaviors.

Negative influences may be more powerful than positive influence in social networks (Marlatt, & Donovan, 2005). Negative influences include people who offer drugs or alcohol, use around the person in recovery, show behaviors that stimulate craving, and produce cues for using. *If you have many positive people in your social network and still include one drug or alcohol using person, you are placing yourself at a high risk of relapse, particularly in your early recovery.* A safe environment for the person who successfully completes treatment and rehab *does not* include people who use alcohol or drugs or who are involved in the drug economy.

Get Real Motivation!

What are your reasons for quitting? Are they strong enough? Revisit page 18.

Becoming Mentally And Physically Healthier To Build Healthy Relationships

The healthier you become mentally and physically, the more you will increase your coping skills and energy. This will make it easier for you to attract positive people into your life. We tend to attract people who are similar to us. As your emotional and physical health improves, you will attract and surround yourself with other healthy, positive people.

Families Need Help Too

For your family to move on from your addiction experience, you may have to help them. Families experience a wide range of emotions such as anger, fear, anxiety or depression during their family member's addiction. They may need to learn more about addiction and how to get help and support for themselves. It may help them to talk with other families who have experienced similar problems. As your family members are empowered by quality information and acquiring new skills, their negative emotions will lessen toward themselves and you. Helping your family members to acknowledge their feelings may be uncomfortable for you and them, yet it's important to their and your recovery (Daley, & Marsili, 2005).

Family members need to understand and support your plans to prevent lapse and relapse. Involving supportive family to some extent in your plans contributes to a better outcome for you (Daley & Marsili, 2005). Family members need an understanding of addiction and recovery so they can develop behaviors that will support you as well as help themselves to effectively manage their own feelings and behaviors.

Take a few minutes and make a list of all your current family relationships. For each person on your list, make an assessment of your relationship. For each relationship:

- First list strengths and then weaknesses that may impact your relapse prevention plan. Underline the weaknesses you think are not changeable in the short term, such as a family member who is currently using and has no desire to change.

- Check mark relationships that have positive qualities and that you want to maintain and increase, such as *your relationship with your mother who is a good listener and uses humor to cheer you up.*

This is going to form an important part of your social support plan.

Family Relationship:	Strengths and Weaknesses:
☐	_____
☐	_____
☐	_____
☐	_____
☐	_____

You can succeed and make your last relapse the last!

Social Support And Relapse Prevention

Social support is not the same as a support group. Support groups are structured managed meetings. A social support network is a circle of people who increase your sense of belonging, purpose, self-worth, and promote your positive mental and physical health. People with varied and strong social supports live longer (MayoClinic.com, 2005). Talking with a non-using friend over coffee can help you through difficult times. Your non using friends and social contacts can encourage you to stay free of drugs and alcohol and support you to manage stress and depression. They can also be there to celebrate your successes and you can be there to celebrate theirs. Sometimes, just knowing someone is there for you is enough to reduce stress and let you get on with living your new life.

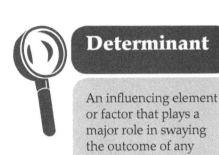

Determinant

An influencing element or factor that plays a major role in swaying the outcome of any given situation

Social support plays a critical role as a determinant of relapse. Positive social support is highly associated with reduced relapse and negative support with increased use (Marlatt, & Donovan, 2005). There is a high probability of your relapse if your network includes people with whom you have high levels of conflict and people who use. To reduce your relapse risk, *you need to seek out people who will support you in your decision to stop drinking and using and avoid those people who will not support you.*

Your social support network needs to include friends, colleagues, and acquaintances you can turn to for friendship or help in times of crisis. Make sure your life partner is supportive of your abstinence and life goals. Your network can help you achieve your life goals, if you find sufficient people who are able to provide:

- Emotional support.
- Some practical help.
- Share points of view with you (Fairbrother, 2004).

Using a blank piece of paper, take as long as it takes, and list all your family members, friends, work and school contacts. Remember to include your current family relationships that you have already assessed.

Step 1: Weed Out There are people in our lives that by their presence and their actions influence us to make decisions, take actions or view ourselves in ways that are self-harming and self-defeating. Strike these people from your list. First cross out the people who use. During the first few months following abstinence, it is imperative that you limit or eliminate any contact with people who are actively using drugs or alcohol. Contact with people who use should be limited to a safe place and to when they are sober or free of drugs. These people typically have substances in their homes, on their person or have active contacts for accessing drugs and will continue to put you at risk of relapse.

Next review your list and cross out people who are physically or verbally abusive to you. Next, cross out people who may manipulate you. These are people who cause high stress in your life through their behaviors. Planning to stay away from people who may put you at risk is called problem avoidance. By practicing problem avoidance you will be keeping yourself safe.

Step 2: Family and Friend Support Now identify positive family, friends and contacts. Circle the names of the people who are able to provide positive support to you and who have the abilities and resources that match the type of support you need. Use your "Support Network Worksheet" at the end of this chapter and the following categories to help you clarify in your own mind the type of help individuals may be able to provide. Start your list now.

Emotional supporters are people who tell you they care about you, believe in you, and who think well of you. They help you to stay true to your goals and give you the opportunity to help them as well. They give you honest feedback, both positive and negative (Fairbrother, 2004).

Practical helpers are people who care enough to give you help with things like money, food, assistance with cooking or a safe place to stay. These people are capable of giving practical help because <u>they have the resources themselves</u> and they are willing to share them with you. They help you to meet your goals by giving support that directly keeps you on track. They are people who do not hold their help as ransom or expect particular behaviors from you. They are credible people whose help you see as valuable and dependable (Fairbrother, 2004).

People who are able to share different points of view need to be part of your network. These are people whose knowledge, information, and experience can help you to develop your life goals and find success (Fairbrother, 2004). These are people you can turn to in times of doubt, when making key decisions or solving particular problems. Think of the multiple skills you will need to succeed in all spheres of your life, relationships, physical and mental health, work and school, home and community, and communications. You will need credible, knowledgeable people who are willing to offer their honest opinion about how they view particular situations. They will be willing to tell you how they would choose to handle a situation and help you to make your own best decisions. Think of people like your counselor, minister or even your neighbor.

New Habits Are Possible

Addictive behaviour patterns can be changed.

Experts can give you factual information, and are people you turn to for quality information before you take action (Fairbrother, 2004). This area is particularly important when it comes to making decisions regarding your health, future goals or even your past experience of addiction. These people can be doctors, teachers . . . experts in any area you need help.

Make your own resource list of all the sources of information you can use to get additional facts to validate and plan for your life goals. These may include websites, government agencies, and organizations that have factual information available to you in your community.

It is now time to pick your best social support for each area. Try to have at least one person as a support in each of the four areas: emotional support, practical help, sharing points of view, and sharing information. If you have only one support person to cover all areas, eventually, they will burn out. It is easier to find people who have particular skills rather than looking for someone who can be everything for you.

> *The risk of relapse is reduced for those who also engage in providing assistance to people in their support network as well as receiving assistance.*

Your current connections with your family, friends, and others can be improved and enriched to ensure they remain meaningful as you change and grow. Changing your connections with your family requires taking the time to plan in detail how you can relate to them differently and how you can have them see you differently. Think of areas in their lives where you can provide assistance or can recognize their strengths. Do they have interests that you can talk about or participate in that are not related to your old roles? Are there ways you can help them? Everyone needs helping people in their lives.

Our sense of dignity and self worth is reinforced when we can act as helping adults for others and practice compassion and caring. *The risk of relapse is reduced for those who also engage in providing assistance to people in their support network as well as receiving assistance.* Lending support to others is part of building *your* support network and it will increase your sense of personal value (Brooks, & Goldstein, 2004).

Look at relationships as opportunities to help you meet the variety of needs in your life and to provide help to other people. Creating vibrant relationships means ending some relationships, beginning new relationships, and improving others. All relationships require work. You will now want to challenge, change or renew many of your relationships.

Interpersonal Boundary Setting Reduces Risk Of Relapse

Interpersonal boundaries reduce stress, reduce conflict, and help to keep you safe. The purpose of having interpersonal boundaries is to protect and take care of you. You need to be able to tell other people when they act in ways that are not acceptable to you. You need to be self-centered in the sense of *self-care centered*. The addiction lifestyle encourages a blurring and erosion of interpersonal boundaries.

Intoxicated people have sex, share confidential information, experience violence, and allow people into their lives that they would never have considered before the addiction. The addiction lifestyle erodes the individual's ability to set clear boundaries for themselves and for others.

To keep a safe support network, you will need to set up interpersonal boundaries to keep yourself safe, and to reduce the risk of relapse. It is your responsibility to communicate clearly to others when they respect or ignore your choice to stop using drugs and alcohol. Learning to set boundaries is essential to keeping yourself safe and free from drug and alcohol use.

Becoming focused on caring for yourself will support you to uphold your new values and goals. Setting boundaries will help you stay healthy in all areas of your life. It is impossible to have a healthy relationship with someone who has no boundaries or with someone who cannot communicate directly and honestly. If you have family or friends who are still using drugs and alcohol or who are earning a living through some aspect of the drug economy, you will need to decide how to set boundaries to keep yourself safe. Turn now to the end of this chapter and quickly review the "Self Care Recovery Boundaries Worksheet."

To keep an alcohol and drug-free home, you must be able to control who enters your home and how they behave in your home. You will need to set boundaries with others on how you will or will not share information about your past addiction and on the extent you will allow others to comment on your choice to remain drug and alcohol free. You will need to set boundaries on how often you will allow others to bring up negative things you may or may not have done. Does this sound difficult? In the beginning it will be.

What Is An Interpersonal Boundary?

A boundary is a limit, the point at which something ends. An interpersonal boundary is the limit you set on the behavior of others and on your own behavior based on clear and sensible thinking. Boundaries control when and how others approach you or behave around you, such as, *I will not allow a hug from someone I do not like. I will not allow drugs or alcohol in my own home. I will lock the door on my bedroom when I need to be alone. I will not allow smoking in my home or in the presence of my children. I will not allow drinking in my car.*

Boundaries allow you to take care of yourself and live a value-based life. *I believe exercise is my form of mediation and I will exercise each day. I believe that my body is my most important asset and I will not abuse my body with drugs and alcohol. And, I will not allow someone to dictate the time or type of sex I have. Honesty is my basic value and I refuse to allow someone else to talk me into dishonest behavior for whatever reason.*

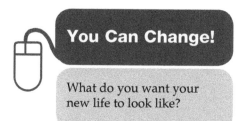

You Can Change!

What do you want your new life to look like?

Boundaries allow you to maintain confidentiality about your personal information and protect yourself from the negative emotions of others. *I will only share information and feelings about my past addiction when it will advance my personal growth. I have my own ideas and I do not have to depend on others for solutions. I can defend with clear information my right to choose not to drink or to use drugs.*

Boundaries can be reinforced by words and action. *Walk away from a person who is trying to convince you to have a drink.* Think and say the words: *I do not drink. Both words and actions can be effective ways of communicating boundaries.* Boundaries are ways to protect you such as refusing to go rock-climbing with friends when you are not trained for this sport; refusing to go to a party where drugs will be used; or refusing to have sex without a condom. Use well thought out boundaries to protect yourself from inappropriate behavior and your self-esteem will grow.

Define in writing the behavior you will or will not carry out to maintain safety and self-respect such as: *I will not get drunk and make a fool of myself. I do not use alcohol and drugs to make friends or have better sex. I do not get caught in a lie, because I tell the truth, even when it's difficult. If I am with someone who becomes violent, I leave. I exercise, get enough sleep, and eat well. I forgive myself for my mistakes.*

Boundaries, when they are clear, specific, and reasonable are enforceable. You tell your ex-wife you will talk with her about financial problems and you will not accept your former addiction as a reason to agree to pay more support. You tell your friend you will go skiing with him, but you will not go to the bar afterwards. You tell your friend you will not go to the club where you used to buy drugs. *When people are unwilling to respect the boundaries you've established based on self-respect, self care, and core values, you end the relationship.*

> **Get Real Motivation!**
>
> What are your reasons for quitting? Are they strong enough? Revisit page 18.

To begin to decide where you need to set boundaries, go back to your stress inventory and look at the situations where clear boundaries would have helped reduce stress and prevent relapse. Circle the ones that require a boundary. Were they boundaries for your own behavior or boundaries you needed to set on behavior of people around you? Think about the other areas in your life where boundaries would have helped to achieve a goal: relationships, school/work, physical/mental health, home/community, and communication.

Return to Chapter 2 and to the list that you made of the names of the people who taught you to use drugs and alcohol and encouraged you to continue using. Add these people to the physical or emotional columns on your "Self Care Recovery Boundaries Worksheet." Develop physical or emotional boundary actions to keep yourself safe from these people, such as "Do not answer phone calls from Sally, my former dealer."

Using your "Self Care Recovery Boundaries Worksheet," at the end of this chapter write your own relapse prevention boundaries. Write them for your person, body, space, home, car, exercise or recreation. Write them for your feelings and how you will manage sharing, intimacy, and relationships. Write them about your knowledge and how you will improve your skills and problem-solving, and use your own solutions for recovery. Write them about your life values that you will no longer ignore or allow others to ignore. What is important to you that will help you meet your life goals and maintain your self respect and your self-care? Make sure you have written boundaries to help you keep on track.

Living and Enforcing Boundaries

Boundaries can be shared and clearly communicated if they are written. Write yours. People share their boundaries by their actions, and verbal and nonverbal communication. Practice behaving in ways that clearly signal your boundaries. You can't share and live your boundaries if you don't know them yourself. Giving confused or conflicting messages during recovery can result in relapse. Discuss your boundary plan with a trusted person or a supportive family member. Ask a friend or a counselor for advice and feedback, then practice, practice, practice. Send clear signals to yourself and others that you do not use alcohol or drugs and that you live your values.

Use the "Support Network Worksheet" at the end of this chapter to identify the positive people who you will invite into your life.

Summary

Your family and friends can be a part of your new life or they can pull you back to your old life. It's up to you to decide who will be part of your social network and who will be limited in their contact with you. Setting boundaries for yourself and others will help you create and keep a positive social network. Setting boundaries will help you manage guilt and shame. Taking action on guilt can result in healed relationships and increased self-esteem for you. Reaching out to help your family and friends increase their knowledge and understanding about your past addiction and its impact on them, can help them heal as well as gradually improve their relationships with you.

Taking the time to identify who will be in your support network and then working to improve those relationships will take you forward to your goals and ensure your relapse prevention plan is strengthened rather than weakened by relationships. It's up to you. You can't change others but you can take action to reduce your guilt and shame and to keep yourself safe from destructive people. You can build positive relationships and enjoy them in your new life.

References

Marlatt, G.A., & Donovan, D.M., (Eds.). (2005). *"Relapse Prevention Maintenance Strategies in the Treatment of Addictive Behaviours."*(2nd Edition). New York. The Guilford Press. 13, 20, 28-29, 78, 233.

Potter-Efron, Ronald & Potter-Efron, Patricia (1989). *"Letting Go of Shame, Understanding How Shame Affects Your Life."* San Francisco. Harper and Row, Publishers. 121-125, 132-141.

Daley, Dennis C. & Marsili, Ricardo (2005). <u>No One is Left Unharmed: Dual Disorders and the Family.</u> *Counselor: the Magazine for Addiction Professionals*. Deerfield Beach, Florida: Health Communications, Inc. February, 2005 Vol. 6. 37-43.

MayoClinic.com Tools For Healthier Lives. (2005). <u>Developing social support: How to cultivate a network of friends to help you through rough times</u>. Mayo Foundation for Medical Education and Research. Retrieved from <u>http://www.mayoclinic.com</u>

Fairbrother, Nichole. (2004) Prepared for BC Partners for Mental Health and Addictions Information. "Who needs social support? We all do!" Wellness Module 3: Social Support. Retrieved from www.heretohelp.bc.ca

Brooks, Robert, & Goldstein, Sam. (2004). *"The Power Of Resilience, Achieving Balance, Confidence, and Personal Strength in Your Life."* New York. Contemporary Books. 181.

New Habits Are Possible

Addictive behaviour patterns can be changed.

Guilt and Shame Stress Inventory Worksheet

Write your personal definition of guilt:

What approach to managing guilt do you use most often and why isn't it effective?

My Stressors and Action Plan
Identify all your guilt stressors. Then identify which are high-risk stressors, those that influenced you in the days prior to your last relapse. Underline or circle the high-risk stressors, and pay particular attention to developing techniques to manage them.

Guilt Stressors	Technique to Manage, Setting Boundaries or Life Change Required

You can succeed and make your last relapse the last!

Chapter Eight: Guilt And Shame Stress Inventory Worksheet

Write your personal definition of shame:

What approach to managing shame do you use most often and why isn't it effective?

My Stressors and Action Plan
Identify all your shame stressors. Then identify which are high-risk stressors, those that influenced you in the days prior to your last relapse. Underline or circle the high-risk stressors, and pay particular attention to developing techniques to manage them.

Shame Stressor	Technique to Manage, Setting Boundaries or Life Change Required

Shame and Guilt Stressors	Technique to Manage, Setting Boundaries or Life Change Required

Self Care Recovery Boundaries Worksheet

Stressors are the result of poor or no boundaries your life. Poor boundaries cause stress, which leads to relapse. Identify areas in your life that require boundaries to keep you safe. Underline as high-risk those areas that led to your last relapse such as your brother sold you drugs, relationship boundary required.

Areas of Self care in your life include:

- self respect
- healthy life style
- value based spiritual growth
- continual search to improve and test personal knowledge

* Pay particular attention to relationships that may require boundaries in all four areas of physical, emotional, intellectual or spiritual.

Physical: keeping myself physically safe from actual physical harm or potential harm

You can succeed and make your last relapse the last!

Chapter Eight: Self Care Recovery Boundaries Worksheet

Self care includes:
- self respect
- healthy life style
- value based spiritual growth
- continual search to improve and test personal knowledge

* Pay particular attention to relationships that may require boundaries in all four areas of physical, emotional, intellectual or spiritual.

Emotional: keeping myself emotionally safe from actual or potential verbal, non verbal and emotional harm

Self Care Recovery Boundaries Worksheet

Self care includes:

- self respect
- healthy life style
- value based spiritual growth
- continual search to improve and test personal knowledge

* Pay particular attention to relationships that may require boundaries in all four areas of physical, emotional, intellectual or spiritual.

Intellectual: keeping myself intellectually safe from ideas and values that are not based on rational information and evidence

You can succeed and make your last relapse the last!

Chapter Eight: Self Care Recovery Boundaries Worksheet

Self care includes:

- self respect
- healthy life style

- value based spiritual growth
- continual search to improve and test personal knowledge

* Pay particular attention to relationships that may require boundaries in all four areas of physical, emotional, intellectual or spiritual.

Spiritual: keeping myself spiritually safe from actions and potential actions that would go against my core values and beliefs

Support Network Worksheet

Contact Information		Emotional Support	Practical help	Sharing points of view	Sharing information
Name:	Relationship:				
Contact @					
Physical Distance:					
Last contacted:	Planned contact date:				
Name:	Relationship:				
Contact @					
Physical Distance:					
Last contacted:	Planned contact date:				
Name:	Relationship:				
Contact @					
Physical Distance:					
Last contacted:	Planned contact date:				
Name:	Relationship:				
Contact @					
Physical Distance:					
Last contacted:	Planned contact date:				

You can succeed and make your last relapse the last!

Chapter Eight: Support Network Worksheet

Support Network Worksheet

Contact Information	Emotional Support	Practical help	Sharing points of view	Sharing information
Name: Relationship: Contact @ Physical Distance: Last contacted: Planned contact date:				
Name: Relationship: Contact @ Physical Distance: Last contacted: Planned contact date:				
Name: Relationship: Contact @ Physical Distance: Last contacted: Planned contact date:				
Name: Relationship: Contact @ Physical Distance: Last contacted: Planned contact date:				

Chapter Nine

Stay on Track, Develop a Personal Vision

Chapter 9

Stay on Track, Develop a Personal Vision

What Causes People To Change?

Humiliation, shame, guilt, and anxiety are not the primary causes of change. These negative emotions can actually have the reverse effect, causing a person to feel that change is impossible and undeserved. Constructive behavior change seems to happen when the person connects the change with something of intrinsic value to them, something important to them, and something cherished by them (Miller, & Rollnick, 2002). *The way to find the motivation to change is to find what truly matters to you. A way to keep changing is to continuously clarify what truly matters to you.*

> *The way to find the motivation to change is to find what truly matters to you.*

All people making life changes experience ambivalence. For you, ambivalence is feeling positive and negative emotions about stopping the use of drugs and alcohol. You can work through your periods of ambivalence by:

- Clarifying and challenging the values that allowed you to use.
- Creating new values that support change.
- Challenging your expectations of what a return to alcohol or drugs will give you.

Exploring Values

Everyone has something that is important in their life, something they are motivated about. Everyone has values and goals, although they may not be voiced, written or even acknowledged (Miller, & Rollnick, 2002). Now that you've stopped using, your mind will become clear enough to allow you to find and define your core values; what is most important to you. Then you can explore and understand how drinking and using are in conflict with your core values and life goals.

You can build and strengthen your own motivation and create the inner resources to sustain change. Values are often contrasted with material things and can mean different things to people. Some view values as beliefs that relate to religion, a higher power or a universal connection to all living things. Some people view discussions about values as a waste of time.

What is a value-driven life? Simply put, it is a life that is lived on the basis of a consistent set of beliefs that advances the pursuit of worthwhile goals. The set of values chosen determines the person's purpose in life. Ultimately, your values and personal beliefs determine your behavior, and that includes whether or not you choose to abuse alcohol and drugs. Values are concerned with the long-term direction of your life. *Attaining a specific goal is not as important as maintaining a continuing commitment to stay pointed in the right direction.*

Why Is Defining Your Values Important?

Values become beliefs. Beliefs become behavior. People may say values are pointless and some might say defining them is a waste of your time. However, when you stop to reflect, it is clear that all meaningful and lasting change and accomplishments in the world occur because someone acted on positive values and beliefs. Your values and beliefs can help you step higher or drop lower.

> *Attaining a specific goal is not as important as maintaining a continuing commitment to stay pointed in the right direction.*

When someone raises their level of expectation for themselves, it is most likely due to an internal value system or belief system that they hold. *The values that count are the standards you hold yourself to when no one else is looking.* Doing the minimum is not enough when you have values that you consciously use as your behavior guide. It is the *core values you choose to live by* that compel you to do better or allow you to slide into indifference (Richmond, 1999).

Advancements in personal life and in the world are made when someone says; *this isn't good enough and I'm going to do it better*. Through pursuing your dream of changing things for the better in your life and in the world around you, your passion for life grows, and improved personal character and lasting fulfillment are achieved. Values and beliefs can guide you on your journey to abstinence and to achieving meaningful life goals.

How Did We Develop Our First Values And Beliefs?

When we were kids, the values and beliefs our parents and families talked about and acted on became a large part of our first value system. Our friends and peer groups were the next major influence. We learned from them about values that were different from our family's beliefs. The beliefs and behaviors of our heroes and people we admired also left a mark on our developing values. Formal institutions like school, media, and organized religion also instilled values within us. Societal values demonstrated through the laws and courts had some influence on developing our value systems. A lot of people helped you form your values and beliefs.

Get Real Motivation!

What are your reasons for quitting? Are they strong enough? Revisit page 18.

Chapter Nine: Stay on Track, Develop a Personal Vision

Some questions for you to ask now are:

1. Who chose your value and belief system for you when you were using? You or the people around you who were also using?

   _____
   _____

2. Will your current value system support you to get to the ultimate destination you want in your life? Will your value and belief system help you to prevent relapse? Or, will it ensure that you will relapse?

   _____
   _____

3. Have you ever written out the basic values and beliefs you use to guide your every day, moment to moment decisions?

   _____
   _____

If your current value system does not positively support you in achieving success in your life, why not change it to one that will? If you aren't clear what your value system is, then it's time to figure it out.

Choose your character and you choose your life. Character is not how much fun you are or your personality traits. Character is how you act and what you do in a time of crisis. It is what you do when no one is looking. *Choose your character and choose your new life.*

Let's start with something concrete. Take a few moments and imagine your ultimate dream job. Think about the kind of person who has that occupation.

Now answer the following questions:

Make Your Last Relapse The Last

1. How would you need to be to fit in that position?

   _____

   _____

2. What values would you have to live?

   _____

   _____

3. In your imagined dream, what character traits do you demonstrate?

   _____

   _____

	Myself Now	Dream Person	Future Self			Myself Now	Dream Person	Future Self
☐ Do you live by high *standards*?	___	___	___	☐ Are you *humorous*?		___	___	___
☐ Are you *honest* and *dependable*?	___	___	___	☐ Are you *kind* and *caring*?		___	___	___
☐ Are you *healthy* and in *good shape*?	___	___	___	☐ Are you *organized* and *diligent*?		___	___	___
☐ Are you *trustworthy* and *respectable*?	___	___	___	☐ Are you *knowledgeable*?		___	___	___

Take a few moments to rate yourself as you are now on a scale of one to ten on each of the above character traits. Then go back and rate each trait from the point of view of being the person who is capable of having your perfect dream job. That is, rate the future you that you want to become. Is there a difference between now and what you want to be in the future?

You can succeed and make your last relapse the last!

Don't you want the person in your dream job to live by high standards, be honest, dependable, trustworthy, respectable, organized, diligent, knowledgeable, and even humorous at times? If you are going to trust yourself to make the required changes in your life, you will need to *develop these traits in yourself and live by them.*

New Habits Are Possible

Addictive behaviour patterns can be changed.

Can You Change Your Values And Beliefs?

In order to become the person of your dreams and achieve your new life goals, you may have to change some of your beliefs and values. Is this possible? Yes, it is. First you must decide what values and beliefs will support your success in your new life goals and your relapse prevention plan. Secondly, you must believe that:

- Everything you need is already inside of you,
- You have a valuable purpose to complete,
- Permanent change is possible, and
- You are always free to make a better choice.

Research has demonstrated *negative attitude predicts relapse while belief in yourself and in your skills leads to abstinence and success in managing life* (Miller, & Rollnick, 2002).

When faced with a crisis people can respond in one of two ways. Some find the inner courage to raise their standards, even to the point of risking their life for a stranger. Others, when faced with difficult challenges, consistently and repeatedly lower their standards and seek the easiest way out. What types of behaviors did you use during your addiction experience? Did you raise your standards every day or did you lower them? Did you do the best you could or did you take the easiest way out? For relapse prevention and to get your life on track, the key is to recognize that *clarifying and changing your value system is a powerful relapse prevention tool.* You can't raise your standards if you don't have any. You can't change your life if you don't have values as standards to live by.

Planned And Controlled Life Change

Unchallenged and unchanged beliefs, habits, and patterns will bring you back to the cycle of addiction. <u>Change by choice</u> happens when you increase your level of attention to what your values are, and prevent your thoughts from being absorbed by destructive old habits and old thinking. Your ability to act and respond differently depends on your ability to develop and maintain focused attention on what you are thinking, what is happening around you, and why you are making certain choices. Defining values requires you to become aware of your actions and to listen to yourself.

How do you define your values? Every time you do something, ask yourself, *why did I do that?* Your values are demonstrated moment to moment by your actions. If you don't show up when you promised a friend you would, then you value something else higher than friendship, your word or integrity. When you identify the reasons for your actions, you will begin to learn your current values. Over the next week, carry a small journal. Jot down the values your behavior says are important to you. Once you know why you behave the way you do, you can ask yourself the bigger question: What values do I want to hold and what values do I want to change? Then just as important ask yourself, "How do I begin to *honor* my values through my actions?"

> *Research has demonstrated belief in yourself and in your skills leads to abstinence and success in managing life*

How Do You Raise Your Values And Standards?

You take the first step and decide this is what you are going to do. Look at what you are doing and what you want to be like in the future. *Every moment, raise the expectation for yourself.* If you want to become more truthful, you start with the phrase, *"I will be more honest with everyone I meet today."* Write it down and carry it with you in your pocket. Say it to yourself. Test each of your actions against your new standard.

Meditation, A Simple Tool

Do you find you can't think clearly about your values? A good way to learn to focus your thoughts and integrate change into your life is through meditation. Meditation is a simple practice that cultivates attention and focus. Meditation is about listening to your own mind and body. It is about improving your health and quality of life.

Life's problems can be seen more clearly through the lens of a clear mind. Meditation is the development of mindfulness. Mindfulness is moment-to-moment awareness. Mindfulness is developed by purposefully paying attention to things we ordinarily never give a moment's thought to. It is a systematic approach to develop a new kind of control in our lives based on increasing our capacity and skills for relaxation, paying attention, awareness, and insight (Kabat-Zinn, 2005).

You Can Change!

What do you want your new life to look like?

We routinely and unknowingly waste enormous amounts of energy in reacting automatically to our own inner experiences and the outside world. Cultivating mindfulness is a way of paying attention. It requires looking deeper into your self with a spirit of self-inquiry and self-understanding. Try the following meditation exercise for five minutes.

Chapter Nine: Stay on Track, Develop a Personal Vision

New Habits Are Possible

Addictive behaviour patterns can be changed.

- Sit comfortably and let your gaze fall on an object, eight to ten feet away. Do not close your eyes in the beginning.

- Breathe naturally, notice when you breathe in and out. Do not try to change your breathing, just notice it.

- Let your thoughts come and go. Do not grab hold of any of them. Let them pass by you like waves on the ocean.

- Always return your thoughts gently to your breath, listening to, and feeling your breath (Kabat-Zinn, 2005).

Informal meditation practice can happen anytime. Just move your thoughts to your breathing and gently follow your breath in and out. As your thoughts flow, acknowledge the thought and let it go. Return to listening and feeling the rhythm of your breathing (Kabat-Zinn, 2005).

Short periods of meditation can help you manage stress, increase insight into self and behaviors, increase optimism, and reduce risk of relapse. Meditation is proven to have a positive influence on your immune system. It is a simple tool to help focus your thinking and help you to find your values. Try meditating for five minutes every morning before you head out the door (Kabat-Zinn, 2005).

Raising your standards is a choice and a decision. When you make a decision to use simple relaxation techniques (like meditation) to help you calm your mind you can begin to live your values and create lasting change in your life. Meditation can help you develop the clarity of thought and find the reasons you need to change and to maintain your new higher standards. Mediation is a way to calm yourself and check back into your values when you are thinking about using again or experiencing frustration or stress.

It is your clear values and higher standards that will form the strongest foundation in your relapse prevention plan. Using the powerful tool of a personal vision is initiated by defining your basic value system. Through developing your value system and increasing your mindfulness, you will begin to lay out the real purpose in your life. With positive values, purpose, and a simple tool to calm your mind, you now have the beginning of a recipe for passion in life, joy in achievement, and lasting fulfillment. Every journey begins with the first step. Your journey can start by simply knowing you want to take the journey.

Creating Your Vision And Establishing Goals

So you can take action to achieve a healthy, successful life and relapse prevention you will need to define your values, vision, and write concrete goals. **To get started establishing your vision and goals use the "Life Plan and Goals for Next Year Worksheet" at the end of** this chapter and write down your vision of what you want in your future:

1. Relationships
2. Work/School
3. Home/Community
4. Physical Health/Mental Health
5. Communication

If you establish at least one goal in each of these areas, you will be on your way to developing the variety of goals you need to achieve and enjoy a higher quality of life and a balanced lifestyle.

Your goals need to be simple and measurable. Set a time when you want to have each goal completed. Include times and a way to measure your goals or your list will be made up of wishes instead of goals. Wishes are: *I would like to quit using, I would like to lose weight, and I would like to find new friends.* A goal is: *I will do aerobic exercise for 20 minutes every day and lift weights three times a week to reduce my weight. I will join an exercise club on Monday and I will take a Spanish course starting the beginning of April to meet new people.* Do you see the difference between goals and wishes? Goals are much more powerful motivators than wishes.

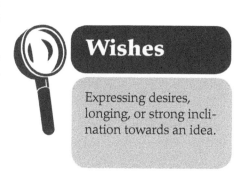

Wishes

Expressing desires, longing, or strong inclination towards an idea.

Remember to make goals that reflect your vision of how you really want your life to be. ***Goals must be important to you.*** Keep them simple. Begin by writing a single sentence that includes what you want to achieve, how you are going to achieve it, and when.

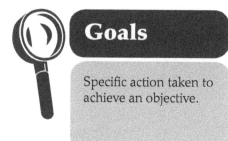

Goals

Specific action taken to achieve an objective.

You will need motivation and personal leverage to keep you on the road to your goals. You must search for the most important things in your life to create your personal growth plan. All change starts inside of you. It is your ultimate <u>desired</u> destination that will determine your direction and give you the power to take your first step. Now take as much time as you need to complete your first draft of your "Life Plan and Goals For The Next Year Worksheet." Don't worry about getting it perfect the first time through, just get out your pencil and start thinking and writing.

Are Your Goals Important Enough To Sustain Change?

Review the vision and goals you have written down for the five life areas and do the following exercise. Imagine this is your last day on earth. You are alone and sitting in front of a window looking out at a garden. You are thinking back over your life and reflecting on the period of time right after you quit using and drinking. You remember creating your first set of life goals.

Take your list of goals and for each one, take a minute and imagine what you would feel like if you did not reach that goal. Do you feel regret? Are you upset that you missed your opportunity? If you don't feel upset, then the goal was not a *must do for you*. Circle the goals **you are sure you will regret not doing**. Take time and do the last day on earth test on each of your goals.

For the goals that pass the last day on earth test, divide your list into two categories, the "I must-do's" and the "I want to do's." To determine your must-do's, consider the ultimate importance of that goal for you. If the goal is a stepping stone for another important goal, such as, *you can't sail around the world solo next year, if you don't meet your goal to first learn navigation,* then where does it fit on your list? Remember to include your health goals. You can't be in construction work if you are too weak to carry a toolbox. Ensure you are working toward a balanced lifestyle and create at least one *must-do goal* in each of the life areas:

1. Relationships
2. Work/School
3. Home/Community
4. Physical Health/Mental Health
5. Communication

Now choose your top three *must-do goals*. Think about how you will have to alter your current lifestyle to devote enough time to each goal to really make a change. What will you miss out on if you don't achieve your top three?

Take a plain piece of paper and make a <u>pocket leverage sheet</u>. This is a motivator to keep physically in your purse or wallet or back pocket. Starting with your three most important goals, identify the cost of not meeting each goal by answering the following questions for each. Starting with the first goal:

1. Write all the things you will miss out on if you don't accomplish this goal.
2. Write the negative things you will have to deal with if you don't follow through.
3. Write all the things your family and friends will miss out on if you don't succeed.

Once you determine what it will cost you to not complete the goal, write a sentence or two on how you would feel knowing you missed out on those things. Here's an example: *If I don't exercise and work out to get my physical health back, I will miss out on walking, biking, and hiking with my wife and kids. I also won't have the energy to follow through on the rest of my goals, which means I will have less success and less money*

> **You Have the Power to Change**
>
> Whether you think you can, or think you can't, you're right. Henry Ford

to support my family and have fun. I'll end up spending more time at the doctors and hospitals as I age because of poor health. I will get weaker and look more and more unattractive. I will get to watch other people having fun. I will feel like I'm just an observer of life, an outsider, looking through a window, seeing things, not experiencing positive action and energy in my life.

Now that you've completed the first part, start again with the first goal.

1. Write all the positive feelings and other benefits you gain when you complete this goal.
2. Then, list all the negative things you *won't have to deal with* when you follow through on your goals.

Now go through each of your top three goals and complete the full process for each. Yes, it will take a bit of time.

Paradigm Shift

A radical change in personal beliefs including values, goals and ways of thinking. The new beliefs replace the old way of thinking with an entirely new, positive, and constructive way of thinking, speaking and acting. Old beliefs are never returned to.

The very next time you don't feel like following through on your commitments, like working out, read your comments on your pocket leverage sheet. Start by rereading the negative things that will happen if you don't follow through and ask yourself: *do I really want to choose all this negative garbage?* Then, reread the positive list and ask yourself: *do I really want to get to my last day on earth and not have accomplished any of these?*

Now re-examine your Life Plan vision and goals. Are they compelling? Are these goals and the differences they will make in your life (and the lives of others) more important to you than anything else you can imagine? When you read what happens by not following through, do you get upset in your very core? If you answered "yes," then you are getting close to your tipping point.

Tipping Points

A tipping point happens when many small events and rational reasons add up and lead to a paradigm shift or a shift in focus so the world never looks the same to you ever again. Here is an example of how a tipping point can happen.

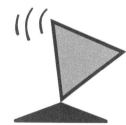

Until the early 1970's, smoking was acceptable everywhere. Nothing happened to change this. Gradually, small pieces of information started forming and circulating. Health problems were made public and restrictions on advertising began. By the mid 1980's many small events and pieces of information added up. People rapidly began changing how they thought about smoking, and then the dam burst. Within a two to three year period, smoking was banned on airplanes and in most public workplaces. Restaurants designated non-smoking areas. On TV shows and in movies, nobody wanted to be seen smoking. It seemed that only the bad guys or immature adolescents still smoked. The world view of the majority of society had gone through a tipping point. Smoking as an accepted behavior was going downhill fast. Every year the number of smokers in Canada and the United States is less. No matter what any advertising firm may try, smoking will never appear so cool to so many people again.

Your Tipping Point

Through your vision of where you want to go and what you stand to lose by not proceeding, you can create a tipping point about drugs and alcohol in your life. Your goals *must be compelling*. The number of changes you make in your daily life must be sufficient to give you momentum. Changing one small thing won't cut it, even if that small thing is a temporary period of abstinence. You need to take action in multiple areas of your life at the same time. The price of not moving forward is brutally high. You can lose self-esteem, self-respect, self-confidence, your spouse, family, friends, and work. You can even experience poverty, prison, physical and mental disease, and ultimately lose years off your life.

> *Find something you want that moves and shakes your very core and make it your goal!*

Have you found your tipping point? Everyone's final tipping point is different and unique. What is most important to you? It could be the dream of driving a car at NASCAR, not losing your kids or getting them back, saving the rain forest or perhaps getting a place to live on your own. It might be that you *just know* you were meant for something better. If you have found your tipping point, write it down now. Copy it. Post it wherever you frequently look. Put it on your fridge, your bathroom mirror, your locker at work or school, and the dashboard of your car. Make it a screensaver on your computer.

If you haven't found your tipping point, look deeper. Find something you want that moves and shakes your very core and make it your goal! Spend more time developing your leverage for each life goal, carefully describing every minute detail of what you stand to lose and all you have to gain. This is such an important step. We all fight harder to protect what we have and what we know than we are willing to risk for something new.

Get Down The Action Details For Each Goal

Using the "Goal Planning Worksheet" at the end of this Chapter, for each goal in your Life Plan, complete a detailed action plan. You will need to work on more than three goals to reach your balanced lifestyle. Once you've completed the best plan you can for your three most important goals, work on developing a top goal for each of the other five life areas. You are creating a clearly defined path to your desired future. Don't overwhelm yourself with more than five goals. Choose your goals carefully and they will be your motivation on difficult days.

How To Set Goals With Important People In Your Life

Why set mutual goals with someone important in your life? So you can get *more* momentum and *maintain* momentum toward your goals. The speed of change in your life is dependant on two main variables: the desire to change and leverage to change.

Imagine an airplane. Think of your ability to change like an airplane. The higher you fly, the faster you will grow and change. Your will and desire are the engines that move the plane. Your barriers to change represent a drag on the speed of the plane. The more you remove barriers, the more streamlined your plane becomes, and the easier it flies. Let's try another example.

When a business is stuck and isn't growing, the owner can call in an outside consultant for a fresh perspective. Most consultants find it is far easier to achieve greater growth by removing barriers to growth than by pushing employees to do more. By removing barriers, growth and change occurs with less effort. As growth returns, the staff morale is higher. *Then* effort is applied for people to give more. As the barriers to growth diminish, the staff's efforts are rewarded with positive results, and a growth cycle is established.

Another example is what you are doing at this very moment. By reading this book and completing the exercises, you have increased your knowledge and removed some of the barriers to your personal progress.

Life Partners Can Power Change

Life partners have the ability to profoundly affect both sides of the success equation when it comes to your life goals. Having a partner on your side, who is your number one cheerleader, is essential to your recovery. By gaining the support of your partner, you will have eliminated a large potential barrier to maintaining abstinence and achieving your life goals. Mutual goal-setting can be a very powerful tool towards growth and achievement. When sitting with your significant other, partner or family member, it is important that you are clear about what you really want in your life. Clarity is critical.

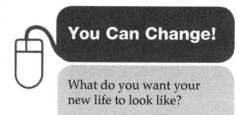

You Can Change!

What do you want your new life to look like?

Some people are very clear about what they do not want. *I don't want to drink again*. However, they are not as clear about what they do want. Wanting fewer problems in your life is not a goal, that's a wish. Sit down and do your goal-setting exercise. Invest the time in yourself to really think about the things you want to accomplish.

You can succeed and make your last relapse the last!

Rate your goals on their importance from the ones you absolutely have to accomplish to the ones that may not be as critical. Do your timelines. Have written reasonable steps to achieve each goal and make them measurable. Now, you're ready for mutual goal setting.

Mutual Goal Setting

Is your partner or spouse ready to participate in goal setting? For this exercise to work both people must examine their life. If your partner doesn't have clarity about what they really want, it won't work. You may have to positively coach them on goal-setting so you can create your vision together. Give them a blank copy of the "Life Plan and Goals For The Next Year Worksheet" and ask them to complete it to get ready for setting goals together. When both of you have written precise personal goals, you are ready for mutual goal-setting.

If your partner is not ready, here are two questions you can ask them to start them thinking in the right direction. "If you could start over again, what would you take in school? If you knew you couldn't fail, what would you do?" Take a few minutes now and write down some other questions you might like to ask your partner.

Mutual goal setting most commonly fails due to a lack of willingness to imagine both of you can meet your most important life goals. These discussions must take place within the context of total commitment to active listening and the belief that both parties can get what they want. Both people need to *honestly identify* what is most important to achieve in their life and bring their goals to the discussion table. The mutual task then becomes one of putting both of your goals together. Both parties need to keep in mind that there is a solution where everyone's values and goals can be met as long as there is cooperation and imagination.

Imagine a scenario where one partner wants to live in the downtown quarter of a very large city. The other partner wants to live outdoors and be involved in camping and backpacking. Don't think a solution is possible? A solution might lie in one person running an outdoors store in a big city where they are around people who like the outdoors, and working with the equipment they love. Or perhaps they run weekend groups for urbanites venturing into the wild.

New Habits Are Possible

Addictive behaviour patterns can be changed.

The key to mutual goal-setting lies in listening to the must haves of your partner and seeing them as components of a joint puzzle. How can you put the pieces together to create a picture you <u>both want</u>? By listening, understanding their motivation, and learning what's important to them, you will be able to find a plan for both of you.

Don't give up or stop the process until there is a plan in place that addresses the values of both parties. Think outside the box. If you are stuck, ask questions. Is there another way we can accomplish these goals? Keep writing, cutting and pasting goals and timelines, until you get a finished product you are both comfortable and happy with. If you get stuck, switch roles. Try to explain out loud, your partner's core values and goals. Defend them harder than you would your own. You'll be able to make valuable and realistic plans together if you move beyond a token understanding of what's important to each other.

This is a tough assignment but the results are very powerful. The benefits include having two people aligned, supporting each other on their way to achieving their individual and joint goals without presenting barriers for each other.

Answer this question, *if you were living the life of your dreams with the person of your dreams and they were living the life of their dreams with the person of their dreams, would there be any room at all for drugs or alcohol to enter this picture?*

Summary

To get moving and to stay on track:

- Clarify and challenge the values that allowed you to drink and use.

- Create new values that support positive change in your life.

- Learn and use simple meditation techniques.

- Challenge your expectations of what a return to alcohol and drugs will give you.

- Define your new values in writing.

- Live your values moment to moment.

- Develop your vision and goals by completing your "Life Plan."

- Find your tipping point for positive change.

- Set mutual goals with significant people in your life to provide motivation and momentum toward success.

References

Miller, William R., & Rollnick, Stephen. (2002). "*Motivational Interviewing, Preparing People For Change.*" (2nd edition)." New York. The Guilford Press. 12, 83.

Richmond, Lewis. (1999). "*Work as a Spiritual Practice, A Practical*

Buddhist Approach to Inner Growth and Satisfaction." New York. Broadway Books. 16.

Kabat-Zinn, Jon. (2005). "Full Catastrophe Living, Using the Wisdom of Your Body and Mind to Face Stress, Pain, and Illness, The Program of The Stress Reduction Clinic At The University of Massachusetts Medical Center." New York. Bantam Dell. 11-12, 25-26.

Get Real Motivation!

What are your reasons for quitting? Are they strong enough? Revisit page 18.

Life Plan and Goals for Next Year Worksheet

1. Relationships:

For your relationships write out the vision that you would like to have of yourself one year from now, i.e. the life you want to be living. Then complete the compelling reasons, goals and tasks to achieve the vision.

My Vision:

• ⎯⎯
• ⎯⎯
• ⎯⎯
• ⎯⎯
• ⎯⎯
• ⎯⎯

Compelling reasons I want to achieve my vision and goals: ....

....

....

Goal 1: .... **Date to be achieved:** ....

Goal 1 Tasks and date to be completed

1) ....

2) ....

3) ....

4) ....

5) ....

Goal 2: .... **Date to be achieved:** ....

Goal 2 Tasks and date to be completed

1) ....

2) ....

3) ....

4) ....

5) ....

You can succeed and make your last relapse the last!

Chapter Nine: Life Plan And Goals For Next Year Worksheet

2. Work/school:

For your work/school life write out the vision that you would like to have of yourself one year from now, i.e. the life you want to be living. Then complete the compelling reasons, goals and tasks to achieve the vision.

My Vision:

- _____
- _____
- _____
- _____
- _____

Compelling reasons I want to achieve my vision and goals: ....

Goal 1: _____ **Date to be achieved:** _____

Goal 1 Tasks and date to be completed

1) ....
2) ....
3) ....
4) ....
5) ....

Goal 2: _____ **Date to be achieved:** _____

Goal 2 Tasks and date to be completed

1) ....
2) ....
3) ....
4) ....
5) ....

Life Plan And Goals For Next Year Worksheet

3. Home/community:

For your home/community write out the vision that you would like to have of yourself one year from now, i.e. the life you want to be living. Then complete the compelling reasons, goals and tasks to achieve the vision.

My Vision:

- ....
- ....
- ....
- ....
- ....

Compelling reasons I want to achieve my vision and goals: ....
....
....
....

Goal 1: .... **Date to be achieved:** ....

Goal 1 Tasks and date to be completed

1) ....
2) ....
3) ....
4) ....
5) ....

Goal 2: .... **Date to be achieved:** ....

Goal 2 Tasks and date to be completed

1) ....
2) ....
3) ....
4) ....
5) ....

You can succeed and make your last relapse the last!

Chapter Nine: Life Plan And Goals For Next Year Worksheet

4. Physical health/Mental health:

For your physical health/mental health write out the vision that you would like to have of yourself one year from now, i.e. the life you want to be living. Then complete the compelling reasons, goals and tasks to achieve the vision.

My Vision:

- _____
- _____
- _____
- _____
- _____

Compelling reasons I want to achieve my vision and goals: _____

_____

Goal 1: _____ **Date to be achieved:** _____

Goal 1 Tasks and date to be completed

1) _____
2) _____
3) _____
4) _____
5) _____

Goal 2: _____ **Date to be achieved:** _____

Goal 2 Tasks and date to be completed

1) _____
2) _____
3) _____
4) _____
5) _____

Life Plan And Goals For Next Year Worksheet

5. Communication:

For your communication skills write out the vision that you would like to have of yourself one year from now, i.e. the life you want to be living. Then complete the compelling reasons, goals and tasks to achieve the vision.

My Vision:

• _____
• _____
• _____
• _____
• _____

Compelling reasons I want to achieve my vision and goals: _____
_____
_____

Goal 1: _____ **Date to be achieved:** _____

Goal 1 Tasks and date to be completed

1) _____
2) _____
3) _____
4) _____
5) _____

Goal 2: _____ **Date to be achieved:** _____

Goal 2 Tasks and date to be completed

1) _____
2) _____
3) _____
4) _____
5) _____

You can succeed and make your last relapse the last!

Chapter Nine: Goal Planning Worksheet

Goal Planning Worksheet

✓ To acheive your vision in each of the 5 life areas, you will need to develop new attributes and skills. For each attribute or skill, decide where you are now and where you have to go. Use this sheet to help you prioritize, plan, and schedule to reach your goals. Use one sheet for each goal. You can prioritize your goals by stacking the sheets in order of importance.

GOAL: Attribute or skill to be achieved _____

What changes would have to occur?

What courses might you have to take?

What books would you have to read?

What mentors would you have to find?

ACTION PLAN TO ACHIEVE GOALS- Write a detailed description of the steps you will take to acquire this skill or attribute:

Chapter Ten

Meaningful Work And Relapse Prevention

Chapter 10

Meaningful Work And Relapse Prevention

To reduce the risk of relapse following treatment or rehab, it is important to add structure to your day. Risk of relapse is higher on days when you experience boredom, loneliness or a sense of meaninglessness in your life. Individuals who do not have skills to cope with boredom and loneliness frequently return to drugs and alcohol as their solution. Positive structure reduces exposure to cues and is effective in managing and reducing the incidence of cravings.

New Habits Are Possible

Addictive behaviour patterns can be changed.

Positive structure is more than just being busy. It is having meaningful things to do on a regular and consistent basis that create a personal benefit for you and others. Work is the most common way to positively structure a large portion of your time. Work provides meaning, purpose, and exposure to a different social group. Besides earning money, it can be a source of prestige, personal responsibility, praise, respect, and self-worth. Work provides opportunities for: learning, new experiences, accomplishments, fun, travel, and change.

The stress of unsatisfying work and a stressful work place can set you up for relapse. That's why it's so important to find the right work for you.

Work impacts all the different areas of your life. Devoting time to work requires juggling commitments with friends, family, and children. It involves managing the expectations of coworkers, superiors, customers, and deadlines. Some types of employment create disappointment, boredom, monotony, fear, and fatigue. Work particularly impacts the time and energy available for: exercise and social activities, personal and spiritual growth, reading, relaxation and meditation, hobbies and fun, and sleep and rest (Bond, Thompson, Galinsky, & Prottas, 2002). So it is important to seek meaningful work that fits into and advances your life plan.

Finding, creating or keeping meaningful work will be a critical goal in your Life Plan. Many people are not satisfied with their work and feel nervous and stressed due to their work life (Bond, Thompson, Galinsky, & Prottas, 2002). The stress of *un*satisfying work and a stressful workplace can set you up for relapse. *That's why it's so important to find the right work for you*. Remember, anger, interpersonal conflict, depression, and anxiety are common triggers of relapse which can easily be magnified by stressful, meaningless work.

Mental Roadblocks To Finding The Right Work for You

Some of the most common mental roadblocks to making changes in our lives include fear of success, resistance to change by friends and family, and being in a rut (Yost, 2004). Mental roadblocks are really distorted thinking that gives you reasons *not to try* to change. They are common in people who have experienced addiction.

The **fear roadblock** occurs when you allow your fear of failure to stop you from taking *any* action. It is being paralyzed by distorted thinking (Yost, 2004). Some examples are:

- **All or nothing thinking:** "I will not be able to pay my bills if I go to school so I can't go."

- **Negative labeling:** "I'm not good enough, I'm not smart enough."

- **Fortune-telling:** "I will never get accepted into that training program."

Do any of these sound familiar to you? *Write down some of the negative language you use when you talk to yourself about making changes.*

_____

_____

_____

_____

If negative, fearful self talk is a common experience for you, you may find some good tools to manage this type of dysfunctional thinking in *"The Feeling Good Handbook"* By Dr. David Burns.

The **resistance roadblock** exists when you <u>stop</u> trying to change your life whenever *other people resist and prot*est (Yost, 2004). Some examples are:

- **Parents:** "How will you ever pay your bills if you do that?"

- **Friends:** "That sounds pretty risky." or "It doesn't pay well, I wouldn't do it".

- **Wife:** "The last time you tried something like that it didn't work."

- **Others:** "How can you do that, aren't you an addict?"

In the resistance roadblock other people use their cognitive (thinking) distortions and dysfunctional thinking to convince *you not to take*

Chapter Ten: Meaningful Work And Relapse Prevention

action. Have people in your life discouraged you from changing? Improving your communication skills and learning to manage interpersonal conflict will help you to deal successfully with the people who create barriers for you. *List the people whose opinions you will have to manage or for whom you will have to set boundaries because they don't believe that you have the power to change.*

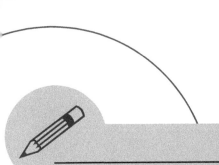

Being in a rut occurs when you can't see any possibility of change (Yost, 2004). You have been thinking negatively about your life, yourself, and work for so long you just can't see it any other way. Your continuous negative self talk may include:

- "It's the only thing I know how to do."
- "I never was good at school and never will be."
- "It pays the bills."

To stay in a rut, you actually use a lot of energy to keep up the negative attitude and distorted thinking. Do you think your work life is in a rut? To get out of the rut, you will need to work to raise your self esteem and self confidence. You will need to practice and use the new thinking skills you will be learning through your reading.

Finding Meaningful Work

To prevent relapse, you need to make sure the largest part of your day is organized, prescheduled, and positive. That means you need to find work that is meaningful and rewarding *to you*. Your work will need to keep you away from drugs and alcohol, so tending bar or being a wine taster is not an option. Creating a great work life starts with asking yourself questions and creating a picture in your mind of your dream job.

You Have the Power to Change

Whether you think you can, or think you can't, you're right. Henry Ford

You started this work in Chapter 9 when we looked at "choose your character; choose your life" and the qualities of the person in your dream job. *Now give yourself the freedom to answer the following questions as if anything was possible and you had your whole life ahead of you. Take enough time to think through and answer the following questions.*

1. What do I really love to do? What is my dream job?

   _____

   _____

2. Where would I love to live?

   _____

   _____

3. What kind of people would I like to work with?

   _____

   _____

4. What types of people would I like to serve?

   _____

   _____

5. What great work accomplishments do I want to achieve?

   _____

   _____

Use Creative Thinking

What do you want your new life to look like?

Thinking creatively about yourself can be fun and easy if you simply turn off the negative voice in your head. Let's try an example of using creative thinking. You love basketball and you're 45 years old and 5 feet tall, so making the NBA as a pro-basketball player is an unrealistic dream job. You can still make a wonderful living in basketball as a community coach or running a company that holds basketball camps. Dream up other possibilities that build on your love and knowledge of basketball.

Considering the above example, go through your answers about your dream job a second time. Ask yourself what you *really* love to do and take time to think of the many different ways you might be able to use that passion. Now, look at each answer for the third time and ask, "Is this what I *really want* or is it closer to what I think I can get?" If it's not what you really want, cross it out, write what you really want and do the process over again.

The next step is to imagine your perfect day in your dream job. Imagine that day now as you close your eyes and picture yourself at work. You are actually doing it, having fun, and doing it well! Imagine your surroundings. Imagine who is there with you on that perfect day. Imagine what it will feel like to be that person having that perfect day and accomplishing what you dreamed of doing. If you actually were that person, in that job, how would it be better for you, your family, and friends (happier, more money, more pride)?

Create Your Written Vision Of Meaningful Work

Now create your vision of meaningful work for you by taking about 10 minutes to write a brief description of your perfect day in your dream job. *Use your answers to the previous five questions about your dream job and describe yourself in a real world work situation. Describe the benefits that would result for you and those around you. Try to capture your vision in one or two short forceful paragraphs.*

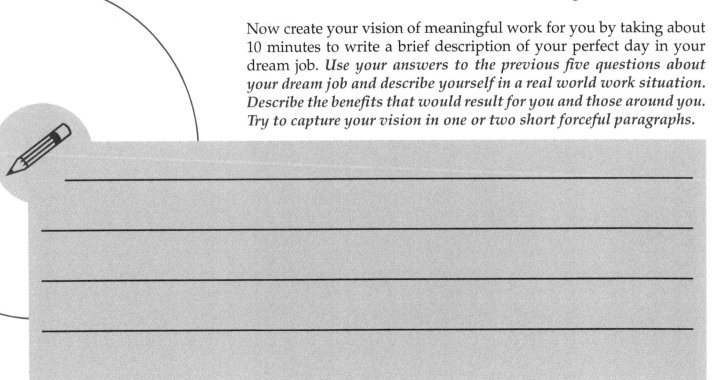

Making Dreams A Reality

You now have your vision of the perfect work for you. To make your dreams a reality you need to make an assessment and list the:

- Skills your dream job requires
- Skills you currently have
- Skills you need to acquire to match your dream job

To start this assessment, go to the library or use the internet to find job descriptions that match or are close to your dream job. Check out the websites of companies that hire people like the *person you are going to become*. Check government and company websites that post positions like your dream job. Check the job descriptions for the qualifications and skills required. You can use this information to make your plan to get your perfect job. You will need to know the specific education, skills, and experience required. Talk to people who have your dream job. Talk to people in the human resources

Chapter Ten: Meaningful Work And Relapse Prevention

or employment departments at some of the companies who have positions like your dream job. Find out what type of people they hire. This process can be tedious and somewhat time consuming, yet it is essential if you are going to take your dream job from just a wish to a set of concrete goals in your Life Plan.

Once you have completed at least some of your job research, you can use the information to make a list of the skills and education required for your future job. Now compare that list with the skills and education you currently have. Once you know what skills and education you will need, you can add specific goals and tasks to your Life Plan in the section under work and school. *To help you define the goals for getting ready for your dream job answer the following questions.*

1. Are there ways to change my current job into my dream job or do I need to find my dream job elsewhere?

   _____

   _____

2. What courses will I have to take?

   _____

   _____

3. What topics do I need to read up about?

   _____

   _____

4. What mentors do I have to find and where?

   _____

Make Your Last Relapse The Last

_____

5. What are at least two different ways to gain the skills needed to get my dream job?

_____

_____

5. What changes will have to occur in my life to allow me to do these things?

_____

_____

_____

You are now starting to create a realistic and concrete plan to achieve your dream job. Remember, even if it will take you ten years to achieve your ideal work, ten years will still pass anyway. You can choose to be ten years older and still in a rut or you can be ten years older and living your dreams.

Achieving Goals

You will need to make commitments to achieve the personal vision and goals you are listing in your Life Plan, at the end of Chapter 9. The five key areas you have goals in by now are:

- Relationships
- Work/school, *which now includes your dream job*
- Home/community
- Physical health/mental health
- Communication

You have started looking at some of your core values and beliefs,

New Habits Are Possible

Addictive behaviour patterns can be changed.

and are exploring the idea of strengthening and changing your value system. You have begun to define purpose in your life and think about the ideal work that will fulfill you. Using your Life Plan, you have begun creating specific plans for growth and learning. You may have bravely shared with others some declarations of where you are headed. Perhaps, you have been thinking about mutual goal setting with one or two key people in your life.

Putting it all together, means you start taking action on your goals and keep on taking action, every day. Everyone has good ideas and good intentions. Everyone wants to follow through on their plans. But what happens? Why do people start with high hopes and then slow down, fizzle, and wilt?

The Catalysts Of Change

There are two things that are crucial if you're going to follow through. After the initial euphoria of deciding where you want to go and realizing you *can* change, some of the not so glamorous work begins. What two things will keep you going until the results start to take shape and you will never want to stop?

1. High personal energy level
2. Momentum

Change occurs by carrying out a series of tasks. These tasks are easier to accomplish with a lot of energy. When you are learning something new, which is easier, the 1st, 2nd, 30th or the 45th day? Change is work. The more change you want, the more work is required over a longer period of time. To follow through on your commitments, you need to increase and boost your personal energy levels.

Increase Your Energy

There are three basic ways to rapidly increase your energy levels:

1. Daily physical exercise
2. Daily nutritious diet
3. Daily positive mental diet.

<u>Physical exercise</u> elicits critical alertness. It makes you more aware. Good aerobic exercise puts your nervous system in a state of moderate arousal which is ideally suited for mental tasks. Exercise also relaxes you after experiencing stress. So, working up a good sweat gets your brain ready to work and it decreases the energy robbing effects of stress (Howard, 1999).

A healthy diet is fuel for the body. How can you have lots of energy with poor fuel? A 1996 study of 2,000 children found being undernourished resulted in lower levels of achievement and social interaction because of low mental energy. After providing the children with a healthy diet, the researchers observed reverses in poor academic performance and social interaction. They attributed the children's improved performance to their healthy diet (Brown, & Pollit, 1996). You will be able to study better, learn more, and socialize more readily with a balanced, healthy diet. This alone is an excellent reason to include healthy eating as part of your relapse prevention plan.

Negative attitude and emotional states are associated with relapse. For a positive mental diet, plan and schedule opportunities to read books and attend programs that advance your knowledge and skills. Learn more about people who have the traits you want to acquire. You will be able to complete more mental work if you schedule time formally with yourself to accomplish these activities. You can read books about people who have experienced struggles and succeeded. You can attend programs that focus on how people solved some of the same issues or concerns you may be experiencing. Remember "garbage in, garbage out." Stay away from negative reading, movies, and people that do not contribute *positively* to your life. Your time is valuable and so is your brain. Don't waste either one.

> *By preplanning and scheduling these 3 strategies into your day, you will have greatly improved your odds of succeeding at relapse prevention and achieving your life goals.*

Combine all three of these strategies simultaneously: exercise (especially first thing in the morning); eat a healthy diet; and provide yourself with a positive mental diet daily. By doing all three you will have greatly improved your odds of succeeding at relapse prevention and achieving your life goals. Each strategy must be preplanned and scheduled into your day. Get a daily organizer, write things down, and use it to plan in advance. You will want to include the times you get up, eat, work, exercise, and attend mentally nourishing events. Unless you plan in detail and in advance, your goals will turn into wishes instead of actions. Relapse prevention means taking concrete action daily so you have the personal energy and the drive to succeed without drugs and alcohol.

Get Real Motivation!

What are your reasons for quitting? Are they strong enough? Revisit page 18.

Increase Your Momentum

Now add the power of momentum. *Momentum is the power to increase your pace toward success.* Action is the process of *doing* in order to achieve a purpose. Doing is not thinking or talking about doing.

Chapter Ten: Meaningful Work And Relapse Prevention

Doing is taking action! **Action leads to increased motivation, which leads to increased action, which results in increased motivation. This is the power of momentum.** While you plan your exercise, get walking. Go to the grocery store and buy fresh fruit to munch on while you make your menu for the week. Get the idea? A body in motion tends to stay in motion until acted on by an outside force. Sir Isaac Newton figured this out over 300 years ago.

Action always comes before motivation. Start today and build your winning streak through action.

Action always comes before motivation. Start today and build your winning streak through action. Get high energy and momentum through taking many small actions. With energy and momentum on your side, your life goals and your relapse prevention plan comes alive. Your life then begins to feel and look brighter and brighter.

Handle Your Mental Objections To Taking Action

Mental objections will start to surface. There are always three objections to making change:

1. **Money:** *I can't afford it.*
2. **Time:** *I don't have enough time.*
3. **Pain:** *It's too hard for me.*

Most beginning salespersons learn how to handle these objections easily, so use a tried and true sales technique to overcome your objections.

Not Enough Time:

The next time you want to change something in your life and the voice in your head says, *yes, but I don't have the time to exercise every day.* Answer very politely, *Mr. Voice, I know how you **FEEL** about not having enough time. In finding time to exercise, many others have **FELT** the same way. What they **FOUND** was they gained so much energy by working out first thing in the morning; they got more done during the day and actually had more time.*

Not Enough Money:

Your brain objects that it will cost you too much. Reply, *Mr. Voice, I understand how you **FEEL** about the cost. Many others **FELT** exactly the same way. What they **FOUND** was that it wasn't a cost; it was an investment in their life.*

Too Hard For Me To Do:

Your brain objects and tells you going back to school and writing papers is too difficult for you. Reply, *Mr. Voice, I understand how you* FEEL *about writing all those papers. Many others* FELT *exactly the same way when they went back to school. What they* FOUND *was because it was their choice to go back to school, and the subject was of their own choosing, they were capable and actually enjoyed writing papers.*

Using **FEEL, FELT, and FOUND** is one way of breaking though your own thinking distortions. Many, many other people in your situation have succeeded in finding meaningful work, changing their lives, and so can you. Try using this technique to help you break through dysfunctional thinking barriers.

Take Action To Get Ready For That Dream Job

You have learned you can get the extra personal energy to follow through on your plans by regular exercise, a balanced diet, and a positive mental diet. Creating momentum by linking each day's activities together puts the laws of physics to work for you. A lack of money or time and the possibility of discomfort will not deter you because **you are a barrier breaker**.

Think back to your dream job and imagine the person in that job. What was their level of physical health? Did they have the body of your dreams as well as your dream job? Now think of *your* physical health. What is your level of physical health at this moment? What areas do you want to improve? Are there areas you think it is urgent for you to change such as: weight, blood pressure, physical strength, energy level or overall fitness? Put your energies into developing a balanced and realistic exercise plan that motivates and inspires you to keep moving forward. Take time now to re-examine your "Exercise, Recreation, and Social Activities Plan" at the end of Chapter 5 and strengthen your exercise plan to improve specific areas of your physical health.

To succeed in your dream job and in your new life, you must develop your mind. A healthy and creative mind has many tools and knowledge about a variety of subjects. What new skill would you like to learn that has nothing to do with your current occupation, your dream job, or your past addiction? Do you want to learn another language? Or . . . ?

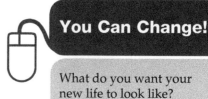

You Can Change!

What do you want your new life to look like?

Again, thinking of that person at work in your dream job, what mental talents and skills do they possess that have *nothing* to do with their chosen occupation? What personal relationships do they have? Where do they live? Examine where you are at in your life compared to that person in your dream job and where you want to be. **Add goals to the appropriate section in your "Life Plan and Goals for**

Next Year Worksheet," at the end of Chapter 9.

Summary

Meaningful work can be paid or unpaid. Meaningful work can have different qualities at different times of your life. Unless you take the time to define your perfect dream job and make a plan to get it, you will always have a large gap in your days, and a sense of loss or missed opportunity.

Having your dream job or working to achieve it can provide you with the self esteem and self confidence to succeed in other areas of your life. Creating energy and momentum can be a catalyst to change your life and to maintain relapse prevention. It always starts with the basics. You need to ensure that you have:

1. A written vision and goals
2. A healthy mental and nutritional diet
3. Regular exercise

Now take positive actions every day to maintain momentum. Cue yourself every day, "I can do this. I am living my dream."

New Habits Are Possible

Addictive behaviour patterns can be changed.

. . . .

References

Bond, James, T., Thompson, Cindy, Galinsky, Ellen & Prottas, David. (2002). "Highlights of the National Study of the Changing Workforce." New York. Families and Work Institute. No. 3. 63, 65, 76.

Brown, J.L. & Pollit, E. (1996). Malnutrition, Poverty and Intellectual Development. *Scientific American*. February. 38-43.

Burns, David D. (1999). *The Feeling Good Handbook*. New York. Plume, Penguin Group. 3-11.

Howard, Pierce. (1999) "The Owner's Manual for the Brain, Second Edition: Everyday Applications from Mind-Brain Research. " Austin, Texas. Bard Press, 138.

Yost, Cali Williams. (2004). "Work And Life, Finding The Fit That's Right For You." New York. Riverhead Books, Penguin Group. 100.

Chapter Eleven

Reducing the Risks of Using Again

You can succeed and make your last relapse the last!

Chapter 11

Reducing The Risks of Using Again

Relapse is a breakdown or failure in an attempt to *maintain change* in behaviors. Relapse prevention training combines learning to change behavior and thinking. It is an approach that emphasizes self-management and rejects labels like alcoholic or drug addict.

> ***Relapse prevention training assists you to increase your resilience to stress and increase your capacity to solve problems without drugs and alcohol.***

Relapse prevention training assists you to increase your resilience to stress and increase your capacity to solve problems without drugs and alcohol.

Effective relapse prevention strategies include coping skills training, cognitive or thinking therapy (changing how you think), and lifestyle changes.

1. Coping skills training includes: communication skills, anger management, relaxation techniques, and stress management (Parks, & Marlatt, 2000).

2. Cognitive therapy helps you change negative thinking, reframe the way you think about your habits, manage the stress of changes (even positive ones), and treat errors and setbacks as learning experiences.

3. Lifestyle changes will reduce the risk of relapse and strengthen your overall coping capacity. This means including in your life: meditation, exercise, relaxation, healthy diet, regular sleep, scheduled activities, positive work, and an improved support network (Parks, & Marlatt, 2000).

Relapse is a process that starts with a lapse. A lapse is a single use or one event of using. A lapse can be a learning experience and if managed can increase your strength and capacity to prevent another lapse and prevent progression to relapse or a state of regular using. A lapse signals you to:

1. Use damage control to reduce negative consequences of the lapse.

2. Stay engaged in your recovery.

3. Continue to take actions that help you make progress toward your life goals.

4. Renew your focus on your new, more balanced lifestyle.

5. Review the situations, emotional states, and events that preceded the lapse and make changes in your life based on

what you find in your review of the lapse.

6. Take actions to prevent further use (Parks, & Marlatt, 2000).

In most relapse episodes, the first lapse occurs in a high-risk situation that individuals report they were not expecting and were poorly prepared for. They found themselves in rapidly escalating circumstances they could not deal with effectively. The lapse or subsequent relapse appears to be the last link in a chain of events that led to exposure to the high-risk situation itself. It seems as if individuals set themselves up for relapse, because they did not or could not see the early warning signs (Parks, & Marlatt, 2000).

> *A lapse is a single use or one event of using.*

> *Relapse consists of conscious acts. An act is something you do.*

Detecting Your Relapse Setup

Thinking distortions, such as denial and rationalization, make it easier to set up your own relapse episode. The process is started by participating in or setting up a number of events or activities that lead you to expose yourself to high risk situations. This can also allow you to deny any responsibility for relapse. There is no such thing as a relapse caused by things external to you (Parks, & Marlatt, 2000). It results because of your actions or lack of actions. This is *good news* because you have the power to be proactive and make changes.

The choice to use again is strongly influenced by the level and variety of skills you develop to manage your life. Choosing to use is the final decision in a series of small decisions that led you to an opportunity to choose to pick up that glass of alcohol, swallow that pill or inject that drug. Relapse is the act of returning to your previous condition: a former mood or way of life, especially a bad or undesirable one, after coming out of it for a while. It always refers to a return to a negative state.

- **No one says:** *I had a relapse and started exercising again. I don't know what happened.*

- **No one says:** *I had a relapse and started going to school again. I don't know how I got enrolled.*

Get Real Motivation!

What are your reasons for quitting? Are they strong enough? Revisit page 18.

Relapse consists of conscious acts. An act is something you do. A reason is an explanation or justification for doing or not doing something. Unless you are experiencing a serious episode of mental illness such as psychosis or have suffered serious brain damage, you can become more aware of your reasons and motives for acting or thinking in a particular way. To get a handle on your rationalizations and the distorted thinking that supports use or a return to use, cognitive or thinking therapy is often a good resource. It recognizes you are able to control and make changes in your thinking.

Habits Or Conditioned Responses

Thinking precedes every action except for actions which require a conditioned response. A conditioned response is the way we eventually drive a car. We don't think about every tiny part of driving except when we are learning to drive or when we are particularly aware of our actions due to hazardous or unusual road conditions. If we are in a new car that we're not used to, we may reach for the gearshift and realize it is not on a steering wheel, but on the floor. It takes time to change habits.

Using frequently and heavily results in developing a habitual unthinking response to all life's situations by using again. The total environment around the user eventually becomes so cue laden that the user is faced with cues to use at every turn. This can be overwhelming to some people. Take time out at a safe place, to help you stop habitual using behavior. When you are in a safe place away from drugs and alcohol and from people who routinely use, you can learn to become aware of your thinking, feeling, and responses to situations. A timeout allows you to pause, to be away from cues that maintain or reinforce your old thinking habits. This time out gives you the opportunity to build new thinking patterns and responses.

A Time Out From Using

What happens when you are in rehab or at a safe home and not putting drugs and alcohol into your body? You begin eating better. Your body has nutrients to rebuild damaged tissue and normalize nerve function. You begin exercising and you improve flexibility and increase body mass. Your brain begins once again to produce dopamine and other necessary brain chemicals to function normally. As a result, your body's natural mood modulators kick in and are enhanced by your improved thinking patterns, attitude, and behaviors. When you have not used for a period of time, your body physically changes for the better. This is the good news.

The other news you need to be aware of is these changes mean you cannot tolerate the same level of drugs and alcohol you were using when you quit. After a period of abstinence, your body is not the drug and alcohol processing machine it was when you were using heavily. Your body can't immediately tolerate a return to previous high levels of use.

What Is Substance Dependence?

You became addicted to alcohol and drugs in two ways: physically and psychologically. Substances like alcohol, cocaine, amphetamines, and opium cause *both* physical and psychological dependence. Some like cannabis, LSD, and PCP cause psychological dependence even though they are not physically addicting (Frances, & First, 1998).

Dependence is the side effect of drugs and alcohol that results in drug seeking behavior. Your brain and nature never made the extremely powerful, toxic, and highly concentrated substances that can now be purchased and put in your body. When laboratory animals can electrically self-stimulate brain pleasure centers, they do so rather than eating or drinking and they ultimately die of thirst and starvation. Once addicted, humans devote every waking moment to getting the substance, using it, looking forward to the next time, and feeling bad about the last time. They develop severe psychological symptoms and harmful physical consequences (Frances, & First, 1998).

Physical addiction occurs because the human brain is skilled at adapting to new chemical environments. When exposed to drugs or alcohol, your brain adjusts by gradually modifying the number, configuration or sensitivity of nerve receptors for that substance. In this way your brain develops tolerance to the drugs which is a protective mechanism that allows it to become accustomed to the level of the drug you are putting in your body. For example, the first dose of heroine has an intense effect on brain cells. Higher and higher doses are required to achieve the same effects because of increased tolerance. Many drugs, such as alcohol, amphetamines, cocaine, nicotine, opiates, and anti-anxiety medication result in tolerance and therefore higher and higher doses are required to get the same high or effect (Frances, & First, 1998).

When using the same amount of drug or alcohol over time, the high eventually falls flat due to increasing tolerance to the substances in your brain. In an attempt to get the same high back, the individual increases the amount used and the frequency of use. For example, they increase the amount drank at one sitting from two drinks to six drinks, and they shorten the interval between drinking from every six hours to every three hours. The brain once again compensates and develops a higher tolerance to the effects of the larger amounts of alcohol and the other drugs. And, the cycle repeats with the individual consuming larger amounts more frequently.

Going through withdrawal and maintaining abstinence results in a return to lower tolerance levels for drugs and alcohol in your brain. Decreased tolerance means your body now behaves like a non-using adult. If you return immediately to your prior high level of use, you can experience severe side effects including; unconsciousness, respiratory distress, and even death. You no longer have a protective mechanism against high doses. You are at extremely high risk if you suddenly choose to use at high levels again (Frances, & First, 1998).

Get Real Motivation!

What are your reasons for quitting? Are they strong enough? Revisit page 18.

In addition, you may have sustained physical damage to your body during your previous use. You may be at a higher risk of negative effects if you return to using because your organs such as the liver, heart, and lungs are damaged from your past use of drugs or alcohol at high levels. Your physical health is poorer than it was when you first tried drugs and alcohol. If you choose to use again, you need to take precautions or you will suffer serious harm.

Overdose is a high risk if you use drugs and alcohol following a prolonged period of abstinence. If your drugs are illicit (i.e. from the street), they will have varying levels of purity and often contain mixtures of multiple drugs. This means you never really know what you are getting. You don't know the strength or dose. So if you do choose to use, take care of yourself and use extreme caution.

If You Choose To Use Again, Take Precautions

Do not do it alone, do not stock up, make sure the amount you use is small, and treat it as a one time act. Buy or obtain only enough for one hit or one drink. Having larger quantities available is an incentive for you to keep taking more as you get intoxicated. This can push you into an overdose. Make decisions about how to keep yourself safe *before* you choose to use again. Because, once you are high, your judgment is impaired, and you cannot keep yourself safe. Always make sure someone is around you who is not using.

> *Don't pretend using isn't a decision. Do choose to stop using after a lapse.*

Don't mix drugs and alcohol if you choose to use again. Alcohol added to other drugs leads to overdose. People who take heroin, and at the same time also take tranquilizers, alcohol, and cocaine are at high risk for sudden death. Death by asphyxiation in one's vomit is more common among people who mix alcohol with drugs. Alcohol is more likely to cause people to vomit while additional drugs make the intoxicated individual less able to stir themselves awake. Make sure your family or friends know:

- Never to try and guess the level of drunkenness.
- A person who has passed out may die.
- If there is any suspicion of alcohol overdose, call 9-1-1 for help.

You will regret choosing to use again. You can get your life on track quickly after a lapse, only if you are still alive to do so. If you suffer brain damage from an overdose of alcohol or drugs, you have limited all your future possibilities. <u>Don't pretend using isn't a decision</u>. If you choose to use, don't use alone. Don't buy in quantity. Do have people around you who know what to do in emergency. Do choose to stop using after a lapse.

Don't allow one use to be the end of your life goals. If you choose to use again, as long as you keep yourself safe and treat it as a one-time event, *you can* choose to stop. Lapse is not a tipping point to total relapse unless you choose it to be so. Whether you call it a slip or a lapse, you are still in control and you can choose not to continue to use.

1. Identify the things, events, emotional states, and location *cues to use* that were present before your lapse.

2. Check your pre lapse stress level and determine what relaxation or stress reduction actions you can take if a similar situation arises.

> *There is evidence that people who lapse, that is have a single episode of use, do not progress to full relapse if they use their coping skills to identify why the lapse occurred.*

3. Check your anxiety or depression level.

4. Check for negative emotions such as anger.

5. Be honest with yourself and take action.

6. Strengthen your support system.

7. Loneliness and boredom can be ended through action or tolerated for periods of time.

8. Keep exercising.

9. Use relaxation and stress management.

10. Talk to a supportive friend or family member.

11. Keep working towards your important goals.

A Lapse Can Lead To Greater Commitment

There *is* evidence that people who lapse, that is have a single episode of use, do not progress to full relapse if they use their coping skills to identify why the lapse occurred. They do not relapse if they use the analysis of their lapse to implement needed change such as improving stress management or giving up on a high risk friendship. A high level of commitment to abstinence and using effective coping skills results in the person using the lapse as a learning experience. The lapse, when treated as an event to be learned from, results in an even stronger commitment to life goals and a stronger, more effective relapse prevention plan (Marlatt, & Donovan, 2005). A high level of commitment to self-improvement is also linked with a reduced relapse rate when the commitment is supported by effective coping skills. A lapse just means you have more to learn about managing your life, and who doesn't have more to learn?

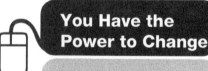

You Have the Power to Change

Whether you think you can, or think you can't, you're right. Henry Ford

Lapse As A Guilt Inducing Event

A full relapse is more likely when:

- The lapse is viewed as confirmation of the individual's personal weakness.
- The lapse is viewed as confirmation of the individual's failure of will power.
- The individual has poor coping skills (Marlatt, & Donovan, 2005).

Guilt and shame are of no benefit to you when you experience a lapse. A self instilled burden of guilt and shame can be used to justify a return to using or drinking. What can you do immediately after a lapse?

> *This book encourages you to look at multiple areas of your life so that at any given time, you are always succeeding and moving ahead in some life area.*

1. *Use rational thinking skills*, to end the *all or none* dysfunctional thinking. "If I lapsed once, I will continue to full relapse."

2. *Stop self-blame*. Learning to maintain abstinence is a process just like learning any other skill.

3. *Remove guilt*. If you must feel guilt use it to stimulate positive action for further relapse prevention.

4. *Stop negative emotions and negative self-talk*. They are counter productive. Use relaxation techniques and physical exercise to clear your mind.

5. *Assess the situation for using cues* that led you to the lapse. Make changes to your environment, behaviors, and your relapse prevention plan.

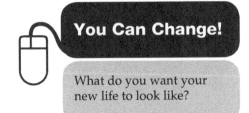

You Can Change!

What do you want your new life to look like?

6. *Practice drug and drink refusal skills* based on scenarios just experienced during the lapse.

7. *Increase exercise, meditation, and relaxation activities* during the days after the lapse (Marlatt, & Donovan, 2005).

The effect that all drugs and alcohol have in common is they impair judgment. Poor judgment can result after taking small amounts, which is why taking a small amount often leads to taking more. One drink leads to two. With impaired judgment, it appears to the user that more is better. Impaired judgment from drugs or alcohol is a high-risk for relapse. In addition to using, if your judgment is also impaired by lack of sleep, chronic fatigue, depression or anxiety, you are at even higher risk for relapse. A balanced life style improves physical and mental health, improves your judgment about using drugs, and reduces the risk of relapse.

It is relatively easy for people to change undesired behaviors temporarily. Maintaining behavior change is much more difficult. This book encourages you to look at multiple areas of your life so that at any given time, you are always succeeding and moving ahead in some life area. Even if you lapse or when one particular life area may be temporarily left on the backburner, you are still moving forward, taking action.

> *Although you can learn from a lapse and even from a full relapse, the most effective learning occurs during daily drug and alcohol-free coping with life's problems and by achieving your goals.*

A lapse is the initial use of a substance after an individual has made a commitment to abstain from that substance. A relapse is a full return to the negative behaviors and the original level of substance abuse. Using increases the intensity of craving. A single dose or use of a drug or alcohol causes your body to react in an anticipatory way. *During your period of addiction, you trained your body to expect that you won't stop at one drink or pill or injection*. When you use once or lapse, your body remembers past patterns of use, and it asks for more through escalated craving.

Expect increased cravings after a single use and use the techniques described in Chapter 5 to reduce craving intensity. Use your coping skills that you learned about in Chapter 6 and from other sources so you can take action to reduce the risk for further use.

Although you can learn from a lapse and even from a full relapse, the most effective learning occurs during daily drug and alcohol-free coping with life's problems and by achieving your goals.

When Can I Go Back To Using Moderately?

Moderate use is defined as use of a psycho active substance that does not generally cause problems either for the user or for society. There is a difference between problem drug use and addiction. Problem drug or alcohol use is at the beginning of a spectrum of experienced negative effects on life and health. A person notices the negative impact of drinking or using in a particular area of their life, and decides to change their pattern of use. Problem use has not taken over the person's life. Problem use can lead to an abuse cycle and addiction or it can be managed and reduced so the person stops using or changes their pattern of use.

Chapter Eleven: Reducing The Risks of Using Again

You have stepped beyond problem use if you have been attending a formal addiction program or receiving extensive addiction treatment. With addiction, your drug and alcohol use changed the way you felt, the way you were treated. It consumed your thoughts and time. It negatively influenced your work and school. It negatively affected your relationships. It caused you to feel worry, shame, guilt, anger, anxiety, and depression. You often experienced symptoms of withdrawal and felt generally sick and out of control all the time. You tried repeatedly to stop or reduce use and you were unsuccessful. This is full addiction, not problem substance use. **If you have experienced addiction, there is no such thing as limited use for you.** Trying to gradually cut down or trying to return to limited use is a fruitless venture once you have been addicted. Each use fuels the craving and desire for more and prolonged using. Repeated attempts to reduce use and return to moderate use postpones the recovery process indefinitely. **If you are in doubt whether you have an addiction, seek a professional assessment**.

How About Using Other Drugs And Alcohol Except My Drug Of Choice?

Limited use or social use of any of the legal or illicit drugs that you can become addicted to is strongly discouraged due to the extremely high rate of relapse when this is attempted.

The use of alcohol and marijuana decreases inhibitions and *decreases* the likelihood that abstinence will be maintained for all other substances, particularly cocaine. The research shows that clients who have been addicted to cocaine will need to stop using all other drugs, including alcohol and marijuana. Social use of cocaine is not safe for people who have been addicted. Once you have become dependant on cocaine, the only way to regain control of your life is to stop using completely. The path to cocaine addiction at some point becomes a one-way street and the road back to occasional use is blocked. Virtually everyone who enters treatment because of cocaine abuse has already tried to cut back dozens and dozens of times. Therefore, complete abstinence, not controlled drug use, is the only option known at this time for cocaine addiction (Weiss, Mirin, & Bartel, 1994).

People who are in the early stages of problem use of alcohol benefit most from controlling their use with the objective being to cut down on their alcohol consumption or stop drinking altogether. For individuals who have progressed to being unable to stop drinking or to decrease their use, and have unsuccessfully attempted several times to decrease or stop use, abstinence is the target as opposed to limiting or decreasing use.

Limited use or social use of any of the legal or illicit drugs that you can become addicted to is strongly discouraged due to the extremely high rate

of relapse when this is attempted. The reason for relapse may be that limited or social use brings you back into contact with <u>all of the using cues</u>, not just the drink or the drug. *Successfully managing a full set of cues, environment, drugs, alcohol, places, people, feelings, sounds, sights, is not possible for long, when you add that judgment is impaired by drugs or alcohol.*

So you have crossed the line biologically and psychologically. Perhaps at sometime in your future, there will be research that demonstrates how to return to moderate use. At the present time, moderating use is only an option for those persons who have experienced early problem use. *Early* is the operative word. If you have been experiencing considerable life problems, **and** negative mental and physical side effects from your drug and alcohol use, your problems have probably progressed to dependence. Problem use is often a wish rather than a reality for people who are addicted, because people who are addicted use dysfunctional beliefs to allow them to keep using, even when they are in trouble.

> **New Habits Are Possible**
>
> Addictive behaviour patterns can be changed.

Testing the Water

Often, it takes several weeks, months or up to a year of abstinence before your sleep, physical health, emotions, and thinking return to a state of balance or normalcy for you. When your thinking is clear enough, you can rationally assess how much damage the abuse of drugs or alcohol did to your life and if it is worth testing to see if limited use will be possible for you. Learn by your past experience. A person in control of their life learns from past experiences, both positive and negative. You have already tried unsuccessfully to reduce use. For some people experimental use led to moderate use, which led to problem use, then abuse, and finally addiction. There is no road back.

Test your rational thinking. *Take ten minutes and write down your reasons for attempting moderate use again. Write down your reasons for not attempting moderate use again.*

1. What are my reasons for attempting moderate use?

   _____

   _____

   _____

   _____

You can succeed and make your last relapse the last!

Chapter Eleven: Reducing The Risks of Using Again

2. What are my reasons for NOT attempting moderate use?

You may find your reasons for not attempting moderate use again are the same as the reasons you wrote in your "Craving Management Plan." <u>They are your reasons for not using at all.</u>

Remember, abstinence is not a goal. Abstinence is a requirement for you to achieve your real life goals in physical and mental health, school and work, recreation, relationships, home and community life, and communications. For you, abstinence is a state of being you have achieved because you are already there. You are clean. You just need to maintain it, enjoy it, and eventually, just like when you became as experienced driver, it will become second nature. You won't even think about it, except when the driving conditions are difficult. And then, you will take extra care and caution to adjust your driving to the conditions of the road. You will be able to keep yourself safe.

Without Drugs And Alcohol, Will My Life Be Perfect?

All people experience life problems. Life problems that are the result of substance abuse are more readily dealt with when the abuse cycle is broken. Some problems actually end with the ending of the substance abuse. Individuals who learn coping skills, and who continue to develop their skills, will be able to face life's problems with less fear and anxiety. They will be better prepared to resolve problems as they occur. Common life problems that will need to be managed even after you've achieved abstinence include:

- Relationship problems
- Financial problems
- Social Pressure To Use
- Daily stressors
- Health problems (Beck, Wright, Newman, & Liese, 1993)

Relationship Problems

All marriages, partnerships, and families have a degree of difficulty. Problems in relationships can be a stimulus for renewing drug or alcohol abuse. Using can provide a temporary false sense of increased self-esteem and a way to exert control in relationships. Using can be an unhealthy way to reduce anger or an escape from relationship unhappiness. Unhappiness and anger in relationships are cues for you to take action and seek specialized help or counseling for your relationship (Beck, Wright, Newman, & Liese, 1993).

During a cycle of drug and alcohol abuse, relationships are often damaged. You have come through withdrawal and are no longer feeling ill, irritable, and depressed. You are no longer using. As a result of reading, taking courses, and some counseling you are developing improved communication skills and rational thinking. You can now talk calmly with your partner or family about how to improve your relationships and move past the addiction. It is time to make a formal plan with your partner or family. Refer to Chapter 9 and the section on mutual goal setting to get started.

New Habits Are Possible

Addictive behaviour patterns can be changed.

Financial Problems

Individuals who have abused drugs and alcohol often face low income due to their limited training, skills, and opportunities. They may be tempted to return to selling or another role in the drug economy. They may return to using drugs and alcohol to manage negative feelings resulting from their low income and limited opportunity to move ahead. Leaving the cycle of abuse will not immediately result in having an increased income. It will result in *increased opportunity* to take better advantage of skills and to plan and work toward a career. Improving one's level of income takes time. This can be particularly discouraging for people who have little tolerance for longer term goal planning (Beck, Wright, Newman, & Liese, 1993).

On the other hand, high-income people who have completed

withdrawal and treatment can once again become involved in a cycle of drug and alcohol abuse to increase energy, confidence, manage pressure or to be part of a lifestyle that includes use (Beck, Wright, Newman, & Liese, 1993).

Facing financial challenges can be a test of your coping and planning skills. Make sure you keep exercising and using relaxation and stress management skills, to get you through the discouraging days. Seek career and financial advice rather than struggling alone.

Peer Pressure Or Social Pressure To Use

A factor affecting both high and low income individuals who have abused drugs or alcohol, is vulnerability to peer pressure (Beck, Wright, Newman, & Liese, 1993). Individuals are frequently confronted by friends and associates who urge them to use, share, and sell drugs. Some people are pressured to prove they're still one of the gang and have the guts to use drugs heavily again. More affluent people may be motivated to use by a need to gain or maintain acceptance with those who use and are powerful, wealthy or have social status.

Individuals may fear they will be deprived of meaningful friendship and employment if they avoid every substance abuser they know. Yet, it is vital to seek and maintain contacts and friendships with people who are abstinent from drugs and alcohol. If peer pressure is a factor in your substance abuse cycle, it will be necessary to look at new ways to meet your need for friendship and to increase your self-esteem. Cognitive training and communication skill training can help you to manage peer relationships. It can help you set boundaries so people who continue to use drugs and alcohol are no longer part of your social network of friends.

Daily Life Stressors

Even though you are abstinent, you will still be faced with mundane problems or stressors that can trigger alcohol and drug use. An accumulation of unmanaged stressful events and negative feelings experienced day after day can encourage a person to return to drugs or alcohol just to get through the day (Beck, Wright, Newman, & Liese, 1993). Even positive changes, such as starting a new life through a new place to live, new work, and new relationships, result in stress and conflict that must be managed. Using rational coping responses is one way to decrease the impact of minor troublesome problems and occurrences, stressors of daily living or any event that triggers a sense of frustration, anger, anxiety, fatigue and loneliness. Your success depends on anticipating stressful situations and learning to manage them, while maintaining your stress resilience through exercise, sleep, diet, relaxation, and a sense of humor. Review your Personal Stress Inventory Worksheet regularly and make new worksheets to keep a current list of stressors and techniques to manage them.

Health Problems

Even when an individual has given up drugs and alcohol, the health consequences from the abuse may linger indefinitely. These health issues may cause mental and physical pain, worry and hopelessness, and a reason to self-medicate using drugs or alcohol (Beck, Wright, Newman, & Liese, 1993). So, get quality medical care. While abusing drugs, individuals do not often seek or comply with medical advice. Now that you are abstinent, it is important to have a regular physician you know and trust so you receive regular healthcare. Untreated diseases are a high health risk for those who have been abusing drugs or alcohol. Have your physician run the required tests to:

- Ensure infections are identified and treated.
- Ensure heart, lung, nervous system, digestive, and liver damage are identified and treated.
- Ensure mental health problems such as depression and anxiety are identified and treated.

Review your Life Plan health goals regularly. Keep taking action on mental and physical health problems.

A Balanced Lifestyle

A balanced lifestyle is about the basics that have been covered throughout this book. Gradually improve your health and well-being through regular exercise, diet, sleep and relaxation. Practice safe sex. Improve your relationships by improving communication, interpersonal, and conflict management skills. Improve your skills to manage depression, anger, loneliness, anxiety or boredom to improve your attitude, reduce negative thoughts, and reduce relapse. You will be better prepared to manage any short-term health problems or chronic health issues you may face. Communication, relaxation, and cognitive skills can help you manage emotions and negative thoughts that accompany illness or decreased health. These same skills will help you face the myriad of life's daily problems you will confront, just like everyone else.

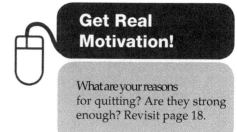

Get Real Motivation!

What are your reasons for quitting? Are they strong enough? Revisit page 18.

Your Future

As a result of your commitment to your new life goals and abstinence, you will be able to make sweeping changes to your life. Positive changes in health and relationships will come quickly when you maintain a drug and alcohol free life that includes balanced lifestyle changes. You'll experience fewer life problems and you will be able to better manage those that do come along. It's not just looking forward to having fewer problems. You can look forward to increased fun, increased health, and improved appearance, greater success in work, school, and relationships. You can experience joy every day.

Summary

Remember to add specific goals to your "Life Plan" to ensure you take actions to:

1. Develop coping skills, cognitive (thinking) skills, and lifestyle balance.

2. Keep yourself safe, if you choose to use again.

3. Treat a lapse as a learning experience and make changes to reduce the risk of further use.

4. Manage relationship problems, financial problems, daily stressors, social pressure to use, and health problems.

5. Reward yourself with positive activities and cues!

. . . .

References

Frances, Allen & First, Michael B. (1998). *"Your Mental Health, A Layman's Guide to the Psychiatrist's Bible."* New York. Scribner. 12, 32, 79, 117-119, 120-122.

Parks, George A. & Marlatt, G. Alan. (2000). Relapse Prevention Therapy: A Cognitive-Behavioral Approach. *The National Psychologist*, Sept/Oct., Vol. 9. No. 5. Retrieved from http://www.nationalpsychologist

Marlatt, G.A., & Donovan, D.M. (Eds.). (2005). *"Relapse Prevention Maintenance Strategies in the Treatment of Addictive Behaviours."* (2nd Edition). New York. The Guilford Press. 28-29.

New Habits Are Possible

Addictive behaviour patterns can be changed.

Weiss, Roger D., Mirin, Steven M., & Bartel, Roxanne L. (1994). *"Cocaine."* (2nd Edition). Washington, DC. American Psychiatric Press. 164-165, 176.

Beck, A.T., Wright, F.D., Newman, C.F., & Liese, B.S. (1993). *"Cognitive Therapy of Substance Abuse."* New York. The Guilford Press. 192-200, 206-209.

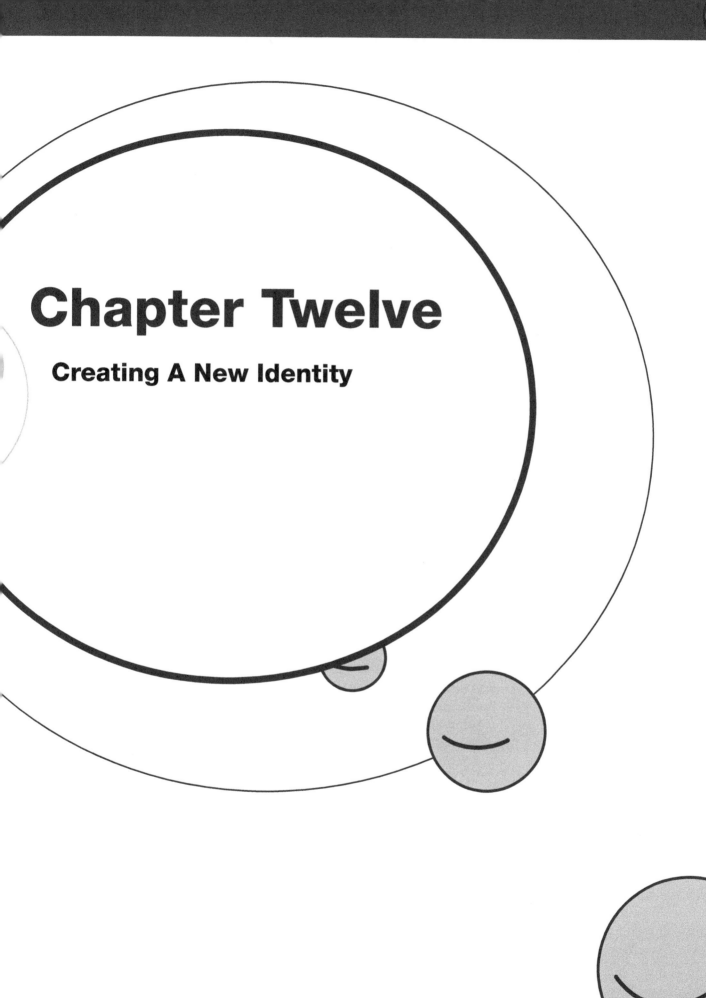

Chapter Twelve

Creating A New Identity

You can succeed and make your last relapse the last!

Chapter 12

Creating A New Identity

Children are told when to eat, sleep, brush their teeth, go to school, who to play with, and what medicine to take when they are sick. For the most part, everything children do is controlled by someone else: parents, teachers, siblings, police, doctors or babysitters. For most children, it feels safe when some one else is in control of their life. Adulthood brings the power to make choices.

Your identity tells you what you deserve.

As an adult, life becomes confusing at times as choices must be made: university, trade school or work; live in a city or town; social activities with or without drinking and drugs; and start or end relationships. You may not have known what you really wanted or what was really important to you. Drinking and using drugs felt like an answer for some of life's problems

When you think about it now, addiction to drugs and alcohol resulted in *giving* up control over many parts of your life. Drug and alcohol use results in dysfunctional thinking, feeling helpless, and letting other people choose the solutions to problems. People, who experience addiction, often ignore or are unaware of the key factors that influence their health and life. In reality, they let someone else be responsible for decisions and outcomes. You have made a choice to gain *new* insights, knowledge, and skill that will help you regain control over your life.

New Habits Are Possible

Addictive behaviour patterns can be changed.

Addict As An Identity

An addict is someone who is physiologically or mentally dependant on a drug and has experienced damaging physiological or psychological side effects. A non-addict is somebody who is *not* physiologically or mentally dependant on a drug and therefore not likely to experience damaging physiological or psychology effects. People are partially identified by the labels applied by self or others, such as the label "addict."

What is identity? Identity is based on what we believe to be true about ourselves. Identity gives us an idea of who we are and how to relate to others and the world we live in. Identity marks the ways we are the same as others who share that vision, and the way in which we are different from those who do not (Woodward, 1997).

Individuality is the awareness that an individual or group has of being unique and having a unique identity. *Take a few minutes now and write down what you thought was unique for you about being an addict.*

That is, how did it make you feel you were different from those who were not addicts?

_____
_____
_____
_____
_____
_____
_____

Identity includes knowledge, beliefs, memories, expectations, and understanding. Each person's identity defines them as a unique individual and also as part of a family and other social groups. Your identity defines you and gives meaning to every aspect of your life. It is shaped by how you interpret, remember and regard events in the past, present, and future (Dombeck, 2006). *Your identity tells you what you deserve. It provides a measure of your worth both to you and frequently to others.*

Identity Expands Or Limits Options

Identity shapes your perspective. It influences what you end up choosing to do or not to do. It directly effects your motivation. When you *don't* believe something is possible to accomplish, you don't persevere at it, no matter how easy that thing might actually be to complete. Identity is the lens through which you look to judge yourself, your options, and the world. Make sure your self-identity is not distorted by mistaken beliefs, faulty understandings, inaccurate memories, and unrealistic attitudes (Dombeck, 2006).

Distorted thinking, based on forever using the identity of an addict, will keep you from seeing yourself, your options, and the world in an objective manner. You will very likely misjudge your options. You will make poorer choices in life and you will end up reliving your past experience of addiction rather than moving into your new life goals.

Strategies To Change Your Identity

Give yourself opportunities to think about what is important to you and what kind of person you want to be. Become involved with different people and activities to get an idea of what you like and what you don't like. Practice communicating assertively regarding who you are now and what you believe about yourself and your future. Other people who have good or bad intentions may tell you how you should think, feel, and act. But, only *you* can decide who you want to be as a person.

The self is made rather than inherited and is not unchangeable. Your self-identity is a work in progress. Each person creates and maintains a set of beliefs about their life, the story of who they are. You can expand your future possibilities. What you tell yourself and others can lead to increased emotional health and reduced risk of relapse. Take the time to honestly find some positive meaning in the past and present events in your life. If you make past negative events the center of your life, you will always find reasons to feel hurt, guilty, angry or defensive. You may be overwhelmed by fear of failure.

> *You can become a different person by thinking, acting, and speaking differently.*

Your future can be limited by the way people talk about addiction and your past ways of doing things as an addict. Your future can be limited by your beliefs about you.

Beliefs Can Be Changed

Beliefs can be changed when you start to ignore them, replace them, and do things differently. You can do this by looking at your addiction as a *past learning experience* rather than as your present and your future. You *can* become a different person by thinking, acting, and speaking differently.

You can change the negative expectations held by you and others, by creating new structure and activities in your life. You can work to find a new way of behaving and believing. Step into the future, and let go of the label of addict and the behaviors that go with that label.

Being honest and positive in assessing past events and what you learned from them will help you create your new life. Your life isn't, never was, and never will be all black and white, good or bad. It is important to take the time to think about how you currently define yourself. Take time to plan for a new vision of yourself and your life. Have the courage to let go of that familiar old you. Make a commitment to yourself, your new life, and relapse prevention by:

1. Redefining your identity beyond the label of addict.

2. Viewing your life in a future-oriented way.

3. Making a public commitment to create that future.

Letting Go Of The Past

Not forgiving has many consequences: emotional pain, suffering, guilt, remorse, revenge seeking, anger, blaming, and negative behavior. Not forgiving creates ongoing conflict. Conflict puts you at higher risk for relapse. To forgive is to act as if the negative event never occurred. To forget is to stop thinking or worrying about the event or person involved. If you can't forgive, then, accept that it happened, and forget it. Move on in your life.

Take five minutes now and write a list of the people whom you can't forgive and describe the event or wrongdoing. Now write down the events or wrongdoing for which you can't forgive yourself.

1. List the people whom you can't forgive:

   _____
   _____
   _____

2. Write down the events or wrongdoing for which you can't forgive yourself:

   _____
   _____
   _____

Forgiving another person happens when you accept they are human, have faults, and make mistakes. You let them know you will not hold hard feelings for the wrongdoing. Forgiving yourself is recognizing you are human, have faults, and make mistakes. Forgetting is putting those events behind you and no longer bringing them up. Forgetting is stopping all negative talk about and negative references to the event or your self (Messina, & Messina, 1999). Are you human? Every

Chapter Twelve: Creating A New Identity

You Can Change!

What do you want your new life to look like?

human being makes mistakes and does things they later regret.

Forgiving is expressing genuine remorse and regret for your actions or words that hurt or disappointed others or yourself. Forgiving is promising your self that this harm will not be done again. Forgetting is making a commitment to let go of the anger and pain (Messina, & Messina, 1999). *Expressing true regret is the first step. The second step is behaving differently. The third is letting go.*

To help you to forgive yourself and others:

- Face conflict head-on, resolve it on the spot.
- Develop skills for open, honest, and assertive communication.
- Get professional help when necessary to resolve problems in relationships.
- Recognize your part in setting up hurtful experiences.
- Replace dysfunctional thinking and irrational beliefs that stop you from forgiving and forgetting.

1. Have you ever been forgiven? How did it feel? What behaviors did the other person use that signaled they had forgiven you?

_____

_____

_____

_____

2. Has anyone ever brought up something from the past to remind you of how you hurt them? How did that make you feel?

_____

_____

Make Your Last Relapse The Last

_____
_____
_____

3. How has the lack of forgiving and forgetting affected your current relationship?

_____
_____
_____
_____
_____

3. If you can't forgive yourself, you need to work on acceptance of what happened. You can't change the past. Take five minutes and write down what behaviors you could use to show forgiving and forgetting in a relationship.

_____
_____
_____
_____
_____
_____

You can succeed and make your last relapse the last!

Chapter Twelve: Creating A New Identity

Get Real Motivation!

What are your reasons for quitting? Are they strong enough? Revisit page 18.

Try Penance If You Can't Forgive Yourself

If you can't forgive and you can't accept, then you may want to try the concept of penance. Penance is self-punishment performed to show sorrow for having committed an act. Punishment is the penalty that is imposed on somebody for wrongdoing. By not forgiving yourself or someone else, <u>you are always punishing yourself</u>. Some people punish themselves by negative self talk. *I'm an idiot. I'm stupid. I'm a jerk.* Some people punish themselves by not trying to succeed. *I don't deserve this.* Some people try to punish others by never forgiving them. In reality, people who never forgive others are only punishing themselves by always remembering the event that caused them pain. What to do? Try the following.

Let your punishment fit the crime. In Canada, the maximum life sentence without the possibility of parole is twenty five years. Both a life sentence and dangerous offender designation are *very rarely* used even when the offender is found guilty of a particularly grievous offence. If you are declared a dangerous offender there is no maximum or minimum sentence. But either way, a parole review occurs every seven years.

Be The Judge

What have you or someone else done that deserves a life sentence of punishment? Have you been berating yourself or someone else for years over a past behavior or event? A judge would provide an opportunity to review your current behavior and revise the punishment or even let you go. Be the judge. Decide on a reasonable punishment. Remember, effective punishments should *help you change and move forward*. Before you try this exercise read the following examples of punishments that support change:

1. Crime: You spent all the money in your family savings account on drugs and alcohol. Sample self punishment: Make a positive life commitment, stop using drugs and alcohol, make a savings plan, get a better paying job, and save double the amount wasted. Then after <u>five years,</u> forgive yourself and let it go.

2. Crime: You got very intoxicated at a family wedding four years ago, started a fist fight, and then vomited on the front steps. Punishment: Make a commitment not to drink or use drugs. Decide to: always dress immaculately to show you value being part of the family; always use behavior that is positive and respectful of yourself and others. After <u>one year</u>, forgive yourself, and let it go.

3. Crime: You had sex with strangers when you were intoxicated. Punishment: Make a positive life commitment. Visit a doctor and get checked for sexually transmitted diseases. Stop

drinking and taking drugs. Don't have sex for 3 months and read one book every two weeks on sexual health and building self-esteem, even if you have to give up other events. Then, <u>after 3 months</u>, forgive yourself, and let it go.

Think of a specific negative event that you can't seem to let go. Then answer the following questions.

1. What have you done?

   _____

   _____

2. What can you do to make amends?

   _____

   _____

3. What can you do to feel you've been punished enough?

   _____

   _____

4. How long will your sentence be?

   _____

   _____

Be specific and make amends by making the punishment match the crime. After all, you really are your own judge. To forgive and forget, be honest with yourself. Remember, the goal is to give up berating yourself. **Always choose activities for your punishment that will help you to learn to better manage your life and to uphold your values.**

You can succeed and make your last relapse the last!

Staying Angry At Someone Else

Next, get specific about how long you're going to waste your energy being angry at someone else's past bad behavior. Accept it happened and then move on. You don't have to be or stay friends with them, but for your own mental health you do have to let it go. Always set a timeline for how long you are *not* going to forgive them: a week, month or year. Limit the time you will allow yourself to think negatively about the person or event to no more than five or ten minutes every other day. Keep reducing the frequency, until you are at once a month. Then stop thinking about it. Assign yourself activities that will help you to better manage your life and control *thoughts* that spoil life *for you*. Then accept it is part of the past and move on.

> *Loneliness is one of the major reasons individuals return to using drugs and alcohol.*

Loneliness And Recovery

Loneliness is one of the major reasons individuals return to using drugs and alcohol. Loneliness is not necessarily being alone. You can be alone for long periods of time and not feel lonely at all. You can feel lonely in a familiar setting without really understanding why. The best way to begin to understand loneliness is to examine some of the ways you experience it. Do any of the following describe your experiences of loneliness?

- Feeling alone and sad?
- Rarely visiting or being visited by others?
- Lacking friends or encouragement from others?
- Having no one special in your life?

Don't Give Up!

It's hard work, but you can finish this book!

Loneliness is a negative emotional state that must be lived through or changed by using positive coping skills. You will feel lonely when you stop drinking and using and have to give up familiar places, people, and activities to prevent relapse. Life change, even if it is positive results in some sense of loneliness. You will naturally miss past attachments and friends as you make these major changes in your life. You may feel there is no one with whom to share your personal concerns or experiences. Or, you may believe that without drugs and alcohol, you are not interesting or desirable. **People, who have completed addiction treatment and are starting a new sober lifestyle, are particularly susceptible to loneliness.**

Loneliness Is Not A Personality Flaw

Misconceptions regarding loneliness can make you feel even worse. Men may see loneliness as a sign of weakness or immaturity while women may see loneliness as a sign they are not desirable or worthy.

You Have the Power to Change

Whether you think you can, or think you can't, you're right. Henry Ford

Loneliness, like all emotional experiences, can be very negative, depending on what you tell yourself it means. *I'm the only one who feels this way.* People who think of loneliness as a personal defect often have difficulty asserting them selves, making friends, sharing about themselves, and are less responsive to others. There is a greater tendency to approach social events with cynicism. Loneliness is a negative experience when you feel excluded, unwanted or not liked by those around you. If you feel that no one wants you around, then you will find it difficult to make friends (Counselling Center University of Illinois).

People who often feel lonely also often feel depressed, angry, afraid or misunderstood. These negative emotions precede relapse. When feeling loneliness plus other negative emotions, people become highly critical of themselves and overly sensitive to whatever anyone says to them. When people feel negatively about themselves, they easily become discouraged, lose their desire and motivation to get involved in new situations, and isolate themselves from people and activities.

Or the reverse may happen. Out of desperation to end the loneliness, they may become too quickly involved with people and activities, without thinking about the consequences. They may become involved in situations that are high risk for using again. Or, they may adopt an "anyone is better than no one" attitude later finding themselves in very unsatisfying and sometimes dangerous relationships.

People, who feel negatively about themselves, often depend on others to build their self-esteem and start activities. They falsely assume nobody likes them. They blame themselves and other people for their loneliness. Loneliness is a signal it's time to take action and put things in perspective.

What To Do About Loneliness?

Loneliness is a common experience. *Twenty-five per cent of all adults experience painful loneliness at least every few weeks!* Loneliness is neither bad nor permanent. It is a signal that you may need to develop a broader circle of friends, learn to do things for yourself without friends, learn to feel better about yourself, and practice being more content about yourself in general (Counselling Center University of Illinois.) You can use relaxation skills and spend more time on your life goals, or do all of the above.

Loneliness can be overcome, it depends on you. Only you can build your self-esteem and learn to feel good about yourself.

- Seek out positive activities that really interest you and situations that allow you to get involved, get to know others, and let them get to know you. Join a sport, car, dance or gardening club or take a course.

- Get involved in organizations and activities by doing volunteer work.

- Check your personal appearance and freshen up your clothes.

- Exercise regularly to look and feel your best.

- Develop casual friendships through the course of your day by looking for simple ways to spend time with other people such as: eating with new people at work, talking to others at the gym, finding a new work-out or exercise partner.

Start new activities in your life that put you in new situations where you will meet people such as at art gallery events or pet shows. Engage in activities that you have a genuine interest in and you will meet people with whom you have something in common. Make use of community resources and check out local organizations and activities. As you can see ending loneliness means taking action. That means doing some research and getting out there (Olds, Schwartz, & Webster, 1996).

Enjoy Being You

Think of yourself as an important person. Just because you are short on friends doesn't mean you can't enjoy being a friend to yourself. Make sure you eat a healthy diet, get regular exercise, adequate sleep, and do a least one positive pleasurable thing every day. Keep up with your interests and make an effort to develop new hobbies and more interests. Use your time alone positively and get caught up on cleaning, reading, improvements to your wardrobe, home, or car. Use your time alone to get to know yourself and avoid just sitting. Actively find creative and enjoyable ways to use your alone time. Keep things around you that cue you to do things you like, or would like to try such as drawing, practicing an instrument, books, puzzles or music. Always have at least one new skill under development. Learn to play a guitar, cook or dance, or do anything that seems fun and enriching. Explore the possibility of doing things alone that you usually do with other people like going to the movies (Counselling Center University of Illinois).

Take a few minutes now and make a list of a least ten things you can do alone.

1. _____   6. _____
2. _____   7. _____
3. _____   8. _____
4. _____   9. _____
5. _____   10. _____

Now make a list of ten things you can keep in your home to use when you are alone.

1. _____   6. _____
2. _____   7. _____
3. _____   8. _____
4. _____   9. _____
5. _____   10. _____

Now go back to your "Exercise, Recreation and Social Activities Plan" at the end of Chapter 3, and add these activities.

Beating Boredom

Boredom is different from loneliness but can be equally dangerous in precipitating a lapse or relapse. Boredom is a feeling of tedium, monotony, dullness, restlessness or world weariness. Boredom can be mistaken for loneliness. It is the weariness that results from predictability in your life. It does not necessarily mean that you are doing nothing. *It means you are doing nothing new.* When boredom is experienced during recovery, it results in excitement-seeking behavior, which may paradoxically lead to a return to drugs and alcohol. Then the repetitive use of drugs or alcohol often results in further boredom and loneliness.

You can succeed and make your last relapse the last!

Chapter Twelve: Creating A New Identity

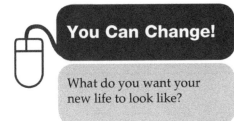

You Can Change!

What do you want your new life to look like?

The cure for boredom is like the cure for loneliness. Try these:

- Find new activities that can be done alone and with others.
- Take the risk of meeting new people in different types of settings than you are used: go to a skating rink, curling rink or swimming pool.
- Take an active interest in other people's needs or welfare and give of yourself: help repair or paint a relative's home, baby-sit a nephew or niece, or plant a garden.
- Check for negative attitudes and dysfunctional thinking and do some self help reading.
- Develop new skills and interests.
- Update your "Exercise, Recreation and Social Activities Plan" at least every two weeks.

You must get physically moving before boredom or loneliness will lift. Don't just sit and wait for better times. Take action. No matter how badly you feel, loneliness or boredom will diminish or disappear when you focus attention and energy on exercising, relaxation techniques such as meditation, learning new skills, and studying to excel at your work or school. Don't wait for your feelings to get you going. Get going on creating your new identity and achieving your life goals, and your good feelings will catch up with you.

Summary

Creating a new identity requires action. It means, challenging old beliefs and changing behaviors. It requires leaving old grudges and painful emotions behind, those you held about yourself and about others. It requires new circles of friendship through new positive and interesting activities. It even requires changing the meaning of excitement in your life and finding different ways to challenge your self and have pleasure and fun. Every living creature changes and so will you, <u>if you let yourself</u>.

• •

References

Counselling Center University of Illinois. *"Loneliness."* Retrieved from http://www.couns.uiuc.edu/Brochures/loneline.htm

Messina, James, J. & Messina, Constance. (1999-2007). *"Tools for Coping with Life's Stressors Handling. Forgiving and Forgetting."* (Coping.org is a Public Service of James J. Messina, Ph.D. & Constance M. Messina, PhD). Retrieved from http://www.coping.org/relations/forgive.htm#Negative

Olds, Jacqueline, Schwartz, Richard & Webster, Harriet. (1996). *"Overcoming Loneliness in Every Day Life."* New York. Carol Publishing Group. 166-183.

Woodward, Kathryn. (Editor). (1997). "Identity and Difference," Culture, Media and Identities Open University Series. Thousand Oaks, California. Sage Publications USA. 1-2.

New Habits Are Possible

Addictive behaviour patterns can be changed.

Chapter Thirteen

Taking Charge of Your Health And Your Life

You can succeed and make your last relapse the last!

Chapter 13

Taking Charge of Your Health And Your Life

Everyone has been to a doctor at some time to get advice. After hearing the doctor's recommendation, have you ever thought *I'm not sure about this drug or treatment?* Then, have you gone for information from another source, perhaps another doctor, a pharmacist, a nurse, the library or the internet, before agreeing to take a prescription or have surgery? This is an example of self-management at work: getting quality information to make your own health decisions in consultation with a professional such as your doctor.

> *To be in control of your health you need to continue to educate yourself about all aspects of your overall health and about relapse prevention.*

People who practice self-management of their health intentionally use coping skills. They manage their own situations by exercising deliberate conscious control to improve the outcome of the situation. They recognize their own strengths and weaknesses and work to overcome them. They take the time to find meaning and value in their life. They are always searching for new knowledge.

Self-help for mental health and addiction issues consists of learning about the nature of your problems, learning how to measure or assess those problems, and learning how they can be resolved. Self help then involves choosing and following a course of action that will help you to resolve those issues (Dombeck, 2006).

Some health problems are simple to solve and have only one or two options. Complex health problems often have more than one option for treatment, require more than one action, and involve more than one health professional. Addiction is a complex health issue.

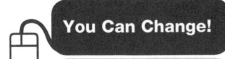

You Can Change!

What do you want your new life to look like?

You know the most about your personal experience of addiction. You have proven that you *can* make good decisions. You have stopped using. You have proven that you want to get and stay mentally and physically healthy. You are reading this book and beginning work to improve your health. You are the best person to manage your life and its problems.

By stopping use you have made a commitment to your own health. Now it's time to create a concrete plan for your health issues and to decide who will be on your health team. To be in control of your health you need to continue to educate yourself about all aspects of your overall health and about relapse prevention. You can be the leader of the people helping you to succeed and prevent relapse. No matter who is on your team: doctor, therapist, family member, personal trainer or meditation coach, you can be actively involved in all of the decisions that affect you.

To be effective at self-management, you first need to make decisions about who is on your team. Then make sure your team members are aware of *your* life plan. Choose people with whom you are comfortable and who challenge you, but also understand and are willing to support your new life plan which includes abstinence. Choose people who are not threatened by your challenges to them and who will support you to reach your goals. Make sure you read enough to know more than anyone else on your team about addiction and are at least familiar with recommended treatments or life style actions for your other health problems. Choose key members for your team who have some knowledge about addiction and who share a similar belief as yours about addiction treatment. You will be effective at self-management of your health if you keep learning from credible sources, treat your health as important as any other part of your life, learn to recognize when you need help, and learn where to go to get it.

When you are free of alcohol and drugs, you can become the expert on your health needs. Take the time to choose and use tools which are effective for you such as screening tools for depression. Become assertive about your needs and take responsibility for your actions and your health. Many health professionals are not experts or even knowledgeable about addiction. To obtain quality health care and lead your health care team, you will always need to continue learning.

> *When you are free of alcohol and drugs, you can become the expert on your health needs.*

When Self-Management Doesn't Work

Self-management doesn't work when your health problem is so severe that it has surpassed your ability to cope, such as prior to detoxification or after a serious injury. Self-management may not be effective for short periods of time if you have a flare up of a serious mental illness. You can plan ahead for what you want done if you are too ill and may need to relinquish some important decisions to others. Written health directives are becoming very common and are important for people with a history of mental health and addiction issues to keep themselves safe.

An Example Of Self-Management

A person with the past experience of narcotic addiction is booked for surgery. He knows he will require some type of pain relief after the surgery. He does not wait and hope the doctor will do the right thing. He asks the surgeon about the types of pain relief medication he normally prescribes. He makes clear his decision to have non-narcotic pain relief. He researches the options on the internet. He is clear with his nurses and physician that he will not be accepting narcotic pain relief. He chooses to use a non narcotic pain relieving drug and relaxation techniques. He researches and practices those techniques. He explains his decision using quality information. He makes sure his family understands and supports his choices. He succeeds in managing his health and he does not return to the addiction lifestyle.

Self-management of your health requires work, responsibility, accountability, negotiation, and communication skills. It results in ownership of your own health. It creates solutions that fit with your knowledge, skills, and value system. It's worth it, if you want to stay in control of your life. Self-management is more effective than letting others manage your health and your new life goals for you. You cannot, by default, not manage your health. You can only manage it well or poorly. If you decide not to engage in healthful behavior or not to be active in managing your health, this behavior actually reflects a decision on your part. Unless you are totally ignorant of healthful behaviors, it is impossible not to manage your health (Lorig, & Holman).

> *Self-management has been documented as effective for addiction.*

Key Tasks To Manage Chronic Health Problems Including Addiction

Self-management is particularly important for those people who have had the experience of addiction, because only they can be responsible for their day-to-day self-care decisions. There are basically three tasks to manage your health (Lorig, & Holman).

1. Medical management of any health condition, such as taking medication or following a special diet.

2. Maintaining, changing or creating new meaningful life goals such as finding a job that reduces exposure to cues and high risk situations to use.

3. Dealing with the emotional aspect of having a chronic condition. Emotions such as anger, fear, frustration, and depression are commonly experienced by everyone with a chronic health condition. Learning to manage these emotions is part of the work required to manage addiction.

Get Real Motivation!

What are your reasons for quitting? Are they strong enough? Revisit page 18.

What is important in self-management of health is that you identify what is most important to you (Lorig, & Holman). If you have arthritis, it might be pain control. If you have diabetes, it might be blood sugar level control. If you have the experience of addiction, it might be stress management, cues and cravings control, or loneliness and boredom reduction. Self-management will work for you, if you take the time to identify your health goals to manage your past addiction and prevent relapse. You will need to make sure you seek professional advice about your physical and mental health.

Self-management programs have been proven to significantly improve health behaviors. Some include: an increase in the amount of exercise, an increase in skill level and practice of symptom management, and improved communication with physicians. Self-management has been documented as effective for arthritis, asthma, cardiovascular disease, depression, diabetes, chronic back pain, anxiety, *and* addiction. Self-management of health has also been documented as improving health status generally, and reducing disability, fatigue, and worry about health conditions (Lorig, & Holman). Self-management is effective when you (Lorig, & Holman):

1. Develop problem solving skills.
2. Make decisions based on information.
3. Effectively use the internet, library and community resources to find quality information.
4. Use communication skills to develop positive partnerships with health professionals.
5. Take action on your health.
6. Feel more in control of your condition or illness.

So, What Does The Evidence Mean To You?

Children learn to manage their diabetes, including severe restrictions on diet and requirements for regular exercise. Teenagers learn to manage serious life threatening allergies and the accompanying diet and lifestyle restrictions. And *you* can learn to manage your; alcohol and drug restrictions, exercise, diet, sleep, and the lifestyle changes required to improve your health and achieve your goals.

> *Research shows that people who make a public commitment are much more likely to succeed and to persevere than those who don't make a public commitment.*

Commitment, as you read in earlier chapters, is a responsibility, something that takes up time, energy. It is an obligation. <u>Commitment is always previously planned.</u> Research shows that people who make a public commitment are much more likely to succeed and to persevere than those who don't make a public commitment. When we are ready to start a new and major phase in our lives; we share our plans and our commitment to succeed. It requires commitment on your part to learn and practice the skills and behaviors you need to succeed in improving your health and your life.

How To Identify The Resources Required For Your Life Plan

Whether working on relationships, work, school, home, community, physical, mental or spiritual areas of our lives, we all sometimes need to access specialized knowledge or skill. To help you overcome the problems that remain from your experience of addictions or to take on the challenges you set for yourself to achieve your goals and new lifestyle, you may need assistance. There are two common sources of assistance, professionals and families or friends.

Professionals

The best advisor is someone who is sympathetic to your goal and who remains detached and can give you realistic answers to questions and not just the answers you may want to hear.

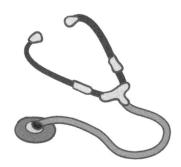

Take time now to go through your "Life Plan and Goals for Next Year Worksheet" at the end of Chapter 9 and identify which goals may need one time or ongoing professional advice or assistance. Sometimes, it's smart to save money and use a *do it yourself* approach. Or you may decide it is best to spend the money to hire a pro to help when starting your own business or a new career. Bear in mind you're putting your goals, health, and safety in someone's hands. So, choose advisors you can trust.

Referrals can direct you to trustworthy advisors. Get referrals from people you know and trust, who have obtained assistance in the same areas where you need help. Ask them who they have used, if they are or are not satisfied, and why. Recommendations from others aren't enough. Take the time to interview candidates. Ask about their general experiences, because you will want an advisor with lots of experience in the services you need. Many professionals specialize. Always discuss cost and ask about any additional fees that might be charged. Find out what you will get for your money. Ask if your advisor has insurance that covers error or loss. Check local community services, some expert advice may be found free of charge.

Then, make a decision and try them out. If it isn't working, give them feedback. If it's still not working, find someone else. Your goals are too important to be slowed down by working with an advisor who isn't helpful or compatible. Remember to check your hidden agendas to make sure you are not sabotaging your own plans by frequently changing advisors.

You may have discovered, as you were doing your life plan that you need to address some complex emotional issues. You may need the help of a uniquely skilled professional for issues such as: violence and anger management, experiences of abuse or abusing, and complex family dysfunction. If you are seeking a therapist, check out the professional organization websites for information on how to find help. Interview your counselor first, before diving into therapy. A therapist should be willing to answer *any* questions you may have about their methods, training, experience, approach, length of treatment, and fees. If a therapist is reluctant to answer your questions or if you do not feel comfortable, find someone else.

Family Or Friends Who Help

Your Life Plan goals may require planned and committed assistance from a friend or family member, such as: participating with you in exercise or sports, assisting you with school or work goals, removing cues or finding a place to live, assistance with relapse prevention, family crisis planning, managing a mental illness or dealing with anxiety and stress. Using a formal approach with family or friends for critical assistance can lessen disappointments and confusion.

Make a detailed, written plan when requesting help from a specific friend or family member. And when you request help, expect that the person helping you will want some specific behaviors on your part as well. Get your commitment in writing and signed so both you and your family member or friend will be very clear about mutual expectations. Taking the time to clarify with family and friends is just as important as taking the time to clarify what you expect from professional advisors.

Clear Communication With Professionals, Family And Friends

Meeting your Life Plan goals requires clear communication with your support network. Make a page with all your life goals and share your vision. Have professionals, family and friends sign for the assistance you both agree they can provide. Sign for what *you* are willing to do for yourself, and for them in return, for their help. Then you are truly on the road to a new life.

> *By making rational decisions, we take charge of our lives and move closer to meeting our life goals. Some decisions seem unimportant but they are important.*

Problem Solving Skills For Health And Life Goals

Life is a constant series of decisions. By making rational decisions, we take charge of our lives and move closer to meeting our life goals. Some decisions seem unimportant but they are important. Every minute or two, we answer through our behavior the questions: What is important to me and what is the best use of my time right now? Any one decision about the next couple of minutes in our lives may seem trivial, but, together the cumulative effect of making these millions of decisions, determines the outcome of our lives.

Chapter Thirteen: Taking Charge of Your Health And Your Life

Important decisions are often made impulsively and without much thought: selection of a mate, friend, doctor, career or health care. Relatively less important decisions are often carefully made. What shirt or dress to buy? What car should I buy? What appliances? What movie to watch? Some decisions are made alone and under tremendous social pressure. When to have sex? What religion to accept? What to do socially with peers, coworkers or family? Whether or not to return to alcohol or drug use?

No Time For Problem Solving?

You can increase your speed, effectiveness, and confidence to solve problems. The goal of good decision making is to make decisions more rationally and wisely. We really do have a choice about many important things in our lives and can avoid making decisions sloppily or by default. We can avoid the irrational ideas, false assumptions, fears and emotions that block good problem solving.

> *A problem well stated is half-solved.*

A problem well stated is half-solved. Use your negative feelings to let you know you may have a problem. Recognize problems early. Decide if there is a problem or if you are exaggerating or minimizing the problem. When in doubt, ask someone you trust. When you have consciously decided on a new philosophy of life, most decisions are much easier. What should take priority in your life? What are your goals? You can't be outstanding at anything without some commitment. You set priorities and make decisions, either consciously or simply by how you spend your time (Malouff, 2006).

Revisit your "Problem List Worksheet," at the end of Chapter two. Clarify each problem and add to your list. Take the time to list all the problems you are facing, including high-risk and general health problems. First tackle the things that are likely to turn into bigger problems if you don't take action. You are ready to solve a problem, if you've defined the problem, determined your goal, and decided to deal with that particular problem. All good problem-solving methods require you to stop reacting impulsively, slow down, and recognize the problem. At this crucial point in your life, take time to define and understand each life problem and your goals clearly.

Generating Solutions

Now create as many possible solutions as you can to each problem. Try brainstorming and consulting experts. Give yourself time and let your unconscious work on a problem while sleeping or in the shower (Malouff, 2006). And keep on trying. Avoid thinking in terms of either/or. *I should* stay or *I should* go. Change your environment for problem-solving. Try going outside or sitting in a peaceful room at a museum or art gallery. Guard against the common decision-making pitfalls of:

- Being out of touch with your own feelings and values.

- Continuing to play the last game. *"This will be my **last** party. My **last** binge. My **last** drink."* Making the same decisions because of past bad decisions.

- Allowing emotions to rush decisions. *"I have to decide right now about having sex with Joe or he'll never see me again".*

- Allowing emotions to drag out decisions. *"I'll think about it later."*

Once you've generated some alternatives, consider the pro's and cons of how you feel about the future implied by each choice. Collect all of the information available and information about the probable outcome of each course of action. Check your values, assets, resources, and limitations. Write them down. Use the facts and give yourself time to imagine what each decision result would be like. How ashamed or proud would you be? How bored? How energetic? Use your intuition. Your feelings, needs, and wants must be given serious consideration along with the facts. Weigh the pros and cons of each action or solution. Then, decide on one you can fully commit to. Now, make your choice, write it down, and take action (Malouff, 2006).

> *Problems are often opportunities. Addiction, conflict, anger, depression or anxiety can be problems. Or, they can be opportunities to change your life for the better.*

Problems are often opportunities. Addiction, conflict, anger, depression or anxiety *can* be problems. Or, they can be opportunities to change your life for the better.

New Habits Are Possible

Addictive behaviour patterns can be changed.

Addiction Results In Negative Stereotyping

People who have had the experience of addiction have often been involved in situations where they are subject to condemnation, moral outrage, and ridicule. Everyone has heard jokes about drunks. They aren't as funny if you're the one who has lived through the pain of detox. Being on the receiving end of gossip and negative stereotyping is a risk-factor for relapse. Stigma increases stress, decreases self-esteem, and can affect the opportunities open to you in relationships and careers.

Responsible Sharing Of Information

Responsible communication starts with each conversation, word, and body language signal. There is a phenomenon in early recovery where people may feel compelled to share every last detail of their addictive behavior. They want to share all the secrets that have burdened them for so long. And while this may feel wonderful at first, it can be a source of regret later.

Choose with care the people with whom you share details of your past. When you err, err on the side of sharing too little information. You can always give more information later. But, you can't take it back. Generally, provide only enough information to support your personal growth and to assist your understanding of your self and others. When discussing your past behavior, talk in terms of how your behavior is changing, rather than focusing only on how bad it was at one point in your life.

Share parts of your total self, not just your past addiction. Concentrate on your future, not your past. Concentrate on your strengths, not your mistakes. When you talk of lapses, talk in terms of what you have done since that lapse in terms of personal growth. Except during treatment or rehab, try to limit your daily conservations about your past addictions. Talk about your successes, your interests, sports or job, whatever is part of your new life. Gradually take your life's focus off your past experience of addiction and put it on the challenges and joys of daily living.

You are the only person who is responsible for monitoring your conversations and the amount of information you share. Honest communication does not require microscopic details. Contrary to what your partner, friend or family member may believe, it is not always in your best interest, nor is it the best interest of relationships to discuss in detail every behavior of your past addiction lifestyle. Doing so may result in destruction of the relationship or your self-esteem. Your mother does not need to know the details about every time you stole money or had sex for money in the past decade. Honest communication requires taking care of yourself and others. Your partner does not need to know the details of every sexual encounter you ever had in your life. But, your partner does need to know that you are going to use a condom, get tested for sexual transmitted diseases, and share the results with them, because your addiction caused you to exhibit poor judgment.

There is no better way to make amends for past actions than to make a complete recovery and achieve your life goals.

As in all things, communication about the past requires a balanced approach. Distorted communication is not the goal. Lying or avoidance is not the goal either. It is possible to be honest and share what you feel comfortable sharing while maintaining your pride and dignity. It involves requesting respect for your privacy and the support to pursue your sincerest desire to change your life. Those who truly care about you and your recovery will respect your emotional boundaries when it comes to your past addiction lifestyle.

Sometimes individuals believe that describing in detail the horror of the addiction lifestyle, is evidence of their sincere intention to stay clean. It may feel good momentarily to confess such burdens to others, but confessing to the wrong people or at the wrong time can stimulate further isolation. Continual confession does not allow you to move on. You have the right to put the addiction lifestyle behind you and nobody has the right to stop you. It is up to you to communicate that right to others. Accept that in some situations, the consequences of your past behaviors will be life long. This is no different than serious mistakes made by other people who have different experiences than addiction, such as financial failure due to poor judgment. **There is no better way to make amends for past actions than to make a complete recovery and achieve your life goals.**

> *You have the right to put the addiction lifestyle behind you and nobody has the right to stop you.*

Practice What You Will Say

Practice answering the big communication questions. Take five minutes and begin making a list of the questions *you* believe you will be faced with from your friends, partner, family and children, co-workers or school associates.

Here are some sample questions and responses to stimulate developing your list:

Question: How can I know you will never use or drink again?

Sample responses:

- *You can't know that.*
- *I intend to stay clean. I'm working every day to bring good things into the lives of those around me.*
- *If I lapse and use I may need your understanding and help to figure out what I can change and do to keep my life on track.*

Question: I hear you have a problem with drinking?

Sample responses:

- *No, that is not true. I did drink too much at one time in my life. Not now.*
- *I choose not to drink because I have found healthier ways to enjoy myself.*

Write down the most likely tough question you will get when you enter a social situation. Work on your response until you're satisfied and say it aloud.

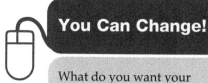

You Can Change!

What do you want your new life to look like?

Chapter Thirteen: Taking Charge of Your Health And Your Life

1. The most likely tough question you will get when you enter a social situation:

   _____

   _____

   _____

2. My response to that tough question:

   _____

   _____

   _____

   _____

   _____

Once you are done, share your response with a trusted friend. Practice it. Keep it short and to the point. Responsible communication is up to you. Practice your answers to tough questions to keep yourself safe, emotionally and physically.

To keep yourself safe, ask yourself before you share details of your experiences or another person's experiences: *Why do I want to share this? Why are they asking? Do I care if other people hear this information third or fourth hand? Does sharing this help me in building my image of myself or does it hurt me? Am I being honest and balanced?* If you are satisfied with your answers go ahead and share. Just remember, when in doubt, less is better. You can always share more at a later date as long as you are honest, don't distort the facts, and communicate your boundaries clearly.

The Stigma of Addiction

Stigma is discrimination or prejudice. Stigma is treatment based on class or category rather than individual merits. Instead of bringing or holding people together, prejudice and discrimination pushes them apart. Prejudice and discrimination always implies some sort of relationship between groups of people. Prejudice is an example of interactions based on hatred, fear or a perceived threat (International Online Training Program On Intractable Conflict, 1998). Prejudice occurs when a group of people defines itself in terms of what it is not, such as, "not an addict" and when that group holds negative stereotypes of the other group, such as "addicts always lie."

People who are stigmatized are not given the opportunity to prove the belief is wrong. Prejudice toward people who have experienced addiction is wide spread. They may be seen as untrustworthy, lazy, violent, emotionally unstable, unpredictable, or undependable. These negative beliefs reflect prejudices that people who have experienced addiction will need to challenge and overcome.

Where Does The Stigma Around Addiction Come From?

Stigma comes from opinions and beliefs based on incorrect and limited knowledge. People hold a view that there is little hope of recovery from addiction because their neighbor still uses. They hear extensive media coverage about violent crimes committed by people who are using drugs or alcohol. They use cultural or family beliefs that may not be accurate or they believe oversimplified public messages. Stigma continues in part because quality research about addiction is distributed to a narrow audience.

Some stigma is reinforced by behaviors of people who are intoxicated. People's beliefs are confirmed by personal experience. They have seen or experienced an intoxicated person being out of control, violent to themselves or others, or behaving unpredictably. Erroneous beliefs about addiction are strengthened through these negative individual experiences.

Health care providers, family, partner, employer, teachers, police or even friends may discriminate against you because of your past addiction. You may experience avoidance, exclusion, blame, and a greater focus on your flaws or errors.

New Habits Are Possible

Addictive behaviour patterns can be changed.

What Actions Can You Take To Break Stigma Barriers?

Stereotype breaking actions are actions a person can take to prove they have stronger character than what is being assumed about them (International Online Training Program On Intractable Conflict, 1998).

You can succeed and make your last relapse the last!

You can visit your detractors and be more reasonable, friendly, agreeable or helpful than they expect. When this happens, they are likely to revise their image at least a little bit, concluding that you are more reasonable than they thought you were. Many stereotype breaking actions are possible. You must simply determine what the other person or group thinks or expects of you. Then do the opposite. If you are expected to be closed to new ideas, express an interest. If you are expected to be selfish and aggressive, use your listening skills. Hear their concerns.

> *Stereotype breaking actions are actions a person can take to prove they have stronger character than what is being assumed about them*

This demonstrates your good will. *The goal is simply to contradict the negative images people have of you and to begin to replace these negative images with more positive ones* (International Online Training Program On Intractable Conflict, 1998).

Establishing personal relationships with people at work, school or places where you may experience discrimination can go a long way toward breaking down inaccurate and hostile stereotypes. These relationships can also increase understanding. Through personal relationships, people come to see the "enemy" as a real, living, breathing, feeling, and caring person, not just an abstract, hostile or evil person. Once this change of attitude takes place, mutual understanding and trust can slowly be developed (International Online Training Program On Intractable Conflict, 1998). *The goal is to have people see you in a different light.*

> *Building your knowledge increases your power to improve your health and life; to beat discrimination and prejudice.*

Storytelling is useful in reducing discrimination and prejudice. By telling your story in respectful and strength-based ways, people can decide for themselves what their real concerns are about you. By telling their stories, they can explore their inner feelings and fears. Storytelling lets people get to know each other better and understand why they feel the way they do. People will often say to themselves, *Oh, I understand. That has happened to me too.* Or, *Yes, I can see how that would have made you feel that way.* It makes people's beliefs and ideas have more reality or validity. Storytelling is a way of opening people up, both to talk and to listen and to pave the way for improved communication and understanding (International Online Training Program On Intractable Conflict, 1998).

Negative Stereotyping Can Be A Two Way Street

Take some time to reflect on your beliefs and to answer the following questions. Do you hold prejudices and stereotypes that may affect your goals and how you treat others around you? Could some of your beliefs and behaviors be increasing the negative reaction of some people toward you? What do you believe about non-users? What do you believe about professionals involved in your health care? Challenge your own beliefs and actions to find and change the negative prejudices and stereotypes that you hold.

You Have the Power to Change

Whether you think you can, or think you can't, you're right. Henry Ford

The Best Tool For Improved Health and Stigma Reduction

Taking charge of your health and your life requires taking action based on good information; developing and using knowledge and skills. The strongest tool to improve your health is you. Only you can take action to make the best use of professionals, family, and friends to meet your goals. The strongest force against prejudice is your actions, your appearance, your self-respect, and your tolerance for other's differences.

Building your knowledge increases your power to improve your health and life; to beat discrimination and prejudice.

Summary

Taking control of your health and life requires specific actions on your part. Self-management of your health requires problem solving skills, quality information, communication skills, and taking action.

Your health plan is part of your life plan and requires you to make an honest assessment of the assistance you require from professionals, family, and friends. This assistance will be reciprocal in that you may need to help others or behave differently. It's time to put those mutual expectations in writing and get on with your goals. As you proceed you will need to communicate wisely and act as a stigma breaker, to overcome barriers to your success. Remember, public commitment leads to increased success in meeting your goals. What are you waiting for? Share your life plan and move ahead.

. . . .

References

Dombeck, Mark, Director of Mental Help Net (2006) "Psychological Self-Tools An On-line Self Help Book." Retrieved from http://www.mentalhelp.net/poc/center_index.php?cn=353

International Online Training Program On Intractable Conflict. (1998). *"Prejudice and Discrimination."* (1998). Conflict Research Consortium, University of Colorado. Retrieved from http://www.colorado.edu/conflict/peace/problem/prejdisc.htm

Chapter Thirteen: Taking Charge of Your Health And Your Life

New Habits Are Possible

Addictive behaviour patterns can be changed.

Lorig, Kate, & Holman, Halsted, "Self-Management Education: Context, Definition, and Outcomes and Mechanisms." Stanford University School of Medicine, Stanford Patient Education Research Center. 1-15. Retrieved from http//www.stanford.edu/group/perc

Malouff, John. (2006). "Fifty Problem Solving Strategies Explained," University of New England School of Psychology. Armidale, Australia. Retrieved from http://www.une.edu.au/psychology/staff/malouffproblemsolving.php

Chapter Fourteen

Putting All The Pieces Together

You can succeed and make your last relapse the last!

Chapter 14

Putting All The Pieces Together

What Is Structure?

Creating daily structure is a powerful way to constantly cue you for success and cue yourself away from using. Structure is a system of interrelated parts functioning as an orderly whole. The different parts are linked and work together. You give structure to your life when you consciously organize or arrange all parts so that they work together as cohesive whole. **For relapse prevention, structure is the way in which the different parts of your life link and work together to give positive form to your life on a daily, weekly, and yearly basis.**

> *Creating daily structure is a powerful way to constantly cue you for success and cue yourself away from using.*

Structure dictates behavior. Structure can produce the desired behavior even if the resulting behavior in the beginning feels wrong or totally disagreeable (Senge, 1990). <u>Positive life structure is the single most powerful tool you have to change addictive behavior patterns.</u>

An Example Of The Use Of Structure

The armed forces deliberately use the power of structure by getting everyone up at the same time, getting everyone to dress the same, giving everyone the same haircut, having everyone do the same basic training, and giving soldiers the same messages day after day after day. Each soldier's activities are scheduled in advance and someone ensures they complete them. A culture of action is created and soldiers learn to respond with speed and efficiency using the skills and knowledge they were trained to use. <u>The result of all this structure is predictable behavior</u>. Leaders in the armed forces are masters of using structure to create constant and predictable behavior in individuals, even when those individuals are placed under great stress.

What Makes Up Structure?

Structure is concerned with key factors that influence people's behavior over time such as money, information, knowledge, rituals, rewards, cues, and time. People from any point on the globe when placed in the same structure will eventually act in much the same manner. The pervasiveness and momentum of structure places enough pressure on individuals to force change (Senge, 1990).

Let's say for example, you grow up in a small town and learn to drive in a relaxed, courteous manner. Because of the local town structure, you know, at least marginally, most of the people in town. You always slow down to let other drivers change lanes or turn. And because of the great connection to those around you, it's highly likely you will stop to let a pedestrian cross the street, even if they're not at the corner or in a cross walk. Then, you move to a large city like Montreal with very busy and congested traffic. The traffic structure consists of traffic jams and little or no personal connection to those around you. Now, when you drive in a slow, courteous manner, people cut you off and honk at you. When you try to change lanes, you put on your signal light and wait, and wait, and wait, and no one lets you in. The Montreal traffic structure influences your behavior with cues and rewards that almost go unnoticed. Before long, you find yourself forcing your way into lanes of traffic and cutting other people off so you can get to work and get home on time. Gradually and over time, you become a more aggressive and less courteous driver because the reinforcing structure of big city traffic makes life too difficult for you any time you try to go against it.

Get Real Motivation!

What are your reasons for quitting? Are they strong enough? Revisit page 18.

Can Structure Create Helplessness?

The drug and alcohol culture is a pervasive structure that erodes problem solving skills and increases negative behavior. Drug and alcohol abuse reduces thinking ability, increases impulsiveness, and perpetuates a belief in the inability to stop using. The structure of the addiction lifestyle perpetuates irregular sleep, erratic activity, and poverty. These in turn decrease self-confidence and self-esteem. The addiction lifestyle structure reinforces hopelessness.

Positive Structure Can Change How You Behave

Structure reinforces accepted behaviors and limits what behaviors are viewed as possible. If you choose to work at a health and fitness club, you start your day at 6 AM, work all day with clients who want to get healthy and fit, and eat at the clubhouse food bar. You listen to people's success stories and use the equipment for free. It is very likely you will get more healthy and fit, like your clients, and the other staff. Sitting, smoking, and over eating are no longer acceptable to you.

Structure is neither inherently good nor bad but it is a powerful force in life. It's important for you to use the power of structure in your life to prevent relapse and achieve your goals.

Structure is neither inherently good nor bad but it is a powerful force in life. It's important for you to use the power of structure in your life

Chapter Fourteen: Putting All The Pieces Together

to prevent relapse and achieve your goals. Individuals experience reduced stress, reduced rates of lapse and relapse, and increased success in all areas of their life, when they actively plan and schedule positive structure and activities into their lives after stopping use and after detox or rehab (Marlatt, & Donovan, 2005).

Some of the characteristics and behaviors you demonstrate are the outcomes of past structures in your life. An example could be that your family always read together after supper (structure) and as a result you developed a great love of reading (outcome). *Now, take a moment and think of two characteristics or behaviors you currently*

1. Write down one *good* characteristic you currently demonstrate:

   _____

   _____

   Write down the structure and outcomes or behaviours: _____

   _____

   _____

   _____

2. Write down one *bad* characteristic you currently demonstrate:

   _____

   _____

   Write down the structure and outcomes or behaviours: _____

   _____

   _____

   _____

demonstrate, one good, one bad. Are they the outcomes of structure in your current life? Write down the structure and the outcomes or behaviors.

Structures Can Support Or Deter Sobriety

Where you choose to live and what you choose to do are two structure choices that have a huge impact on your life and relapse prevention. If those structure choices don't support your sobriety, then change them. It is virtually impossible to stay clean in a work or living environment that reinforces an addiction lifestyle. Once you have dealt with these two big choices, you now need to put positive structure into your daily life to reinforce the behaviors that will support you to meet your life goals.

Positive Structure

Pre-scheduled commitments to support positive, constructive activities or attitudes. Can include positive peer pressure, such as plans to complete activities with other people.

Structure Can Cue You To Succeed

Now, that you understand the concept of structure, take a look at your Life Plan goals. If you have a goal to work out every day, in what ways could you add structure to this goal? You could join a running club that meets and runs two or three times a week. This is considered positive structure because the <u>time for running is preset</u> and there is no need for you to decide to exercise, and less chance for you to change your mind. Because <u>times are regular</u> and set in advance there are no opportunities for you to be double-booked. The second reason this is positive structure is that three times a week, you are <u>surrounding yourself with the culture</u> of fitness and consciously or not, you will start to conform to the expectations of being fit. You are surrounding yourself with people who have fitness as a goal and who are actively pursuing this goal. <u>You will be talking with and learning from others with similar expectations</u>.

Take the time to put structure behind each of your goals and they will never be just wishes. For example, you can even add more structure to your fitness goals than a running club. Sign up with a fitness trainer or a disciplined friend to meet at certain prearranged times to work out and build the muscles required for running. <u>If they will call you when you don't show up, it's structure</u>. If they don't care or even notice if you don't show up, it's not structure. Now you have two events happening that work together to help you meet your goal of physical fitness. For more momentum, add a third related scheduled activity such as enrolling in a sports nutrition course. Put the money down as a commitment and write the times in your calendar. Then to reward yourself, join a club or group that takes advantage of the byproduct of increasing physical fitness from running, such as a hiking club or biking club. Now, you have four activities that provide structure and cue your behavior to your fitness

Take the time to put structure behind each of your goals and they will never be just wishes.

goal.

You are now running three times a week, meeting a friend or trainer, attending a course on nutrition, and hiking or biking once a week. You are building momentum and creating interrelated activities that focus on that one priority goal: your fitness goal. And, the by products of those activities are: meeting new people, having fun, getting in shape and being outdoors. They all help you prevent relapse. Take a look at your ``Life Plan and Goals For Next Year Worksheet`` at the end of Chapter 9. Review your physical health and mental health goals and add structure.

<u>*To succeed in preventing relapse you need to add formal positive structure to your days, which requires planning in advance and making commitments to all your goals.*</u>

Now, examine your education and learning goals in the same light to add more structure. Instead of just reading a book about leadership whenever you think of it, have the time set aside and write it in your daily planner, half an hour every night at nine thirty before bed for reading. You could also find a group of people from work who are willing to meet regularly and discuss the book. That way you have added more structure to your life and goals because you are publicly committed to finish your readings and have another opportunity to socialize without the use of drugs and alcohol. Are there other related activities or courses to take that again, would add momentum and involve a regular time commitment and advance your goals? Always write the activities in your calendar with times and places.

Next, take the time and put structure into your relationship goals. Family goals are another area where organized structure can help. For example, instead of just dropping your kids off at soccer practice, arrange to stay and help out on a regular basis. Organize structure within your family by scheduling weekly events like Sunday dinner together or Tuesday movie night. Write the events in your calendar with the time allotment. Don't allow yourself the old excuses, "I forgot" or "I got busy." Own your family commitments and use structure so people learn to trust your word.

Volunteering is a wonderful way to add structure to your life. It is a way to improve your own mental health, make new relationships, gain valuable work experience, and create opportunities that might not otherwise be available. You can use your current skills and build new knowledge or skills. So stop now and insert a date and time into your schedule to investigate volunteering opportunities. Continue on and review all your life goals for opportunities to insert positive structure into your life.

When Is It Real Structure?

Structure in our daily life goal boils down to three simple points:

1. It is regular and preset in advance, at least weekly.

2. It places you in a culture of like-minded people seeking the same result.

3. It requires some sort of external and visible commitment beyond just to your self.

Creating good structure reduces stress and increases commitment. By filling your life with structured commitments that you have chosen, you will benefit because:

1. *You won't have to always depend on will power to keep you away from drugs and alcohol and to keep you on track to your life goals.* It is easy to tell yourself that you can do it later, but it's much harder to let others down.

2. *You don't always have to decide.* Sometimes, choice is a burden. We get tired of constantly having to figure out what to do with the rest of our day. Having a reasonable portion of your life preset with good things allows you to give your brain a rest once in a while.

Creating Positive Life Structure Keeps You Safe From Risk

Filling your life with structured commitments that you have chosen, helps keep you safe from lapse or relapse. Reducing stress through structured positive activities reduces the risk of relapse. If you have a brutal day at work, worrying and stressing over it all night will not be healthy. Going after work to a pre-booked meeting with your running club will break the negative train of thought and emotion leftover from your workday. It is much harder in the middle of negative thinking and negative events to make a sudden positive decision to go for a run all by your self.

New Habits Are Possible

Addictive behaviour patterns can be changed.

Make inserting structure into your daily life a habit to reduce the risk of relapse. Using the "3 Month Weekly Planner" at the end of this chapter, start inserting dates and times for activities you need to do to achieve your Life Plan and Goals. You will need to plan ahead for at least three months at a time to insure you have sufficient structure in your life to keep your positive motivation and momentum rolling. Always use your calendar to structure your life. Plan your activities in advance and write them down. Get committed to your schedule and to planning ahead. Written commitments are harder to ignore.

To prevent relapse it is essential to organize your life structure and to include at least two positive activities each day in addition to work or school. Book one morning activity to gives you something to look forward to and ensure you have a good reason to get up early and start the day. Constantly sleeping in will result in relapse, losing your job or failing at school. Even if you don't have work or school in your life right now, get up anyway and start your day with a positive activity!

Always book one positive activity every evening. Having nothing planned to do after work or school is unhealthy for you. This is true especially during early recovery. Idle time is a cue to using. Having prescheduled positive commitments **every evening** will keep you focused on where you want to go and it will keep you away from drugs or alcohol.

Don't depend on will power. There will be times when your desire to succeed and motivation will be low. Some peaks and valleys are normal in life. It is at these times that structure is invaluable. **When you don't have the energy to decide to do the right thing, having that activity locked into place will ensure success.**

1. _____
2. _____
3. _____
4. _____
5. _____
6. _____
7. _____
8. _____
9. _____
10. _____

Stop now and think of three ways to add structure to your daily life. Write them down now and start doing them today. Add to this list in

the next day or two, but don't close this book without at least three ideas.

Key Points For Your Success

If you plan, arrange, and schedule healthy, growth-oriented structure into your daily life, you will stay sober, healthy, and goal-focused. Regular structure will reduce the impact of depression, anxiety, anger, and daily frustrations. Regular structure will help you cope with the unexpected such as a layoff from work, relationship breakup or just the bad weather. Regular structure reduces the level of stress in your life and gives you something concrete to look forward to.

Remember, regular structure sends a clear message to your friends and family! You know where you are going each day, you know what you need to do to reach your goals, and you are committed to change. **Every day it sends a clear message to yourself mentally and physically that you are on the road to success.** Regular structure cues you every day: **you are succeeding and managing your life.** It cues you every day that **you are in control of your life.**

> *A commitment is a promise either to our self or others to deliver a specific result or behavior by a certain period of time and FOR a certain period of time.*

Structure Requires And Reinforces Commitment

A commitment is a promise either to our self or others to deliver a specific result or behavior by a certain period of time and FOR a certain period of time. A real commitment is a <u>very firm decision.</u> In Latin, to decide means to cut off. So, think of a commitment as a choice to cut off other options and give all your efforts to your chosen path. Commitments have two purposes:

1. Personal growth
2. Building trust

The purpose of personal growth is obvious. The purpose of building trust is more subtle and far more important. Guard and treasure commitments that build trust like you would care for a precious small child.

Commitments allow us to grow. We see where we are now, we visualize our desired destination, and we mentally deal with the fear of the unknown by committing to our new path. We invest energy in preparing to meet our commitments and getting the necessary actions done. Our commitment gets us through those first steps before there is any positive feedback. Our commitments give order and purpose to our life.

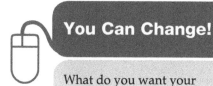

You Can Change!

What do you want your new life to look like?

Commitments Build Trust

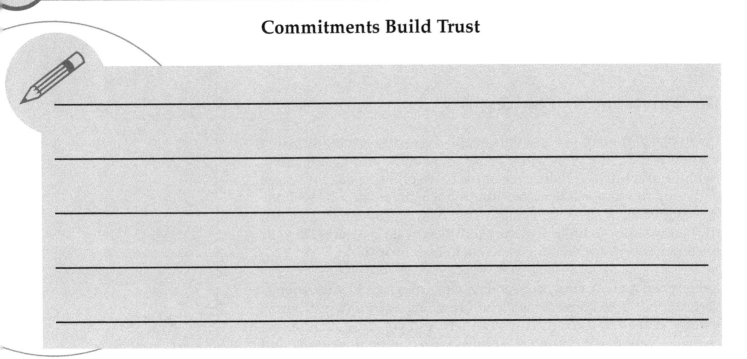

The real power and value of commitment lies in the fact that making and fulfilling commitments is the only way to build trust between people. It's through the process of making and delivering on our commitments that we build trust within ourselves and with those around us.

Repeat this and write it down: *Making and fulfilling my commitments is the only way to build trust.*

Relationships work when there is a high trust level. When trust is low relationships fail, remain very superficial, and damage the participants. If the core relationships in your life are not working, it is most likely because you or the other person is not honoring commitments. In the most valued and beneficial form of relationships, both parties receive what they ultimately want and expect. Without the practice of honoring commitments, successful relationships can't happen and are reduced to manipulation.

Do not make commitments lightly. The size of the commitment doesn't matter. The fact that you made it matters. For example, *I'll help you with that assignment tonight* turns into you watching a movie and avoiding the person with whom you made the commitment. *I'll pay you back that cigarette tomorrow* turns into you never returning the cigarette. *I'll exercise every morning* turns into you sleeping in again. *I'll take care of the kids tonight* turns into a no show. *I'll honor our marriage or partnership* turns into secret affair. Spend your honor wisely. Keep your commitments to a number you can honor. If you find you can't keep a specific commitment, find a way to honor it anyway through another route. You have worked hard to make meaningful goals and plans. Now are you ready to commit? Are you ready to build back the trust in your relationship with yourself?

The Commitment Cycle

Making a promise to yourself and keeping it, leads to inner integrity. Inner integrity leads to increased strength and courage. Increased strength and courage leads to more responsibility. More responsibility leads to larger commitments and success in your life.

Monitoring Your Progress On Your Life Goals

The purposes of monitoring your progress in meeting your commitments to your life goals are simple. Monitoring your progress gives you a chance to:

- Self correct your efforts in both direction and intensity to ensure you arrive at your intended result, at the right time.
- Give yourself motivation to meet your commitments and encourage yourself to continue.

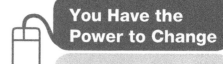

You Have the Power to Change

Whether you think you can, or think you can't, you're right. Henry Ford

Monitoring Too Late Is Costly

You are flying a plane from coast to coast. When would errors in monitoring your direction be most costly to you? When you are 2,500 kilometers away from destination, 500 kilometers away from your destination, or 50 kilometers? If you are going the wrong direction from the start, you will run out of gas before you get even close. If you are only 50 kilometers away, you can make a small correction and still arrive at your destination. The farther you are away from your goal, the more costly the errors and miscalculations will be.

Monitor your progress frequently in the beginning. When beginning a new goal or task, monitoring is far more crucial than when you are close to completion. For something important, monitor your actions both at the beginning and at the end of each day. Once a goal is well underway, a gradual transition to weekly monitoring may be warranted. But for now, monitor your changes in exercise, sleep, and diet every day.

Monitor progress against your written plans. Check off items on your list each time you meet the task and timelines in your written plan. This is the reason for breaking the steps into several "by when" dates. All the tasks and steps must be clearly written and dated or you will get lost.

When beginning a new goal or task, monitoring is far more crucial than when you are close to completion.

You can use formal tests or surveys to monitor progress toward health and learning goals. There are lots of examples of self-assessment tools for health. The BMI or Body Mass Index is a self-assessment tool to measure progress towards healthy body weight and physical health. Comparing your results over time will help you track your improvement and provide the motivation you will need to continue or to adjust your plan.

Get an expert's opinion to monitor your progress. Use a mentor, personal coach or an independent third party to provide an unbiased viewpoint. When you know you're meeting with someone weekly whose job it is to help you assess your progress, it's much easier to stay focused. No one wants to show up and admit they did nothing. Monitoring leads to adapting your plans based on information. Then, you monitor the new plan, which leads to more change. Through this cycle, you both achieve the desired change and ensure you arrive at the targeted time and place.

Managing Slips, Lapses And Relapses

The best way, of course, to manage slips and lapses is not to have them. The best way not to have them is by finding your tipping point and having enough leverage to make better decisions every day. A great way to avoid slips is by having many coping skills and lots of positive structure, positive reinforcement, and positive cues. The lapse can take the form of a single drug or alcohol use just like a return to smoking by having a single cigarette. The slip can be the missed commitment you made to others or yourself such as failing to show up at a booked exercise session. Slips can lead to a lapse if you allow them to build up. Lapses can lead to a relapse.

Remember, if a lapse happens, it's what you do immediately after that determines if it becomes a learning tool to strengthen your relapse prevention plans or a step toward relapse. Remember to get out your leverage lists for your goals. Review and read out loud your reasons for wanting to achieve your goals and the list of things that will happen or not happen if you don't achieve your goals. Review the list of your commonly used cognitive distortions and stop yourself from slipping back into any of those dysfunctional patterns of thinking such as all or nothing thinking, labeling or fortune telling. These simple actions will dramatically reduce the risk of a lapse turning into relapse.

Learn Through Honest Appraisal Of The Lapse

Write out the distortions present in your thinking when you used and write the statements to refute those distortions. Do not hide the lapse or throw "should haves" or shame on yourself. That's just more cognitive distortion. Be honest. Immediately discuss your lapse with a counselor or a trusted friend. Be open to help. Stay confident that you can get back on your path. Reward yourself to keep on track.

Reward Yourself For Both Small And Large Successes

Surprisingly, many people have trouble with the concept of rewarding their own efforts. *The result should be reward enough. I'm not a trained dog that needs a biscuit every time I do something. Isn't that rather childish and simplistic?* This type of thinking misses the reasons for a reward system. A reward is a celebration. We celebrate weddings, graduations, birthdays, and anniversaries. Achieving a worthy goal, like any other milestone in your life is worthy of your recognition. Celebrate your milestones.

How Much Time Is Enough For Your Life Plan?

What is time? It is the continuum of experience in which events pass from the future through the present to the past. It consists of 86,400 seconds per day. It consists of 31,557,600 seconds per year. A period of time is a valuable resource under your control. And, it is sufficient to accomplish something or not: "Take time to smell the roses." "I don't have time to finish." "It took more than half my time." Try the following exercise using your own hourly wage and additional costs to calculate how much your time is worth.

If you work the average amount, you work about 200 days a year, at 7 ½ hours per day. That would equal 1,500 hours per year. At $10/hour for example, that would be (10 times 1500) about $15,000 per year. Total all of your salary ($15,000); add an amount for benefits, taxes, and the cost of your office, workspace or equipment you personally use. Add in the cost of your transportation to and from work, your work clothes, and the cost of any training or education. Take this total and divide by 1,500. This is an approximate cost of your time. This is an estimate of what your time is really worth in dollars and cents.

Once you have an estimate of what your time is worth, you can use it as a simple tool to decide if something is a wise use of your personal as well as work time. For example, if a company is willing to spend a total of $40/hour to purchase your time, are you generating $40 worth of value to yourself with the action you are contemplating? If not, maybe it's not a wise use of your time.

<u>In reality your time is worth way more than that. Your time is irreplaceable. You cannot get more time. You can only spend it as wisely as possible.</u>

Check How You Spend Your Time

Calculating The Value Of Your Time

200 x 7.5 = 1,500 hours / year

Hourly Wage $_____ x 1,500

= Per Year $ _____

+ Benefits $ _____

+ Taxes $ _____

+ Other $ _____

+ Transportation $ _____

+ Work Clothes $ _____

+ Training $ _____

+ Education $ _____

= $ _____

/ 1,500

Value of YOUR Time

= $ _____

ଞ *Note* ଊ

Time May Only Be Spent Once

Chapter Fourteen: Putting All The Pieces Together

Most of us have no idea of the number of hours in a year we spend doing different things. Since you cannot make extra time, you can only manage your time better. The best place to start is to find how you spend your time now. Get a journal and start an activity log. This is a fast way to find out the truth about how you spend your time. Carry this journal with you and write down everything you do in the day log, from the moment you wake until you sleep and round it to the nearest 15 minutes. Keep a record for at least one week (2 to 3 weeks would be ideal), and try to ensure there are no time gaps. For every 15 minutes, quickly jot down what activity you are doing. For every activity note the start time, finish time, and complete a quick rating of the activity. Here's your rating scale:

- Place a minus sign (-) if the activity <u>wasn't</u> useful and meaningful or productive.

- Do not place a sign beside the item if it was a neutral activity like laundry or chores.

- Place a plus sign (+) if the activity was valuable and productive.

- Place two plus signs (++) if the activity was fun, valuable, and productive.

At the end of one week, tally up and see how you're spending your time. Calculate what percentage of your time was spent in ++ activities, fun and valuable and productive. Calculate the percentage of time spent poorly or wasted. Most of us are shocked to find how much time is wasted on TV, going through junk mail, smoking or even just laying in bed thinking about getting up. This wasted time is the extra time you have available to make changes you want to make in your life.

Here's a moment of truth. Now, pull out all of your goals you have set. Look at the ones that are most important to you. What percentage of your time did you actually devote to activities required to accomplish your goals? Compare that to the percentage of time you spent on unproductive activities. Are you happy with what you see?

What else can you learn from your activity tracking journal? It shows you how much time things realistically take in your life. Before you completed the time log exercise, you probably had no idea of how much time most activities actually take. Now you can schedule so much more effectively when setting goals and planning your days. Truly knowing how much time activities take allows you to preserve your time for your absolute *must do's*. Before you agree to do something, check your activity log to gain a more accurate idea of the time commitment something might take. It will give you information to realistically decide whether to say, *yes* or *no*.

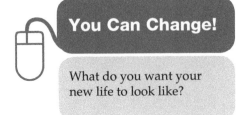

You Can Change!

What do you want your new life to look like?

By eliminating drugs and alcohol from your life, how many hours a week do you have available to devote to your goals, your family, and your health? Take time now and write down the activities you engaged in for two typical days during your addiction when you were most actively using. Write out the whole 24 hours, from when you got up until you went to bed. Use 15 minute increments. Remember to add the time that was spent planning for using and covering up your alcohol and drug use. What percentage of time do you not even remember? Now put in the plus/minus rating beside each activity. Minus signs mean the activity wasn't useful or meaningful. One plus is valuable and meaningful. Plus/plus is valuable, productive and fun. Once you've finished, tally them up. What do you see?

You can make excuses or, you can devote your time and efforts to actions that will improve your life and the lives of those connected to you.

It's your choice.

Making Up For Lost Time

You may feel remorse or anger over the time lost to your addiction. How do you make up for time you have lost with your partner, spouse, children, family, and friends? If you view it in a purely physical sense, you can't get the time back. It is spent, gone forever. If you reframe the problem slightly, there is a solution, even if it is not the perfect one. A relationship with a partner, spouse, family member or a friend is a commitment or promise. It can be seen as somewhat like a debt. A debt even if in arrears can be repaid with interest. The best solution is to complete these time-management exercises and

1. How much time has my addiction cost me and those in my family?
   _____
   _____
   _____

2. How will I make up for lost time?
   _____
   _____
   _____

2. How much time each week will I now devote to my Life Plan?
   _____
   _____
   _____

Chapter Fourteen: Putting All The Pieces Together

find out how to maximize the time you have available. Redirect that found time to the projects and people you choose. Repay those time debts.

Again, it boils down to choice. You can choose to be sad, angry or depressed over the past. You can make excuses: *It's too much work. I have too many things to do. It's a waste of time.* Or, you can devote your time and efforts to actions that will improve your life and the lives of those connected to you. It's your choice. *Now answer these questions and make your commitment to life change:*

Don't Give Up!

It's hard work, but you can finish this book!

Then, schedule your days with activities that advance your goals, reduce risk of relapse, and increase the fun and joy in your life. Put the power of structure in your life for continuous motivation and forward movement. To guide you in completing your detailed schedule of daily activities for your next three months, use your completed relapse prevention plan documents:

- A clear commitment statement and written life goals for the year ahead with compelling reasons for each goal
- A stress inventory with strategies
- A guilt and shame inventory with strategies
- A defined support network with strategies for connection
- A clear boundary-setting plan
- A communications skill improvement plan
- An exercise, recreation, and social activity plan
- A cues and a craving management plan

Your Time For Recovery

*"Recovery takes time. A lifetime.
And that's good, not bad, because recovery is more
than just getting clean and sober.*

*In its broadest, most meaningful sense,
recovery is the process of becoming
the person you want to be . . .*

The person you are meant to be."

(Ketcham, & Pace, 2003).

You Have The Time

You have the time. Instead of asking: *Why did I waste all that time? How can I make up for the lost time?* A better question is: **What can I accomplish with all the extra time I now have since I have changed my life?** It is that extra time you now have available to use for your new plans. It is that extra time that will allow you to work out, take courses, and succeed at your goals. It is that extra time that will allow you to restore relationships and build new stronger ones. It is that extra time that will allow you to go through all the exercises in this book and to complete the many other learning experiences you have planned for yourself.

You know the truth. So, while the rest of the world complains they have no time, as someone who has been through the experience of addiction, you know that is not true. You know there are hours and hours of wasted time to redirect to activities that support who you really are and where you really, really want to go. It's up to you. You have more than enough time to follow your plan. The question is: "Will you?"

• •

References

Senge, Peter. (1990). *"The Fifth Discipline."* New York. Bantam Doubleday Dell Publishing Group, Inc. 40.

Marlatt, G.A., & Donovan, D.M. (Eds.). (2005). *"Relapse Prevention Maintenance Strategies in the Treatment of Addictive Behaviours."* (2nd Edition). New York. The Guilford Press. 5, 74-78.

Ketcham, Katherine, & Pace, Nicholas A. (2003). *"Teens Under The Influence, The Truth About Kids, Alcohol, and Other Drugs_ How to Recognize the Problem and What to Do About It,"* New York. Ballentine Books. 317.

You can succeed and make your last relapse the last!

3 Month Weekly Planner

Chapter Fourteen: 3 Month Weekly Planner

Plan your next 3 months to prevent relapse by filling in the schedule below to create structure. Your counselor will assist you to make a plan.

Day	S(/ /)	M(/ /)	T(/ /)	W(/ /)	T(/ /)	F(/ /)	S(/ /)
Wk 1 - Morn							
Wk 1 - Aft							
Wk 1 - Eve							

Day	S(/ /)	M(/ /)	T(/ /)	W(/ /)	T(/ /)	F(/ /)	S(/ /)
Wk 2 - Morn							
Wk 2 - Aft							
Wk 2 - Eve							

3 Month Weekly Planner

Day	S(/ /)	M(/ /)	T(/ /)	W(/ /)	T(/ /)	F(/ /)	S(/ /)
Wk 3 - Morn							
Wk 3 - Aft							
Wk 3 - Eve							

Day	S(/ /)	M(/ /)	T(/ /)	W(/ /)	T(/ /)	F(/ /)	S(/ /)
Wk 4 - Morn							
Wk 4 - Aft							
Wk 4 - Eve							

You can succeed and make your last relapse the last!

Chapter Fourteen: 3 Month Weekly Planner

Day	S(/ /)	M(/ /)	T(/ /)	W(/ /)	T(/ /)	F(/ /)	S(/ /)
Wk 5 - Morn							
Wk 5 - Aft							
Wk 5 - Eve							
Day	S(/ /)	M(/ /)	T(/ /)	W(/ /)	T(/ /)	F(/ /)	S(/ /)
Wk 6 - Morn							
Wk 6 - Aft							
Wk 6 - Eve							

3 Month Weekly Planner

Day	S(/ /)	M(/ /)	T(/ /)	W(/ /)	T(/ /)	F(/ /)	S(/ /)
Wk 7 - Morn							
Wk 7 - Aft							
Wk 7 - Eve							

Day	S(/ /)	M(/ /)	T(/ /)	W(/ /)	T(/ /)	F(/ /)	S(/ /)
Wk 8 - Morn							
Wk 8 - Aft							
Wk 8 - Eve							

You can succeed and make your last relapse the last!

Chapter Fourteen: 3 Month Weekly Planner

Day	S(/ /)	M(/ /)	T(/ /)	W(/ /)	T(/ /)	F(/ /)	S(/ /)
Wk 9 - Morn							
Wk 9 - Aft							
Wk 9 - Eve							

Day	S(/ /)	M(/ /)	T(/ /)	W(/ /)	T(/ /)	F(/ /)	S(/ /)
Wk 10 - Morn							
Wk 10 - Aft							
Wk 10 - Eve							

3 Month Weekly Planner

Day	S(/ /)	M(/ /)	T(/ /)	W(/ /)	T(/ /)	F(/ /)	S(/ /)
Wk 11 - Morn							
Wk 11 - Aft							
Wk 11 - Eve							

Day	S(/ /)	M(/ /)	T(/ /)	W(/ /)	T(/ /)	F(/ /)	S(/ /)
Wk 12 - Morn							
Wk 12 - Aft							
Wk 12 - Eve							

You can succeed and make your last relapse the last!

Chapter Fourteen: Putting All The Pieces Together

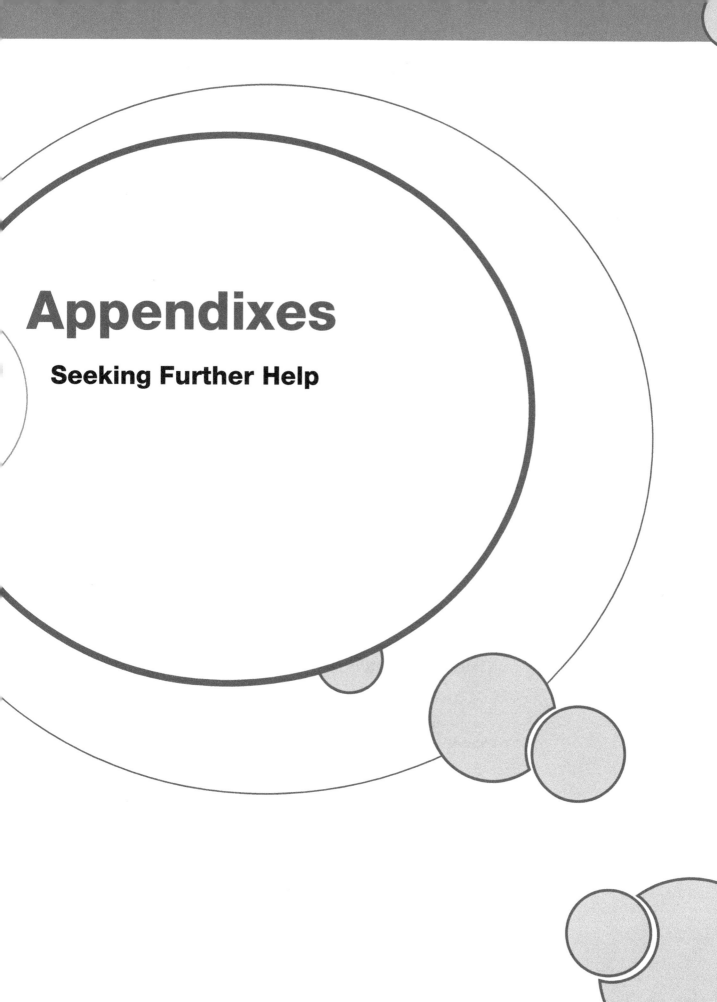

Appendixes
Seeking Further Help

Getting More Help - Reading List

Depression, Anxiety, Worry, Relationships

The Feeling Good Handbook
by David D. Burns
ISBN-10: 0452281326

Feeling Good: The New Mood Therapy Revised and Updated
by David D. Burns
ISBN-10: 0380810336

http://www.feelinggood.com/

You Can Change!

What do you want your new life to look like?

Communication

PeopleSmart, Developing Your Interpersonal Intelligence
by Melvin L. Silberman
ISBN-10: 1576750914

Stress & Relaxation

The Relaxation & Stress Reduction Workbook,
by Martha Davis, Matthew McKay, Elizabeth Robbins Eshelman,
ISBN-10: 1572242140

Anger Management

The Anger Control Workbook (Paperback)
by Matthew McKay (Author), Peter Rogers
ISBN-10: 1572242205

Our Research, Our References

We again wish to thank the experts who created the extensive body of research available in the area of relapse prevention and health care which was used to create this book.

"2004 Alberta Recreation Survey." Highlights of Results. 1. Retrieved from http://tprc.alberta.ca/recreation/ars/surveypdf/2004_Survey_Highlights.pdf

Beck, Aaron T., Wright, Fred D., Newman, Cory F. & Liese, Bruce S. (1993). *Cognitive Therapy of Substance Abuse.* New York. The Guilford Press. 22-23, 31, 34-35, 160-168, 192-200, 206-209.

BC Ministry of Health. (2004). *Every Door Is The Right Door, A British Columbia Planning Framework to Address Problematic Substance Use and Addic*tion. 71-75.

BC Partners for Mental Health and Addictions Information. (2006). "Depression Fact Sheet." Retrieved from http://www.heretohelp.bc.ca/factsheet/managing-depression

Bond, James, T., Thompson, Cindy, Galinsky, Ellen & Prottas, David. (2002). *"Highlights of the National Study of the Changing Workforce."* New York. Families and Work Institute. No. 3. 63, 65, 76.

Brooks, Robert, & Goldstein, Sam. (2004). *"The Power Of Resilience, Achieving Balance, Confidence, and Personal Strength in Your Life."* New York. Contemporary Books. 181.

Brown, J.L. & Pollit, E. (1996). Malnutrition, Poverty and Intellectual Development. *Scientific American.* February. 38-43.

Burns, David D. (1999). *The Feeling Good Handbook.* New York. Plume, Penguin Group. 3-11.

Burns, David D. (1999). *Feeling Good, The New Mood Therapy* (revised). New York. Harper Collins Publishers. 29-30, 87,121.

Chopra, D. (1997). *"Overcoming Addictions, the spiritual solution."* New York, Harmony Books. 100-101.

Counselling Center University of Illinois. *"Loneliness."* Retrieved from http://www.couns.uiuc.edu/Brochures/loneline.htm

Daley, Dennis C. & Marsili, Ricardo (2005). No One is Left Unharmed: Dual Disorders and the Family. *Counselor: the Magazine for Addiction Professionals.* Deerfield Beach, Florida: Health Communications, Inc. February, 2005 Vol. 6. 37-43.

Getting More Help

Davis, Martha, Eshelman Robbins, Elizabeth, & McKay, Mathew. (2000). "*The Stress Relaxation & Stress Reduction Workbook.*" Oakland California. New Harbinger Publication, Inc.

Dombeck, Mark, Director of Mental Help Net (2006) "Psychological Self-Tools An On-line Self Help Book." Retrieved from http://www.mentalhelp.net/poc/center_index.php?cn=353

Fairbrother, Nichole. (2004) Prepared for BC Partners for Mental Health and Addictions Information. "Who needs social support? We all do!" Wellness Module 3: Social Support. Retrieved from www.heretohelp.bc.ca

Frances, Richard J., Miller, Sheldon I. & Mack, Avram H. (Eds.). (2005). *Clinical Textbook of Addictive Disorders* (3rd edition). New York. The Guilford Press. 12, 13-14, 21-32, 259-251.

Frances, Allen & First, Michael B. (1998). *Your Mental Health, A Layman's Guide to the Psychiatrist's Bible.* New York. Scribner. 12, 32, 79, 117-119, 120-122.

New Habits Are Possible

Addictive behaviour patterns can be changed.

Goodwin, Donald W. (2000). *Alcoholism, the facts.* Oxford. Oxford University Press. 91.

Gordis, Enoch. (1998). *Alcohol And Sleep – Alcohol Alert #41, Alcohol and Sleep – A Commentary.* Retrieved from http//www.niaaa.nih.gov/publications

Jiwani, Gulrose & Somers, Julian. (Winter 2004) Concurrent Disorders, Considerations for Evidence Based Policy. *Visions: BC's Mental Health and Addictions Journal, Concurrent Disorders,* Vol. 2 No.1. 10.

Howard, Pierce. (1999) "*The Owner's Manual for the Brain, Second Edition: Everyday Applications from Mind-Brain Research.* " Austin, Texas. Bard Press, 138.

International Online Training Program On Intractable Conflict. (1998). "*Prejudice and Discrimination.*" (1998). Conflict Research Consortium, University of Colorado. Retrieved from http://www.colorado.edu/conflict/peace/problem/prejdisc.htm

Kabat-Zinn, Jon. (2005). "*Full Catastrophe Living, Using the Wisdom of Your Body and Mind to Face Stress, Pain, and Illness, The Program of The Stress Reduction Clinic At The University of Massachusetts Medical Center.*" New York. Bantam Dell. 11-12, 25-26.

Ketcham, Katherine & Pace, Nicholas A. (2003). *Teens Under The Influence, The Truth About Kids, Alcohol, and Other Drugs-How to Recognize the Problem and What to Do About It.* New York. Ballantine Books. 304-309, 317.

Kendall-Reed, P., & Reed, S. (2004). "The Complete Doctor's Stress Solution, Understanding, Treating, and Preventing Stress and Stress-Related Illnesses." Toronto, Ontario. Robert Rose Publishing. 83-85.

Lavery, Sheila. (1997). *The Healing Power of Sleep, How to Achieve Restorative Sleep Naturally.* New York. Simon & Schuster Inc. 16-17, 34, 37, 94-125.

Lorig, Kate, & Holman, Halsted, "Self-Management Education: Context, Definition, and Outcomes and Mechanisms." Stanford University School of Medicine, Stanford Patient Education Research Center. 1-15. Retrieved from http//www.stanford.edu/group/perc

Malouff, John. (2006). "Fifty Problem Solving Strategies Explained," University of New England School of Psychology. Armidale, Australia. Retrieved from http://www.une.edu.au/psychology/staff/malouffproblemsolving.php

Marlatt, G.A., & Gordon, J.R. (Eds.). (1985). *Relapse prevention: Maintenance Strategies in the Treatment of Addictive Behaviours* (1st edition). New York. Guilford Press. 39.

Marlatt, G.A., & Donovan, D.M., (Eds.). (2005). *"Relapse Prevention Maintenance Strategies in the Treatment of Addictive Behaviours."*(2nd Edition). New York. The Guilford Press. 4-5, 7-21, 28-29, 71-72, 74-78, 138, 158.

You Have the Power to Change

Whether you think you can, or think you can't, you're right. Henry Ford

MayoClinic.com Tools For Healthier Lives. (2005). <u>Developing social support: How to cultivate a network of friends to help you through rough times</u>. Mayo Foundation for Medical Education and Research. Retrieved from http://www.mayoclinic.com

McKay, M., & Rogers, P. (2000). "The Anger Control Workbook, Simple, innovative techniques for managing anger and developing healthier ways of relating," Oakland, California. New Harbinger Publications, Inc.

McKay, M., Rogers, Ph.D., & McKay, J. (1989). "When Anger Hurts, Quieting the Storm Within." Oakland, California, New Harbinger Publications Inc. 24 - 32, 218, 220- 221.

Medina, J. (1998). "Depression. How it happens. How it's healed." Oakland California. New Harbinger Publications Inc. 6-7, 32-33, 82-87.

Messina, James, J. & Messina, Constance. (1999-2007). *"Tools for Coping with Life's Stressors Handling. Forgiving and Forgetting."* (Coping.org is a Public Service of James J. Messina, Ph.D. &

Constance M. Messina, PhD). Retrieved from http://www.coping.org/relations/forgive.htm#Negative

Miller, W.R., & Rollick, S. (1991). *"Motivational Interviewing, Preparing People to Change Addictive Behavior,"* New York. The Guilford Press. 12, 14, 21, 29, 38, 40-41, 45, 83.

National Center For Chronic Disease Prevention and Health Promotion. (1996). *Physical Activity and Health, A Report of the Surgeon General.* Chapter 4. Retrieved from http://www.surgeongeneral.gov/library/reports.htm

NIDA InfoFacts: Science-Based Facts on Drug Abuse and Addiction. Retrieved from http://www.nida.nih.gov/Infofacts/Infofaxindex.html

Olds, Jacqueline, Schwartz, Richard & Webster, Harriet. (1996). *"Overcoming Loneliness in Every Day Life."* New York. Carol Publishing Group. 166-183.

Parks, George A. & Marlatt, G. Alan. (2000). Relapse Prevention Therapy: A Cognitive-Behavioral Approach. *The National Psychologist*, Sept/Oct., Vol. 9. No. 5. Retrieved from http://www.nationalpsychologist.com

Patterson, K., Grenny, J., McMillan, R., & Switzler, A. (2005). "crucial confrontations, Tools for resolving broken promises, violated expectations, and bad behavior." New York. McGraw-Hill. 84-85.

Peele, Stanton. (2004) "Tools to Combat Addiction." New York. Three Rivers Press. 41.

Potter-Efron, Ronald & Potter-Efron, Patricia (1989). *"Letting Go of Shame, Understanding How Shame Affects Your Life."* San Francisco. Harper and Row, Publishers. 121-125, 132-141.

Richmond, Lewis. (1999). *"Work as a Spiritual Practice, A Practical Buddhist Approach to Inner Growth and Satisfaction."* New York. Broadway Books. 16.

Rosenstein, D.I. (Spring 1975) Effect of long-term addiction to heroin on oral tissues. *J Public Health Dent.* 35(2). 118-22.

Schiraldi, G.R., & Hallmark Kerr, M. (2002). "The Anger Management Sourcebook." New York. Contemporary Books. 3, 4, 7, 12-13.

Senge, Peter. (1990). *"The Fifth Discipline."* New York. Bantam Doubleday Dell Publishing Group, Inc. 40.

Silberman, Mel & Hansburg, Freda, (2000). PeopleSmart, Developing Your Interpersonal Intelligence. San Francisco. Berrett-Koehler Publishers Inc. 12-18, 37-39.

Simpson, Carolyn. (1997). *Methadone*. The Drug Abuse Prevention Library. New York. The Rosen Publishing Group, Inc. 20-23.

Tjosvold, Dean. (1993). *"Learning to Manage Conflict, Getting People to Work Together Productively."* New York. Lexington Books. 4-5, 7-8.

University of Colorado, International Online Training Program On Intractable Conflict (1998) *"Active Listening."* Retrieved from http://www.colorado.edu/conflict/peace/treatment/activel.htm

Wainwright, Gordon R. (1999). *"Body Language."* Illinois. Contemporary Publishing. 1, 21-32, 58-68, 70-82.

Weiss, Roger D., Mirin, Steven M., & Bartel, Roxanne L. (1994). *"Cocaine."* (2nd Edition). Washington, DC. American Psychiatric Press. 164-165, 176.

Wilson, S.J., Sayette, M.A., & Fiez, J.A. (2004). Prefrontal responses to drug cues: a neurocognitive analysis, *Nature Neuroscience*, Vol. 7 (# 3), 211.

Woodward, Kathryn. (Editor). (1997). "Identity and Difference," Culture, Media and Identities Open University Series. Thousand Oaks, California. Sage Publications USA. 1-2.

Yost, Cali Williams. (2004). *"Work And Life, Finding The Fit That's Right For You."* New York. Riverhead Books, Penguin Group. 100.

Get Real Motivation!

What are your reasons for quitting? Are they strong enough? Revisit page 18.

Getting More Help

How To Find Professional Help

Counseling & Psychiatry

United States Listings:

The Association for Behavioral and Cognitive Therapies
http://www.aabt.org/

Academy of Cognitive Therapy
http://www.academyofct.org

Mental Health America
http://www.nmha.org

Canadian Listings:

The Canadian Mental Health Association
http://www.cmha.ca

Canadian Psychological Association
http://www.cpa.ca/

You Can Change!

What do you want your new life to look like?

Helpful Web Links

The US Drug Rehab Centers directory

http://www.usdrugrehabcenters.com/

...is committed to providing the most comprehensive resources currently available for those in need of information on residential treatment programs and outpatient rehabilitation programs nation-wide. Our directory contains a wide-ranging selection of the most up-to-date listings for drug and alcohol rehab centers.

Canadian Drug Rehab Centres

http://www.canadiandrugrehabcentres.com/

The Canadian Drug Rehab Centres directory was created to address the increasing demand for current and comprehensive resources relating to residential treatment programs and outpatient rehabilitation programs in Canada only.

New Habits Are Possible

Addictive behaviour patterns can be changed.

Index

A

Abstinence
  Allows You Time to Learn 34
  Maintaining 56
Acceptance 130
Acknowledging fear, difficulty in 98
Action 85
Active Listening 122
  Practice 123
Addiction
  Addiction As An Identity 202
  And Your Mental Health 46
    More likely to have a mental health problem 47
  And Your Physical Health 48
    Physical Damage 189
  Changed How You Think 34
  Family history 101
  Impairs Judgment 192
  Learning The Addiction Lifestyle 28
  Manage Chronic Health Problems Including Addiction 220
  Negative Structure 235
  Physical Addiction 189
  Self-help For Addiction 218
  Stigma 228
  Tolerance 189
Addiction lifestyle, Impact Of 49
  Guilt and Shame 129
Afraid To Quit Using 32
Ambivalence 86
Anger
  As a defense 98
  Chronic anger 97
  Physical response of the body 97
Anger Management
  Managing Anger, Coping Skill 97
  Reducing Emotional Cues 65
Angry
  How Long To Stay Angry At Someone 210
Antidepressants 101
Anxiety 47
  Managing Anxiety 101
  Managing To Reduce Emotional Cues 65
  Treatment for 102
Appearance, effects communication 120
Assault 101
Automatic
  Automatic Reactions 155
  Thoughts 45
Automatic Thoughts 45
Awkward Questions, Practice Handling 227

B

Balanced Lifestyle 76
Becoming Stress Resilient 108
Behavior Model 35
Behaviour, effects communication 120
Beliefs 72. *See also* Urges
  Changing Your Beliefs And Values 154, 204
Benefits Of Not Using 188
Body language 120
Boredom 83
  Beating Boredom 213
Boundaries 20
  Interpersonal Boundary Setting Reduces Relapse 136
Brain Will Recover 50

C

Caffeine
  Side effects of 103
Change
  Causes Of 150
  Change beliefs 77
  Life Partners Can Power Change 161
  Maintaining Change 180
Character 152
Clothes 120
Cocaine
  Side effects of 103
Cognitive behavioral therapy 102
Cognitive therapy 101
  To Prevent Relapse 186, 187
Commitment 58, 221
  Commitment Cycle 242
  Commitments Build Trust 241
  Lower Response To Cues 58
  Reduce Craving 58
  Structure Reinforces Commitment 241
  Taking Commitments Seriously 242
Communication Skills 20, 96
  Active Listening 122
  A Relapse Prevention Tool 119
  Clear Communication 223
  How You Look, Talk & Act 120
  Physical Appearance
    Body language 120
    Change your image to improve communication 122
Compelling Reasons
  To Exercise 84
Compelling Reasons Not To Use 77
Competition
  Increases conflict 117
Composure 120
Conflict 116
  And Relapse 116
  Conflict resolution 116
  Cooperation 118
Continued Use 30
  Afraid To Quit Using 32
  Be Part Of A Group 31
  Boosts Confidence 31
  Makes Life Seem Better 31
Cooperation 118
Coping Skills 20, 76, 96
  Poor Coping Skills Lead To Relapse 192
  Preventing Relapse
    Coping skills training 186
Coping skills 56
Coping Skills, Preventing Relapse
  Anger Management 97
Craving Recognition 56
Cravings
  Get Weaker If You Don't Respond 77
  High Sugar Foods During 52
  Irresistible 74
  Management
    Balanced Lifestyle 76
    Change Beliefs 77
    Compelling Reasons Not To Use 77
    Control Craving By Using Reasoned Thinking 74
    Craving Management Plan 75
    Exercise And Relaxation Plan 80
    Permission Refusal Thoughts 74
    Pocket Helper 76
    Positive Self-image 76
    Practical Techniques 78
      Cue Cards 78
      Distraction 78
      Imagery 79
      Record rational response 79
      Relaxation 79
      Schedule Activities 79
    Practice Refusal Skills 75

Index

Rebuttal Statement 75
Recreation Activities 83
Role-play 76
Reducing 59
Crisis
　Handling 154
Cues 27, 30, 44
　Cues Do Not Last Forever 66
　Eliminating Cues 59
　　Removing Items That Cue You To Use 61
　Emotional Cues 64
　Four Kinds Of Cues 59
　How To Manage Them 58
　Location Cues 63
　Management 56
　　Creating New, Positive Cues 61, 65
　　　Adding Positive Cues 65
　　Emotional Cues 65
　　Location Cues 63
　　Managing Situation Cues 63
　Many cues to use drugs or alcohol 57
　Personal Belongings 61
　Situations Or Events 62
　Structure Can Cue You To Succeed 237
　What Are They 58
Cumulative Effect, Drugs Add Up 46

D

Damage
　Physical Damage 189
Decision-making 74
Decision To Quit 32
Dependence
　Substance Dependence 188
Depression 47
　After Using 73
　Managing as a coping skill 100
　Managing To Reduce Emotional Cues 65
　Risk factors for depression 101
　Treatment Of
　　The Feeling Good Handbook, by Dr. David Burns 103
　Vitamin B6 101
　What Causes Depression 100
Diet pills
　Side effects of 103
Digestive disorders 97
Disease Model 35
Distorted Thinking 203
Divorce 101
Dizzy 102
Dr. David Burns. *See* The Feeling Good Handbook
Dreams
　Make Your Dreams A Reality 177
Dysfunctional Beliefs 73
Dysfunctional Thinking 45, 102

E

Eating Irregularly 52
Emotional Cues 64
　Physical Activity Reduces Frequency Of 65
　Relaxation Techniques Reduces 65
Energy
　Increase Your Energy 180
Erroneous Belief 73
Exercise
　Benefits
　　Improved Physical Appearance 82
　　Increase your strength 82
　　Manage cravings 82
　　Manage Negative Thoughts 82
　　Meet new people 82
　　Provides conversation 82
　Exercise And Relapse Prevention 52, 53
　Self Esteem, and 52
Exercise And Relaxation Plan 80
Expectations 56
　Expecting Not To Use 59

F

Facial expression 120
Failure 192
Families
　Families Who Help 223
　Impact Addiction Behavior 127
　Need Help Too 132
　Negative Family And Friend Support 127
　Positive Support 128
　Resisting Your Positive Life Changes 173
Family history
　Addiction 101
　Creating Your First Values And Beliefs 151
　Mood Disorders 101
Family problems 101
Fear 173
　Fear Mechanism 101
Feeling Badly 42
Feeling helpless or trapped 98
Feelings 76
Fight or flight response 102
Financial Problems 197
Finding Needed Resources 221
　Finding Professionals To Help You 222
Forgiving
　Forgiving Others 205
　Forgiving Yourself 205
　　Making Up For The Past Penance 208
Friends
　Friends Who Help 223
　Resisting Your Positive Life Changes 173
Frustration 76
Future 199
　That you want to become 153

G

Generalized anxiety disorder 101, 103
　Treatment for 103
Getting Healthy 49
Goals
　Compared To Wishes 157
　Establishing Goals 156
　Life Goals
　　Monitoring Progress 243
　Must be compelling 160
　Mutual Goal Setting 162
　Set Goals With Important People 161
Guilt 98, 129
　Lapse Induces Guilt 192

H

Habits 188
Headaches 97
Health
　Health Problems 199
　　Manage Chronic Health Problems 220
　Self-management 219
　Taking Charge Of Your Health 218
Heart disease 97
Heart races 102
Help
　Families Need Help Too 132
　Helping Other People To Prevent Relapse 136
Helplessness 235
High-Risk Situations 57
　Avoiding 58
High risk for relapse 29
High sugar foods during recovery 52

Index

Holistic Model 36
Hypertension 97

I

I Can't ....
   Handling Your Mental Objections To Change 182
Identity 202
   Creating A New Identity 202
   How To Change Your Identity 204
Immune system 156
Impaired Judgment 192
Increase Motivation 85
Infections 97
Influences 26
Information To Prevent Relapse, Using 35
Intensify Anger 97
Intention. *Intention,* See Urge
Irresistible Cravings 74

J

Jobs. *See* Work

L

Lapse 186
   Lapse Induces Guilt 192
   Managing 244
   Positive Side Of Lapse 191
Learning to be addicted 28
Learning To Manage Symptoms 50
Leverage
   Personal 157
   Pocket Leverage Sheet 158
Life Partners 161
Life Plan 221
   How Much Time Is Enough For Your Life Plan? 245
Life Story, Your
   Sharing Your Information 225
Lifestyle 76
   Balance 96, 199
Location Cues 63
Loneliness
   Loneliness And Recovery 210
   Managing Loneliness 211
Loss Of Control 74
Lost Time
   Making Up For Lost Time 247

M

Making Changes 84
Making Up For The Past
   Penance 208
Manage Cravings and Cues 20
Manage Cues 65
Manage Negative Emotions 56
Manage Symptoms 50
Managing Cravings 72
Managing Stress 103
Marital therapy 128
Meditation 155
   And the immune system 156
Mental Health 46
   Self-help For Mental Health 218
Mental Objections 182
Mindfulness 155
Missing Out 158
Moderate Use 193
Momentum
   Increasing Momentum To Positive Change 181
Moral model 35
Motivation 56, 84, 157
   Action Precedes Motivation 85
   And Ambivalence 86
Moving 101
Mutual Goals 161
   Mutual Goal Setting 162

N

Need 72
Negative
   Negative Stereotyping 225, 230
Negative Emotions
   Before Using 64
   Cause feelings change is impossible 150
   Overcoming By Thinking Creatively 176
   Where Do They Come From? 44
New Attitude Toward Your Life 65
New Life Course 17
No Choice 74
Nonverbal 122
Normal Functions Return If 49

O

Obsessive/compulsive disorder 101
Offers Of Drugs Or Alcohol 76, 127

P

Panic disorder 101, 102
   Treatment of 102
Partners 161
   Mutual Goal Setting 162
Past, The 205
   Letting Go Of The Past 205
Peer Pressure 198
Penance 208
Permission Giving Thoughts 74
Personal Appearance 120
Personal Standards 151
Phobias 101
Physical Activity
   Managing Emotional Cues 65
   Reduces Frequency Of Emotional Cues 65
Physical Addiction 189
Physical Appearance
   Change your image to improve communication 122
Physical Health 48
   Fitness Skills 96
Pocket Helper 76
Positive Cues
   Add positive cues to your life 65
Positive Self-image 76
Positive Structure 21
Post-traumatic stress disorder 101
Posture, changing 121
Practice Refusal Skills 75
Predicting Relapse 87
Problems
   Daily Life Stressors 198
   Financial Problems 197
   Health Problems 199
   Peer Pressure 198
   Practice Handling Awkward Questions 227
   Problem Solving Skills 223
   Relationship Problems 197
Professionals 222
Progress
   Monitoring Your Progress 243

Q

Questions, Practice Handling Awkward 227
Quitting
   Feeling Badly 42

R

Rational thinking skills 96
Reacting automatically 155
Reason For Using 75
Rebuttal Statement 75
Recognize

Index

High Risk Situations 57
Negative Emotions Early 64
Recovery
  High Sugar Foods During 52
  Problems During Recovery 51
  Sleep patterns can be disrupted during 51
  Your Time For Recovery 248
Recreation Activities 83
Red Zone 64
Refusal Skills 192
Rehab
  Types of.. 35
Relapse
  And the balance sheet 107
  High-Risk Situations 57
  Is A Choice 187, 190
  Managing Relapse 244
  Relapse Prevention
    Beating Boredom 213
    Belief in yourself and in your skills 154
    Commitment
      Taking Commitmens Seriously 242
    Communication Skills 119
    Concrete plan 96
    Discovering Your Relapse Setup 187
    Exercise And 52
    Food And 51
    Interpersonal Boundary Setting Reduces Relapse 136
    Lifestyle Balance 96
    Lifestyle Changes 186
    Managing Daily Stressors 104
    Managing Loneliness 210
    Managing Stress to reduce risk of relapse 103
      Managing Daily Stressors 104
    Meaningful Work 172
    Planning For Healthy Relationships 131
    Positive Structure 235
      Adding 238
    Providing assistance to your support network 136
    Reduce Guilt And Shame 131
    Reducing The Risks 186
    Reward Yourself 244
    Sleep 50
    Social Support Network 134
    Using Information to Prevent Relapse 35
  Relapse Setup 187
  Research That Predicts 87
  Risks
    Boredom 213
    High Risk 29
    Lonliness And Recovery 210
    Monitoring Progress Too 243
    Peer Pressure 198
    Poor Coping Skills 192
    Predicting Relapse 36
    Reducing The Risks 186
    Unsatisfying work 172
  Triggers 56
Relationships
  And Communication, Trust 242
  Relationship Problems 197
  Relationships And Relapse 126
    Planning For Healthy Relationships 131
  Relationship therapy 128
  Repair relationships 123
Relaxation Techniques 65
  Relaxation skills 96
  To Manage Emotional Cues 65
Removing Cues From Your Environment 65
Removing Items That Cue You To Use 61
Reward Yourself 244
Risk
  Staying Safe From Risky Situations And People 239
Role-play 76

S

Self-care centered 136
Self-esteem, Confidence 52, 96
Self-management 219
Self interest 117
Sensation of dread 102
Shame 130
Sharing Your Information 225
Single, Being 101
Situation Or Event Cues 62
Sleep
  And Relapse Prevention 50
  Improve Your Sleep 51
  Problems During Recovery 51
  Shortage of 50
Slips
  Managing 244
Smoking
  Acceptable 159
Sobriety
  Structures To Support Or Deter 237
Social anxiety 101
Social Pressure To Use 29
Social Support Network 20, 132, 134
Solutions
  Generating 224
Some One Offers You Drugs Or Alcohol 76
Speaking Style, effects communication 120
Speed
  Side effects of 103
Spouse
  Mutual Goal Setting 162
Standards
  Raise Your Values And Standards 155
Staying Away From Places 63
Stereotyping
  Negative Stereotyping 225, 230
  Stigma 228
Stigma 228
  Break Stigma Barriers 229
Stimulants
  Side effects of 103
Stress
  Assigning Meaning To Stressors 106
  Becoming Stress Resilient 108
  Daily Life Stressors 198
  Managing Stress 103
  Multiple Stressful Events 107
Stress management skills 96
Structure
  Definition Of Structure 234
  Is It Real Structure? 238
  Positive Structure 172, 235
Substance Dependence 188
Success
  Key Points For Success 240
  Structure Can Cue You To Succeed 237

T

Temptation to eat sugary foods 52
The Anger Control Workbook, Simple, , by Mathew McKay & Peter Rogers 99
The Balance Sheet 106
The Feeling Good Handbook by Dr. David Burns 65
The Relaxation & Stress Reduction Workbook, by Martha Davis, Elizabeth Robbins Eshelman and Mathew McKay 65
Think About Using
  Causes 60
Time
  How Much Time Is Enough For Your Life Plan? 245
  Making Up For Lost Time 247
  No Time 224
  What Is Your Time Worth 245
  You Have The Time 249
Time management skills 96

Index

...ints 159
...ompelling 160
...ance 189
Traumatic Events 101
Trust
    Commitments Build Trust 241
Types Of Rehab Programs 35

U

Urge 72

V

Values
    Creation Of First Values And Beliefs 151
    Defining Your Values 151
    Exploring 150
    Raise Your Values And Standards 155
Violence 101
Vision
    Creating Your Vision 156
    Making Commitments to Achieve Personal Vision And Goals 179
Vitamin B6 101
Volunteering 83

W

Who Will Relapse 36
Wishes 157
Withdrawing 101
    Causing anxiety 103
Work
    Discovering Your Dream Job 174
    Dream Job 152
    Meaningful Work 172
    Roadblocks To Finding Meaningful Work 172
Worksheets 250
    3 Month Weekly Planner 250
    Commitment To Continued Positive Change In My Life 22
    Craving Management Plan 88
    Exercise, Recreation And Social Activities Plan 92
    Goal Planning Worksheet 170
    Guilt And Shame Stress Inventory Worksheet 141
    Life Plan And Goals For Next Year Worksheet 165
    Personal Cue Inventory And Strategies To Manage Cues 67
    Personal Stress Inventory Worksheet 112
    Problem List Worksheet 38
    Relapse Prevention Planning Checklist 23
    Self Care Recovery Boundaries Worksheet 143
    Support Network Worksheet 147
Worry 103

Y

Your Story
    Sharing Your Information 225
Youth, being young 101